151 Polework Exercises

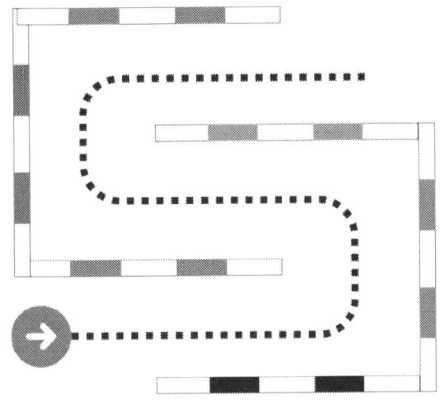

151 Polework Exercises For Horses

Elaine Heney

Copyright © 2024 by Elaine Heney

All rights reserved. No part of this publication may be reproduced, distributed, or transmitted in any form or by any means, including photocopying, recording, or other electronic or mechanical methods, without the prior written permission of the publisher.
First Edition 2024 | Edited by Kas Fitzpatrick
Published by Grey Pony Films
www.elaineheneybooks.com

"The greatest judge in this world is your horse."

Elaine Heney

Horse books for adults

www.elaineheneybooks.com

The Equine Listenology Guide
Dressage for Beginners
The Galway Connemara
The Listenology Guide to Bitless Bridles
Horse Anatomy Colouring Book

Horse books for kids

Listenology for Kids
Horse Care, Riding and Training for Kids
Saddlestone Series for Kids (5 books)

The Coral Cove Series for kids

The Riding School Connemara Pony
The Storm and the Connemara Pony
The Surprise Puppy and the Connemara Pony
The Castle and the Connemara Pony
The Shipwreck the Connemara Pony
The Christmas Connemara Pony

The Connemara Adventure Series for kids

The Forgotten Horse
The Show Horse
The Mayfield Horse
The Stolen Horse
The Adventure Horse
The Lost Horse

Table of contents

Quick start guide 13

Distances guide 17

Training session tips 19

The Training Session Checklist 24

Rider goals & tips 25

Horse goals 29

Suppleness & bend pre-training 36

Groundwork exercises 39

1 - Bending from poll to withers 40

2 - Moving the shoulders sideways at halt 42

3 - Moving the shoulders sideways in walk 44

4 - Moving the hindquarters sideways at halt 46

Collection 48

Collection exercises 52

Backup on the ground (straight line) 54

Backup circle on the ground 56

Halt and backup 59

Trot, halt and backup 63

Shoulder-out (groundwork) 64

Shoulder-out (riding) 68

Shoulder-in 70

Sidepass 71

Sidepass in front of half a pole 72

Sidepass over half a pole 73

Groundwork polework exercises 75

Polework exercises 78

Introduction

Polework schooling sessions can make training and riding a lot of fun for you and your horse. Polework exercises have many benefits - from improved straightness, rhythm, bend and suppleness for your horse, to better posture, focus, confidence and improved balance for the rider.

If you are ready to spice up boring or dull arena sessions, become a confident team with your horse and work together to navigate all sorts of fun polework layouts, then this is the perfect book for you! Polework exercises are a great way to improve your skills with your horse and have fun together. Here are some of the benefits you can look forward to:

Improved coordination and agility.

Navigating through lots of different pole layouts will help your horse to adjust their stride and place their feet more precisely, improving their agility and coordination.

Increased strength and muscle tone.

Regular polework exercises engage different muscle groups, particularly in the back, hindquarters and shoulder areas, leading to increased strength and muscle tone.

Enhanced flexibility & balance.

Manoeuvring around and over poles will encourage your horse to stretch and bend their bodies, which can improve their overall flexibility. Working over poles will also require your horse to balance themselves and you more effectively, especially when changing directions or adjusting stride lengths.

Better accuracy and straightness.

Polework will help you and your horse to focus, have a plan and move efficiently in an accurate straight line, with your horse following your focus and direction.

Improved rhythm and cadence.

Consistent work with poles can help your horse develop a more regular and rhythmic gait, as they learn to maintain an even pace and stride length.

Better collection, posture and lateral work.

Poles are a practical way to help your horse to become more collected and balanced. Incorporating sideways and backwards movements into your polework exercises will encourage your horse to transfer a little weight from their forequarters to their hindquarters, which develops collection, greater hindquarter engagement and improved overall posture.

Mental stimulation.

Polework provides mental challenges that can help prevent boredom and stimulate your horse's mind, which is essential for their mental well-being.

Preparation for jumping.

Polework is an excellent way to introduce and prepare your horse for jumping, by teaching them to judge distance and stride in a manner that is less intimidating for the horse than being faced with jumps straight away.

Enhanced rider-horse communication.

As you guide your horse through polework exercises you are building your horse's confidence and giving them a practical job to do. A considerate rider will be patient with their horse and reward them with regular short rests and praise during the session. This enhances their communication and understanding, leading to a better partnership. Polework exercises, when integrated into your horse's training routine, can greatly improve your horse's performance, health, and relationship with you.

In this book there are over a hundred polework exercises, of all different levels. Some are more simple, and some quite challenging! Under each polework exercise in this book, you will see the benefits of each exercise. Let's see what you need to get started!

Quick start guide

How many poles do I need? Each exercise needs a different number of poles. Most of the exercises in this book used between 2 and 8 poles. A few exercises use up to 14 and 16 poles.

What type of poles are best? I prefer the heavy wooden poles, instead of the light plastic poles. This is because the light poles tend to move around a lot if your horse's foot touches them. If some plastic poles are old they can sometimes shatter when a horse stands on them.

Where can I buy poles? In countries where show jumping is quite common in the UK and Ireland, it's usually easy to find show jumping poles. You can often find them in your local tack or feed shop. If they are not easy to find where you live, you should be able to buy wooden poles in your local hardware shop that will do the job. Ask your local equestrian community for recommendations on where they buy theirs.

What length of poles are required? You can use any length of poles that you have available, but most people use poles between 3 and 3.5 metres long. The shorter the poles the more accurately you will need to ride, but that's not always a bad thing depending on what the focus of your polework training is.

Are these exercises for walk, trot or canter? To start with I recommend starting all exercises in walk. This gives your horse time to figure out the pole setup and what movements you're looking for. When your horse is confident and relaxed in an exercise in walk, working accurately, focused and not hitting their feet on any poles, I would start doing sections of an exercise or two in trot. This is also a great way to work on your transitions. Only when everything is perfect in walk and trot, would I introduce a little canter work, if it is suitable for that layout. Below each exercise you'll see a list of the recommended gaits to use.

What size circles should I use? This will depend on the size of your arena, and your horse. Bigger circles make it easier for your horse to balance, so I would recommend starting with larger circles at first. When you work on smaller circles, in general, a pony will find it easier to work on a 10 metre circle than a 17 hands high warmblood. You can also switch out circles for squares, which allow you to work on straightness and bends.

How long should each session be? No matter what you do with your horse, you want the session to be fun and enjoyable. You don't want it to be long and boring! 5 to 15 minutes of polework training per session is plenty. Remember, it's meant to be fun for you and your horse.

Plus you can get creative and mix it up also. Go for a trail ride and then do 5 minutes of polework at the end. Or do a warm up, 10 minutes of polework and then some jumping! Or if you feel like staying on the ground, or maybe you're waiting for the saddle fitter to visit, do some in hand work or liberty work and then add in some poles at the end to test your skills!

A handy tip - Any time you're training your horse and they do something really good - a very powerful way to reinforce their action and show them how wonderful they are is to end the session, dismount and untack. It's a great way to reward your horse and let them know they did something really special. They really do remember this and will start to look for that great feeling again.

Are there tack adjustments I need to know about? You will be working on collection in many of these polework exercises. To allow collection your horse's jaw needs to be able to move freely and to be relaxed. The horse's jaw, tongue, and TMJ joint are all connected through the fascia to the horse's hindquarters. There are many factors that can restrict the movement of your horse's head and mouth. But by doing that, they restrict the movement of their hind legs. This is something we absolutely do not want! We cannot ask our horses to be more agile, flexible & athletic while restricting the movement of their hind legs.

It can be surprising to realise just how big an impact the bit can have if it is the wrong size, or putting pressure on the tongue, bars or roof of the mouth. The wrong noseband can limit the movement and relaxation of the jaw. So do not use a restrictive noseband such as a flash or grackle to keep the horse's mouth shut. Horses move their mouths for a reason. We should never force their mouths closed. I recommend a plain cavesson noseband, which will allow the horse to move its mouth and breathe freely without restriction.

Secondly, check your saddle to make sure that it fits. I recommend running your hand over both sides of your horse's back before and after each ride. If you find an area where your horse is sensitive, you may have a saddle fit issue. Don't be surprised if you do - saddle fit issues are actually very common and can really impact your horse's health and ability to move freely.

Your horse will benefit from a yearly check-up by a physiotherapist, but be ready to call them out if you spot a suspected pain issue. It is unfair to expect a horse to try their best to improve their rhythm, balance, suppleness and collection if their back is sore.

Distances guide

It's useful to know your horse's stride length so you can set up a sequence of poles they will find easy to travel over. Below you'll find a distance guide for horses and ponies. Use this as a starting point. Your horse's stride length will depend on various factors, including their height, conformation and fitness.

When you are setting up your poles and trying to work out the ideal distance between poles for your horse, it's better to make your distances a bit too long than too short and then reduce them as needed. Look at and feel how your horse is coping with the spacing each time you change it and learn how they feel when the distance is right.

Remember when doing polework, we want to work on impulsion as well as rhythm. So when you are working out your horse's stride, be sure to ask them to walk over the poles in an energetic and forward walk - no slow steps!

Polework distances for ponies

Walk poles: .7m to .9
Trot poles: 1.1m to 1.4m
Canter poles to 2.3m to 2.8m

Polework distances for horses

Walk poles: .8 to 1m
Trot poles 1.2 to 1.7m
Canter poles 2.7 to 3.4m

In some of the exercises in this book, I have included walk, trot and canter poles. Now is a good time to work out your horse's stride length in walk, trot and canter. Follow the instructions above and then write your horse's stride lengths here.

Horse name: _____
Walk poles distance: _____
Trot poles distance: _____
Canter poles distance: _____

Horse name: _____
Walk poles distance: _____
Trot poles distance: _____
Canter poles distance: _____

Horse name: _____
Walk poles distance: _____
Trot poles distance: _____
Canter poles distance: _____

Training session tips

The warm up.

Always warm up before your training session. A warm up is really important for your horse's overall health and performance. Warming up helps raise the temperature of the horse's muscles, making them more elastic and flexible. This increases flexibility and reduces the risk of muscle strains and injuries. A proper warm up improves blood flow to the muscles and joints, delivering essential nutrients and oxygen. This increased circulation ensures that the muscles are well-nourished and ready for the demands of a workout, aiding in performance and endurance.

Get mentally prepared.

Warm up exercises help lubricate the joints, enhancing their range of motion. This mobility is crucial for preventing joint injuries. Just as with humans, a warm up routine can help prepare a horse mentally for the training session ahead. It serves as a transition period from rest to work, allowing the horse to focus and adjust to the demands of the training session, which should improve learning and performance.

Avoid injury.

The combination of increased muscle temperature, improved circulation, enhanced joint mobility and overall mental readiness can greatly reduce the likelihood of injuries during training. The warm up period can also serve as an important time for you to notice any signs of lameness, stiffness, or discomfort in your horse. Begin with 5 to 10 minutes of walking on a loose rein to allow your horse to stretch and relax mentally and physically. Depending on your horse's level of education, you can also include some lateral work, such as leg yields, shoulder-in or simple loops, to enhance suppleness and flexibility.

It's very common to work horses straight out of the stable and often they are kept in rather than being turned out because they will be working later in the day. That may be convenient for the rider, but it isn't ideal for the horse. The movement of a horse when they are out in the paddock or on a track, even if they are just grazing, will gently loosen up joints that have stiffened when stabled overnight. So my preference is to try to avoid working a horse straight from the stable. Even a half an hour turned out will loosen them up before working.

No slow steps.

When you start your ridden work, remember the motto 'no slow steps'. Particularly if you have an energy efficient horse, it's really important to ask for every step with energy and impulsion. This isn't just a physical horse thing; it's actually a rider focus exercise! Can you ask your horse for no slow steps? This begins from your first ridden step, through the entire training session to the end.

Alternatively you can walk slowly with your horse around the arena, and then ask your horse for more energy maybe a minute to two into the session, but this is usually less effective than just asking your horse for impulsion and good energy levels from your FIRST step under saddle.

Impulsion is very important when training. We can't direct our horse to go forwards, backwards or sideways if there is no energy to direct! As a rider it's something we need to focus on. We need energy in the first step our horse takes, and every step afterwards.

Be 100% on or 100% off.

When you are riding your horse, there are two states you should be in. Be 100% focused and working OR take a break and let the horse really relax and be on a loose rein. Do not ride at 50%.

If you want your horse to be 100% focused on you when you are working, you've got to give them 100% of your focus. When riding or doing groundwork, if you put in just 10 minutes of totally focused work, your horse will learn a lot more than they would in 20 minutes of unfocused riding. So don't ride distracted. Riding time is your horse's time. Don't chat to your friends, talk on your phone or daydream about what you need to buy in the shop later.

If you're not mentally 100% focused on your horse I bet you anything they will not be 100% focused on you.

Include regular short rests.

Introduce short rests during your training sessions. A one or two minute rest now and again is very beneficial to horse and rider. Use it to reward your horse for their effort. Allow time for you and your horse to 'soak' and have a think. Horses seem to need a bit more time than we do, so if you've had a break for two minutes and are about to pick up the reins again, just consider waiting until it has been four minutes, call it extra 'horse time'.

Use this time to figure out what your next exercise will be and remind yourself of your goals. Being 100% focused all the time is tricky for the rider, so give yourself little breaks too. When you are on a rest, you can relax your body, loosen your reins, check that your shoulders aren't tense, relax your leg muscles if they feel tight and check your breathing patterns. Give your horse a scratch on their neck, and verbally praise them for their efforts. This break time is also bonding time.

How often for each exercise?

Ride each polework exercise you're working on for a maximum of 2 or 3 times per training session. Even if you are an advanced rider/horse combination, there is no need to keep repeating any exercise - that will bore your horse and make them dull. When you are planning to work in trot or canter, always do each exercise at least once in the walk first to help your horse to figure it out.

Never drill an exercise. If it just isn't working you and your horse probably need to leave it for another day. You may well need to take a step back and practise some of the elements involved in that exercise separately, before approaching it again. If it's going well, bear in mind that your horse can easily get frustrated by the repetition.

Cooling down.

Cooling down your horse after riding is as important as the warm up. It helps to gradually reduce the horse's heart rate, prevent muscle stiffness, and ensure your horse's physical and mental well-being after exercise. Begin the cool down with a walk on a loose rein, allowing your horse to stretch their neck and relax. This period should last at least 10 to 15 minutes.

If the horse is particularly sweaty or has been working hard, you may need to extend this time. The duration of the cool down should be sufficient to ensure that the horse's heart rate and breathing have returned to near-resting levels. Cooling down helps avoid colic, dehydration, and heat stress by gradually bringing the horse's body temperature and cardiovascular functions back to normal.

The Training Session Checklist

1. Don't take your horse straight from the stable to training. Let them have time in a field or paddock to freely move around first.
2. Do at least 5-10 minutes of warmup in walk at the start of every training session.
3. Include some lateral work in walk during the warmup if you can.
4. No slow steps.
5. As a rider, be 100% on or 100% off. Don't be a 50% rider. Don't take a phone call, daydream, not have a plan or chat with friends during your training session. If you expect your horse to focus on you when training, you must give your horse 100% of your focus.
6. Include lots of short rests and praise.
7. Keep it fun. Don't turn this into a drill session. Max 2 to 3 times per exercise.
8. Cooldown your horse in walk for 10-15 minutes at the end of every ride, to keep your horse healthy.

Rider goals & tips

Straight line tips:

- **Ride with equal weight on both seat bones.**

If you look straight ahead your horse is more likely to travel in a straight line. Don't believe it? Ride a straight line and look to the side. Then notice what your horse does! Practise this in your warm up at the walk also. Ask a friend to watch you while you ride, and to tell you if you are doing all of this correctly.

- **Keep your shoulders level, don't drop a shoulder.**

If you keep your shoulders level your horse is more likely to travel in a straight line. Don't believe it? Try riding a straight line but drop one shoulder and notice what your horse does.

- **Look where you're going and don't look down.**

If you look where you are going your horse is more likely to travel in that direction. Don't believe it? Try riding a straight line but look down for a few steps and see what your horse does.

Circle and corner tips:

- Ride with slightly less weight on your outside seat bone. This is a tiny lifting of weight from your outside seat bone. It should not be noticeable to anyone watching you. It's more like just feeling that inside seat bone on the saddle than moving your body. The rule of thumb is that your seat sets the horse's bend, and your legs set the horse's direction.
- Keep your shoulders level.
- Look where you are going and don't look down. Your body will stay tall and vertical.
- Don't lean to one side on circles or corners.

Practise this during your warm up in walk as well as when you are schooling. Also bear it in mind when you are out on a relaxed ride! Ask a friend to watch you while you ride, and to tell you if you are doing all of this correctly.

Posture tips:

- Keep your hands close together inside an imaginary small box over the pommel of your saddle.
- Don't wave an arm or two about in the air, lift your hands high, hold your hands low or pull your elbows back. No one should ever be able to see your hands move. Your rein signals to your horse should be an invisible conversation.

Sometimes riders do these things but are not aware of this habit. I've watched people bring their hands down low to bring the horse's head down in a mistaken belief that it is collection, but it isn't.

Collection is a weight transfer from the forequarters to the hindquarters. It has nothing to do with pulling on your reins to change your horse's head position. That's just uneducated riding.

Too much movement in your hands will give unwanted signals to your horse. This will confuse them and it also negatively affects your balance. Remember the goal is that your cues and signals to your horse should be subtle and invisible to anyone watching.

When travelling over poles, remember to allow your horse to stretch their neck when they need to. Don't use your reins to restrict your horse's head and neck movement. Trust your horse and allow them the freedom to use their body as they need to.

Relaxation and enjoyment.

Smile when you ride. It's supposed to be fun! Can you ride a polework exercise while smiling the whole time? Or while singing the whole time?

Breathing.

Do you end up out of breath or with a red face? Try doing a polework exercise with your main goal being to remember to breathe regularly and not get out of breath. Can you count your breaths while you ride? Try counting - one, two, three - on your 'in' breath, and then your 'out' breath. Does it change how your horse moves?

Horse goals

There are lots of useful goals we can work towards when training our horses. And the great news is that we can use fun polework exercises to help us! Every polework exercise in this book includes a list of benefits.

Straightness

Your horse should be able to efficiently ride from A to B in a straight line. But that's harder than it sounds! Your horse will need to move symmetrically and in alignment. Straightness is needed to achieve balance. A straight horse can carry its weight and potentially that of a rider, more evenly. Straightness training encourages the development of muscles evenly on both sides of the horse's body.

Most horses, like people, naturally have a 'stronger' side, just as people are often right or left-handed. Training for straightness helps to balance this natural asymmetry, leading to better muscle tone and preventing the overdevelopment or underdevelopment of certain muscle groups.

By reducing uneven stress on the joints and ligaments, straightness training contributes to the overall well-being and longevity of the horse.

- In dressage, the ability to move straight and execute movements with precision improves your test results.
- In jumping, straightness ensures that the horse approaches and leaves a fence in a balanced manner, reducing the risk of knocking poles or misjudging distances.

Regardless of the riding discipline, straightness is a foundational skill that supports all others. Whether it's dressage, jumping, eventing or trail riding, a horse that can move straight and in balance is safer, more efficient, and more pleasant to ride.

Bending and suppleness

Training for bending and suppleness is crucial for horses across all disciplines, from dressage and show jumping to western riding and trail riding. Regular bending and suppleness exercises increase a horse's flexibility, making it easier for the horse to perform a wide range of movements. This flexibility is crucial for executing tight turns, extending strides, and performing complex manoeuvres without strain.

Suppleness training promotes even muscle development on both sides of the horse's body. Think of it like yoga for horses! Many horses, like people, have a more dominant side and can develop unevenly if not correctly trained. Balanced muscle development helps prevent injuries and ensures that the horse can perform tasks equally well on both sides.

A supple horse is less likely to suffer from injuries. Flexibility allows for smoother, more fluid movements, reducing the risk of muscle strains, ligament sprains, and joint stress.

Suppleness and bending work improves a horse's balance by teaching it to engage its core and use its body symmetrically.

A well-balanced horse is safer and more pleasant to ride, as it can more easily adjust its stance to accommodate the rider's weight and the demands of different activities. For horses to move on to more advanced levels of training, they must be supple and flexible. Whether it's collecting and extending gaits, performing flying changes, or executing precise patterns in western riding, suppleness is the foundation that allows for these higher-level skills.

Regular bending and flexing exercises help maintain joint health by ensuring a full range of motion and promoting synovial fluid production, which lubricates the joints. This is vital for minimising the risk of arthritis and other joint issues, particularly in older horses.

Accuracy

Accuracy training for horses is essential across all levels and disciplines of riding, from basic groundwork to high-level competition. This form of training focuses on the precise execution of movements, paths, or obstacles - whether it's hitting exact markers in a dressage arena, navigating a course of jumps, or performing complex manoeuvres in western riding disciplines.

Accuracy training for horses is essential across all levels and disciplines of riding, from basic groundwork to high-level competition. For the horse, consistent accuracy training builds confidence in their movements and in their understanding of the rider's cues. For the rider, confidence grows with the knowledge that they can guide their horse with precision. This mutual confidence is crucial for effective performance, especially in high-pressure situations.

Being able to clearly ask for accurate movements from your horse can improve your safety by reducing misunderstandings and accidents, especially in environments with potential hazards or in challenging situations requiring precise navigation.

Rhythm

A consistent rhythm is key to achieving balance. When a horse maintains a steady tempo, it can more easily distribute its weight evenly between all four legs, which is crucial for carrying itself and a rider correctly.

A horse that moves with a regular, balanced rhythm is less likely to suffer from injuries. Irregular movements can lead to uneven loading of the limbs, increasing the risk of strains, sprains, and other musculoskeletal injuries.

For competitive disciplines, rhythm is often directly linked to performance quality. In dressage, for example, the rhythm is a fundamental quality judges look for, indicating the horse's ability to move with grace and efficiency. In jumping, a steady approach rhythm helps in accurately timing jumps and avoiding faults.

Rhythm training requires concentration and mindfulness from both the horse and the rider. This focus has a calming effect, making training sessions more productive and enjoyable. A focused horse is also more receptive to learning and less likely to become distracted or anxious.

For riders, maintaining rhythm teaches valuable riding skills such as timing, feel, and the ability to make subtle adjustments. Developing and maintaining a consistent rhythm requires physical effort from the horse, contributing to its overall conditioning. This includes strengthening the cardiovascular system, developing muscle tone, and enhancing endurance, all of which are beneficial for the horse's health and performance.

By fostering balance, preventing injury, and encouraging proper physical development, rhythm training contributes to a horse's longevity in any equestrian sport. A horse that can move rhythmically and efficiently is more likely to enjoy a longer, healthier athletic career.

Lateral movement and collection

Collection is a weight transfer from the forequarters to the hindquarters. It is never achieved by a fixation or over-focus on head position. Instead it is developed by a series of sideways (lateral) and backwards exercises that change and improve your horse's posture.

Impulsion

Impulsion involves the controlled, forward energy generated from the horse's hindquarters, which is the powerhouse of its body. Impulsion training is crucial in developing a horse's power, engagement and willingness to move forward energetically under control. Training for impulsion helps to develop the horse's muscle strength and flexibility, enhancing its overall athletic ability and performance in any discipline.

A horse with good impulsion is better able to carry itself and a rider with balance and grace. This self-carriage means the horse is not leaning on the rider's hands for support, which unlocks a much higher level of horsemanship. Training for impulsion increases a horse's responsiveness to the rider's aids, making them more attuned to subtle cues for acceleration and deceleration. This sensitivity is crucial for precise movements, whether navigating a complex dressage routine or adjusting stride lengths between fences in show jumping.

Impulsion requires the active engagement of the hindquarters, encouraging the horse to step under itself with its hind legs. This engagement is key to developing the power and thrust needed for advanced movements such as jumping, extended gaits, and collection.

The horse trained to move with impulsion is often a more confident horse. They understand their ability to move powerfully with confidence. This can reduce hesitancy or nervousness, particularly when facing new challenges or environments. Training for impulsion keeps a horse mentally engaged and physically active, promoting overall well-being.

Suppleness & bend pre-training

Some horses have issues when asked to move and bend at the same time. Some horses don't bend their body well on circles. Their body can appear straight, and it doesn't match the arc of the circle they are travelling on. They can often start to lean their whole body into the circle. This is called falling in.

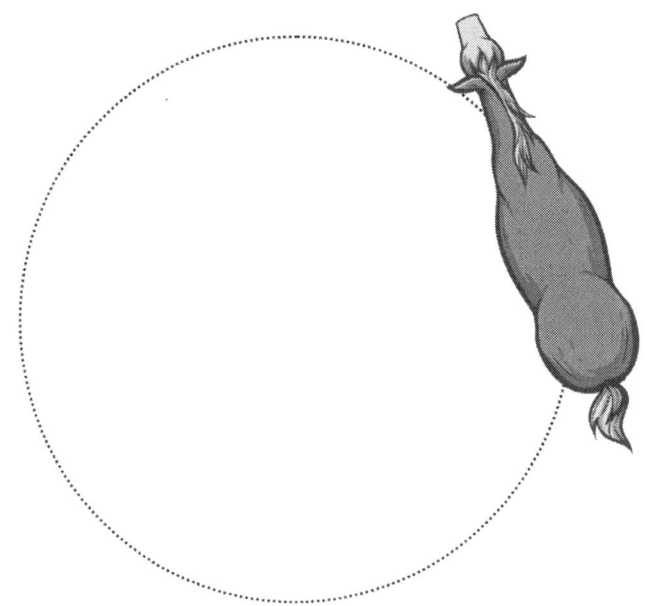

Some horses tend to do motorbike style corners. Their legs are on one track, but their upper body falls in. Imagine a motorbike going around a corner fast, it tips in a little. Horses doing this tend to avoid going deep into corners, or in fact to bend much at all. Their focus is on how to travel around the arena with the smallest bit of physical effort and they are thinking far ahead of where they actually are in that moment. They certainly aren't taking much notice of their rider. Sometimes horses travel on a circle looking out – with the opposite bend to the circle! They are more likely to slip or lose their balance even more – which is not good for horse or rider!

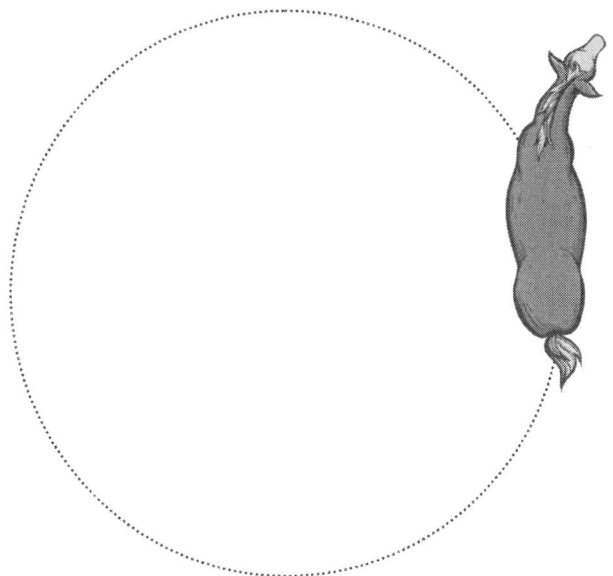

The good news is that this is all normal, and we can help the horse be more balanced and feel better in circles and corners. All we need to do is help them to understand that they can allow a soft bend to flow through their body.

We're not going to force them to change their body shape. Instead we're going to explain our goal kindly, and allow them the time and patience to figure it out. This way they will gain trust and confidence in us and start to feel good using their body in this new way when being ridden. No poles are needed for these preparation exercises!

My philosophy is to break one exercise down into lots of tiny steps. We will use the 'ask and release' method. Release the moment your horse understands what you are asking - and is thinking what you are thinking. This might mean they might have not actually finished the exercise you asked them, but have shown you that they understand the first part of it. For example, they might have changed their weight to prepare for what you wanted them to do. Remember - your patience is the key to helping your horse figure this all out!

Groundwork exercises

Equipment: I use a high quality rope halter and a 12 foot rope without a clip when doing groundwork with my horses. I find a 12 foot lead rope is much easier to use for groundwork exercises than a shorter lead rope.

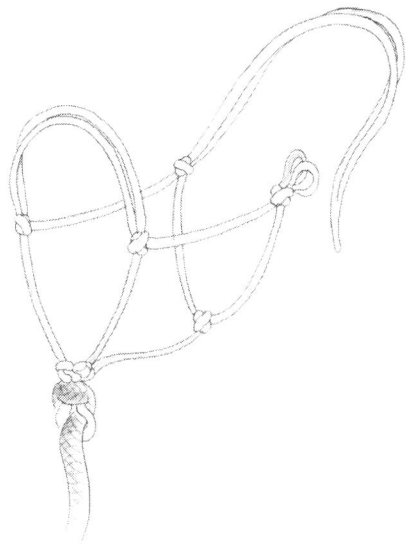

I do not like a clip on the lead rope as it adds unwanted weight to the rope and it interferes with the smooth (and small) signals from the end of the rope that's in my hand. When buying a rope halter, make sure it's of high quality. Many are cheaply made and are too stiff. A rope halter should only be worn by a horse when there is a human holding the end of the lead rope. Never have a horse loose in a field or tied up anywhere while wearing a rope halter.

1 - Bending from poll to withers

Let's start with asking our horse to bend their neck a little from poll to withers. This is also knows as lateral flexion. When we ride our horses we need them to be able to bend their neck a little, both right and left, from a tiny rein cue. You can prepare for this by first working with your horse on the ground.

- Have only a halter and lead rope on your horse.
- Stand beside your horse in line with their shoulder.
- Pick up the lead rope as if it was a rein.
- Ask your horse to turn their head a little towards you using small cues, using your fingers to play on the rein, then release as soon as they make the slightest move.

The slightest move of your horse can be quite subtle at first. Even if you just feel a softening of their neck in your direction, release the rope completely and tell them how clever they are. Initially your horse might not move, but don't release until they make some small change. Just playing with the lead rope gently until there's a tiny change in their thought can often bring about a change.

The goal of this flexion practise is a gentle bend to the side with softness through your horse's neck. But we are not going to make them do this with physical force! Instead we're going to help them to do this by communicating with them and releasing the pressure at the moment they are thinking what we are thinking - when they show in the smallest way that they are starting to understand what is being asked of them.

When we are training our horses, we want to 'help' them, not 'make' them. Changing this one word in your vocabulary can dramatically improve your results and your horsemanship skills.

This is a multi-session exercise. You will find that you have to teach each side of your horse separately. Just because they have learned to follow a feel and bend their neck to the right, doesn't mean they can automatically do that to the left. You need to teach it again from the start on the left. Most horses will find lateral flexion much easier on one side than the other, so if they seem more responsive on one side bear this in mind.

Remember - whatever your final goal is - break down each big exercise into lots of tiny steps. Work on each step individually.

Whatever you are doing, when you see that tiny change, release the lead rope and give them a rest and praise.

2 - Moving the shoulders sideways at halt

To get a nice bend on a circle or corner, we need to be able to move our horse's shoulders independently. This is called a forequarter yield. So let's practise and move your horse's shoulder one step to the side. Your horse just needs a halter and 12 foot lead rope.

A common problem is a lot of horses will do the opposite - they push their shoulder into you, instead of stepping away from you! This encourages falling in and makes balanced circles and corners really tricky. So instead we will teach them to move (yield) their shoulders away from you, beginning when they are standing still. You will do this in both directions, but begin just on one side for a few days, until your horse figures it out.

- Stand in front of your horse and hold the lead rope in your hand - if you are going to ask your horse to move to your right, have the rope in your right hand. Have slack in the lead rope.
- Take your hand out to the side just enough to ask your horse to flex in that direction.

- As your horse starts to flex, walk towards their shoulder and move/twirl the end of the rope in your other hand just enough to encourage them to step over to the side.

Be happy with just one step at first and build up steps from there. This can be a bit confusing for the horse at first and they may start to walk forward.

Generally if you get the timing of lifting your rope for flexion and walking towards the shoulder right, it will all come together. My tip is to try this on a human friend a few times, until you've worked it out for yourself!

3 - Moving the shoulders sideways in walk

Now let's do an exercise while your horse is moving. We are going to ask your horse to move their shoulders away from you while they are walking. Be sure they can already do this at the halt, to increase your chance of success!

Let's give it a try. Your horse needs a halter and 12 foot lead rope.

- Walk forwards with your horse, staying level with their shoulders.
- Hold the lead rope in your outside hand (the hand furthest away from your horse) and the end of the rope in your inside hand.
- Look forward and keep your head up with your focus on where you are going. You will need to feel that your horse is moving forward with some impulsion and energy, because if they are not, they will tend to stop when you ask them to bend. You will be able to use the tail end of the rope to gently encourage them to move forward.
- When you feel that you have enough forward movement, use your outside hand to ask for a soft neck bend and you and your horse will start to walk in an arc.
- Make sure that you stay level with their shoulders.

- If they start to fall in, walk towards them a bit and either touch their shoulder with your fingers, or gently with the rope.
- Now reach over with your inside hand and touch your horse on the girth area, while taking a step sideways yourself towards their shoulder. Try to have a feeling in your body of both of you moving your shoulders together, sideways.

If everything goes to plan your horse will move their shoulder away for a step, while maintaining their forward movement. You will mirror that sideways step with your own body. Your horse will be gently curved around you, looking soft and supple from nose to tail. Asking for this by touching the girth area mirrors your aids when riding. You'll be able to achieve the same result with a gentle touch with the inside of your leg.

Just ask for one step of lateral (sideways) movement first. Then add more steps until you are able to work on a 10 metre circle and yield your horse out to a 20 metre circle, softly, with a gentle bend from nose to tail.

This groundwork exercise will really help you in the saddle. Your horse will find it easier to understand your aids. You will ask gently for the inside bend from the rein, touch your lower leg on the girth area, and 'feel' your inside seat bone - then you will feel your horse yield softly out on the circle.

4 - Moving the hindquarters sideways at halt

It is very useful to also be able to move our horse's hindquarters independently. Maybe we need to open a gate, or step our horse's hindquarters out of the way of a person or car on the road. This is called a hindquarter yield. So let's practise and move your horse's hindquarters one step to the side. Your horse needs a halter and 12 foot lead rope.

Before you start this, your horse must be comfortable with your touching their barrel, sides and back. If you have a horse that is in Any way nervous or is not comfortable with you touching these areas on their body – for any reason from being very green or could have a health issue like ulcers, do not do this exercise. If they are nervous or unhappy – you'll see this from their body language – which could range from pinning their ears back, swishing their tail and stepping away, or threatening you with a hind foot - do not proceed or get hurt!

- This is a groundwork exercise.
- With a halter and lead rope on your horse, ask them to stand still beside you.
- Stand at their shoulder, facing forwards.
- Ask for them to turn their head towards you very slightly.

- Imagine you're riding your horse. Note the area on your horse's body where your heel would be, if you put your leg back a little behind the girth line.
- With your free hand, run your hand from the withers to this area.
- Then very lightly tap this area, slowly and gently.
- Your horse will probably be confused! What on earth are you doing?! That's OK. Don't tap harder or faster. We don't want to use strength to push your horse's hind legs over one step. Instead we want him to learn a new cue.
- So stay there, slowly touch and release. You can help by adding a vocal cue.
- Look for ANY shift of weight to the side from your horse. Then release, reward and praise them. We're not looking for a full step yet.
- If your horse is very confused, you can also help him a little by asking for a little more bend in his neck.
- Again, look for ANY shift of weight to the side from your horse. Then release, reward and praise them. We're still not looking for a full step yet.
- Do this only on one side, until your horse starts to figure it out. It will probably take 1-2 minutes over a few days.
- Then start from the beginning on the other side.
- When both sides are great on the ground, repeat in the saddle at halt.

Collection

People will discuss a horse being on the bit, taking up a contact, being 'round' and working in an 'outline'. It's very common for riders and trainers to be looking for a horse to be in a particular shape, with their head in a certain position, to show that they are collected.

In fact, these days there is a hyper fixation on the horse's head position. *This is incredibly unhealthy for the horse.*

The truth about collection is that it is not making a horse move in a particular shape or forcing their head and neck into an 'outline'. It actually refers to the balance of the entire horse's body.

Collection is simply a shift of weight from the forequarters to the hindquarters.

Collection helps the horse to carry the rider's weight in a way that is more balanced and athletic.

The aim is to have the horse working in true self-carriage without the need for the rider to physically hold them with their hands or legs to maintain that. Horses have no problem working in true self-carriage when they are playing in the field, but they need help to do the same when they are carrying a rider's weight. When the horse's balance shifts more to the hindquarters, a few things happen.

- One or both hind legs step under their body more deeply.
- The angle of their pelvis changes.
- The core muscles engage.
- Their back lifts.
- Their withers lift.
- Finally, the angle of the neck and head changes naturally as a result of all of these other changes. The neck will be flexed softly at the poll, which will be the highest point on the horse. If a horse's neck is flexed behind the poll it isn't being ridden in a collected way, it is being ridden with force.

Their back will stop hollowing, which will enable them to carry their rider more easily and help to avoid them getting back problems. They will be able to carry themselves and they will feel light and relaxed under their rider. There will be no feeling of heaviness in the hands and the horse should be able to carry out the movements we ask easily.

Collection doesn't look the same for all horses, because different breeds are built differently, but all horses can offer it to us if we ask them in the right way. If we concentrate on working through specific exercises that encourage them to step under more deeply with their hind legs, in groundwork and ridden work, and without trying to force a shape on them, they will find collection and self-carriage themselves.

To improve your horse's collection, balance and self-carriage, there are some proven training exercises you can work on that encourage your horse to change their posture and balance, including:

- Backup exercises
- Backwards circles
- Halt and backup
- Trot, halt and backup
- Canter, trot, halt and backup
- Sideways
- Shoulder out
- Shoulder-in
- Spirals
- Teardrops

And the good news is that all of these exercises can be done with poles!

Collection is developed by teaching yourself and your horse the exercises above – and not by pulling on the reins. A forced head position is not collection - it's just a visible indication of a harmful, uneducated and physically damaging horse training method.

I have included many useful and fun lateral work exercises in this polework book that will help your horse to collect and find self-carriage. They are a great way to work on correct muscle development. They will also develop balance in yourself and your horse.

Try them first without poles over a few days. Then when your horse has figured them out, add in poles to spice things up and add more fun to your training!

If anything starts to feel confusing, or you are feeling frustrated or impatient, take a short break. Be ready to go back a few steps. Go slower, and take a few minutes to figure out how you can make the lesson easier for your horse to understand.

It's not your job to force your horse to do any of these exercises. It is your responsibility to be a kind, patient, supportive teacher who is quick to praise, notice when your horse is trying and make your time together fun and enjoyable for both of you.

Collection exercises

In this book I've included quite a few collection exercises you can do with poles. Under each polework exercise, you'll see which ones I designed to help your horse collect, and also what movement is needed - from backup and leg yield, to shoulder in and out and sidepass.

If you already understand how to do these exercises smoothly and lightly, you can skip ahead to the polework exercises in the second half of this book.

But if any of these exercises are new to you, or you'd like to improve them, I have included step by step instructions below for you. No poles are needed at this stage. This is preparation work! Have fun with your horse, and remember it's not about focusing on your end goal - it's actually about enjoying all the little steps on your journey to get there.

****

When a horse backs up smoothly and without hesitation, their posture automatically changes. When you watch a horse doing this correctly, ridden or in the paddock, you'll see their hindquarters drop a little, their back round and their withers lift. This is the result of a shift in weight from the forequarters to the hindquarters, also known as collection. So we're going to ask your horse to do some backup exercises to help him develop collection.

We are going to start on the ground, without poles to keep it simple. All you will need is a halter and a lead rope on your horse. I like the 12 foot lead ropes that do not have a clip, as they are kinder on the horse.

When you have these exercises working well without poles, then you can have fun with the polework collection exercises later on in this book.

Backup on the ground (straight line)

Having a good, soft backup is essential for collection. It teaches your horse to easily and smoothly shift their weight to their hind end. Your horse just needs to be wearing a halter and lead rope for this exercise.

First of all, see if your horse can offer you a 'soft feel'. This means that your horse is able to softly flex at the poll, feeling relaxed and light in your hand. You can't force this, but it's something horses find easy once they understand what is being asked of them.

Stand beside your horse's head, facing your horse's hindquarters. Take hold of the lead rope just under the knot where it attaches to the halter, with your hand closed as a gentle fist, your thumb closest to the ground. Put the tiniest, smallest, downward feeling into your hand and see if your horse responds. Reward the tiniest response by instantly opening your hand completely.

If you feel your horse just flex their poll - release. You are looking to progress to the point where you put the softest feeling into the rope and your horse flexes beautifully from the poll and drops their head slightly. If your horse doesn't understand the slight downward feel on the rope you can softly move your hand from side to side to encourage them to loosen their poll and move their head slightly, then ask for down again.

Next, ask for a soft feel, while looking straight back past your horse's tail. Keep exactly the same feeling in your hand, think about moving backward and gently rotate your hand up towards your horse's jawline, to give them the feeling of asking for a backward step.

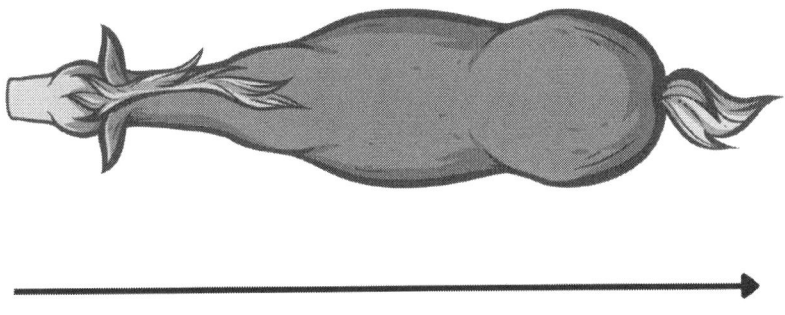

As always, at first reward the thought of back, even if it's just a tiny shift of weight. Release fully. Gradually build up to a point where your horse steps back easily without putting any weight in the halter. A good backup will feel as if there is nothing in your hand, no weight at all. This may take a few days, but take your time, it will be worth it!

This exercise takes feel, timing and patience. You can't rush it or force it.

Backup circle on the ground

When your straight line backup is good, with no weight in your hand, it's time to move on to backing your horse up in a circle. All you need is your horse wearing a halter and 12 foot lead rope.

Your goal is to have your horse walk a circle backwards, with their nose tipped out of the circle a little. If you visualise this in your mind it will help you to carry out the exercise.

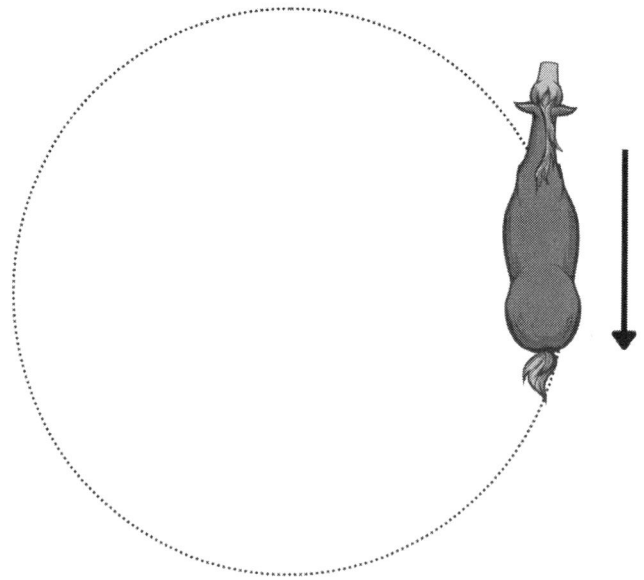

You will be facing your horse's tail and you will be walking forwards. Ask your horse for a couple of steps backwards in a straight line. While your horse is moving use your hand on the rope to tip their head slightly away from you, so they are looking outside the circle. If they are responsive to your hand you should find that they automatically start to walk backwards on a circle. If they are not, that's ok too! This takes a while for the horse to figure out – and that's completely normal!

If you look at their front hooves while you are walking, you want the outside front hoof to take 1 step to the outside, and you want the inside front hoof to take a step backwards.

Be patient, reward the first good step and build up from there. This type of exercise will be new to most horses and it requires them to use their body in a way that is physically demanding, so be prepared to develop the circle over a numbers of days.

At the beginning, the circle is usually quite large. It's often a different size circle on both sides of your horse. As your horse figures it out and more bend naturally begins to develop through their whole body, you'll notice they will find it easier and the circles will become a little smaller naturally.

Backup when riding

- Repeat the straight line backup exercise. Start at halt. Raise your energy in the saddle, sit up tall so your horse can feel you are alert, awake and about to ask him to do something!
- For the first few times, have someone nearby who can help your horse to understand by doing the groundwork version of this exercise with them while you're in the saddle.
- Think backwards, move your shoulders slightly backwards, and wait until you feel a TINY change in your horse's balance. We use minimal reins here. The goal is that the cue comes from your body movement, not your hands. You actually want your horse to backup without using your reins! You don't need a full backwards step yet, just a weight / balance change. Then release the reins, relax, keep breathing, take a rest and praise your horse.

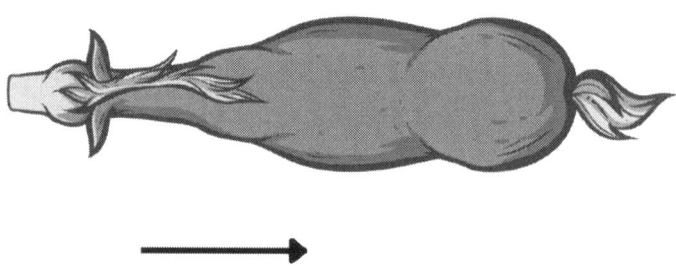

Halt and backup

It's very important your horse stops when you say so - not 2, 3 or 5 steps later. In practical terms, if you see something dangerous, loose wire, an animal or something else unexpected on the ground, stopping at the very moment you ask could mean the difference between a healthy horse, and a horse with their leg badly cut up from wire and/or an expensive vet bill.

Horses can use their bodies in a few ways to halt. Sometimes they stop, but in an un-athletic manner with a lot of weight dumped on their front two legs.

To the rider, they will feel heavy in your hands, and they will not feel ready to do any type of athletic movement. This can be a habit, and this can also be the result of being ridden a lot with heavy hands, and they have got into the habit of leaning on your heavy hands. This way of stopping will not develop collection or improve your horse's balance much.

We've already been working on backup with your horse to develop collection. So we're going to use that exercise to help us with your halt!

The secret to a good halt is a good backup! Most of us find that when our horse halts they push a little into our hands. Some horses push a lot, with others it's more subtle, but it's there. This means that they are still thinking 'forwards' when they have stopped, but also that their weight is mostly on their front end.

When you ask your horse to move forward from a halt like this your horse will set off with their weight on their front end, rather than their hind end. If you're looking for collection you're on the back foot (hoof!) straight away.

Wouldn't it be great to find a way to help your horse to learn to halt without putting their weight forwards and leaning on your hands? A way to have them balanced, with their weight on their hind end before they set off again?

There's a very simple way to teach a horse to halt in balance, and maintain that balance when they depart. It involves teaching them to think 'back' instead of forward when they halt.

To ask for backup, soften your body, relax and breathe out. Keep your shoulders back and actually think 'back'. Keep enough feeling on your reins to discourage your horse from stepping forward, but don't add any rein pressure unless your horse doesn't understand the first cues. If you need to pick up on the rein, think about asking one front foot at a time. Feel for your horse's balance.

When this is easy for your horse, you are ready for the next stage! We're going to try to walk, stop and backup smoothly with feel.

- Pick a spot in the arena you'll use. Maybe it's level with a pole or barrel.
- When you reach that spot in walk, breathe out deeply, think backwards, move your shoulders slightly backwards. Use minimal reins here. It'll probably take your horse a few steps to realise what you're doing. That's fine!
- When your horse stops, don't do anything new with your reins. Instead keep thinking backwards, keep your shoulders slightly backwards. The goal is that the cue comes from your body movement and your thought - not your hands.
- When you get a weight change backwards (maybe not even a full step yet!), release the reins, relax, keep breathing and praise your horse.
- Do this a few times and notice the difference in performance between the 1st time you did this, and the 3rd or 4th time. Praise your horse for being wonderful.

Tip: Each day, pick the same spot in your paddock and arena, and use this as your exact stop to ask your horse to halt. If you do it in the same place two or three times, it makes it easier for your horse to figure it out. But after this, change the spot every day, so it doesn't become a habit. Once your horse has figured it out, you can do it in a different place each time.

Don't use this as just an exercise in your paddock or arena. The key to helping horses is to be consistent. So when you start learning this method, and you go out for a hack - ask for a backup every time you halt. Every single time!

At first this exercise will feel like two elements - first the halt, then the backup. You'll stop and your horse will have a little think before responding to your ask for a backup. When your horse understands what you are asking, this will change and your halt and backup will be one fluid movement.

You should build on this lovely halt and shift of balance and see if you can maintain that feeling when you ask your horse for a couple of steps of walk.

Don't ask too much at first. It's physically demanding for a horse to change their way of going. Just get one or two nice balanced steps then halt, backup and thank your horse for being wonderful.

As time goes on you won't need to physically backup every time you halt, because your horse will understand and you will have such a soft halt. You will be able to feel your horse has their weight on their hind end when they stop. But don't stop altogether. Make sure to add in the occasional backup from halt, so that your horse doesn't forget and fall back into bad habits. Any time you feel that the halt is getting unbalanced, any time you feel that weight in your reins, go back to backing up for every halt. Your horse will remember what's needed very quickly. In fact, they seem to realise that this is a comfortable way for them to do things and seek that softness and balance.

Having a good, balanced halt can save your life. If you have to ride out on the roads, you need your horse to have a good halt and to not be thinking about moving forwards - however long you need to wait at a road junction. If you're out in the countryside you might need to halt because of a hazard you've spotted that your horse hasn't. Horses need to stop with their body and their mind.

Trot, halt and backup

Now we're going to repeat the halt from a trot. So will do a trot, halt, backup. The aim is for this to all be in one movement.

Remember the cues for halt and backup and use them consistently. Aim to halt with as little rein as possible. You might find that when you're going faster it helps to put your feet forward a little, to avoid you coming off over your horse's shoulder if your horse does a very fast halt! Then when your horse halts, immediately, as before, soften your body, relax and breathe out, keep your shoulders back and think 'back'. Only add rein pressure if you need to, and if you do, think about lifting one hoof at a time.

Shoulder-out (groundwork)

Shoulder-out is a lateral (sideways) exercise. Shoulder out is an exercise I like to teach first on the ground and then, once the horse and the human understand it, we can repeat it in the saddle. I teach my horse shoulder out first, as it's easier for them to understand. After shoulder out is good, you can move onto shoulder-in.

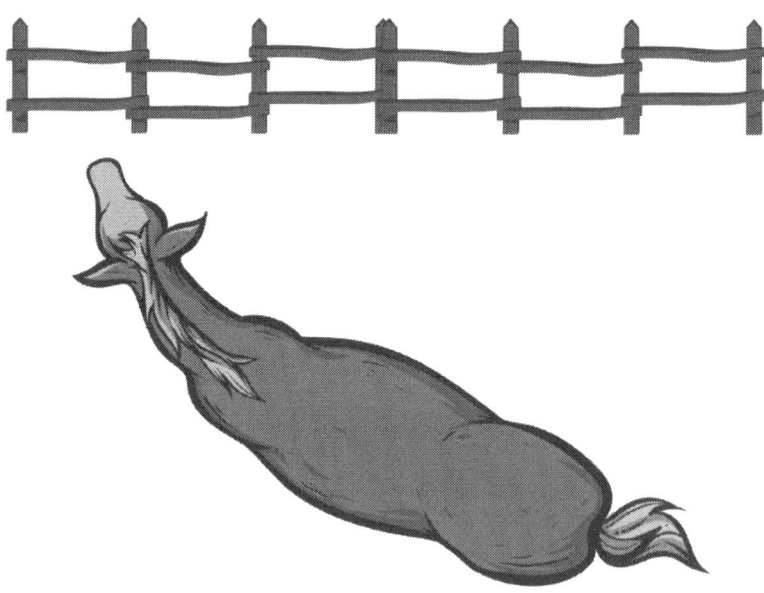

Shoulder out means your horse is looking to the outside – to your arena fence line or along a wall or towards a paddock fence. Looking towards a physical fence really helps your horse with this exercise as it stops them pushing forwards. We are looking for a gentle bend through your horse's whole body - not just in the neck.

Shoulder-in and shoulder-out are very similar. In shoulder out the horse's head is pointing towards the fence line to the outside of the arena, with their hindquarters more towards the inside of the arena. During shoulder-in, the horse's head is pointing towards the inside of the arena, with their hindquarters closer to the fence line.

I also have some good news for you! You do not need a dressage arena to do this! You can do this on trail rides, along a fence line, even with some poles on the ground when your horse figures it out!

How to teach shoulder-out:

- This is a groundwork exercise.
- First make sure that your horse is comfortable with you touching their hindquarters all over and moving close to their back end.
- Check that your horse has remembered their lessons on moving their hindquarters by asking them to move just one step, by touching their ribcage, just behind the girth, where your foot would be if you were riding.
- You are going to work along the fence line of your arena or exercise paddock. Walk along the fence at your horse's shoulder, with you between them and the fence.
- Look ahead and make sure that you are both facing forward.
- Do this a few times in both directions. At the beginning, a fence line helps both you and your horse, as it will naturally

block their forwards movement and help them to move sideways instead.

- Walk along the fence line again, this time allowing your horse to drift ahead of you a little as you go. There should be plenty of room to do this when you are using a 12 foot line.

- As your horse starts to get ahead, they will naturally start to move sideways, looking out of the arena. You will be walking towards their ribs and shoulder, which will help the sideways movement.

- Build this up slowly. Just get one step of lateral movement then ask your horse to go straight. If you ask for too much too soon your horse is likely to get confused.

Common problems:

The most common setback I see when people are learning this exercise is their horse stopping when they start to bend, rather than continuing to walk forward. This is all about impulsion – the horse and human need to be stepping out smartly together, looking forward and with a rhythm about their walk. Bear this in mind if things start to grind to a halt!

Just by doing this shoulder-out exercise you will see a lot of benefits:

- It will improve your horse's balance.

- It will encourage your horse to transfer weight from forequarters to hindquarters.
- It will help your horse become more athletic.
- It will improve your horse's physical posture.
- It is the beginning of collection (which is the healthiest way for a horse to carry the weight of a rider).
- It will help the horse to be able to move and turn with more agility and flexibility.
- When you ride your horse will feel lighter and more responsive to smaller cues.

Now, you might be thinking, do you need some sort of fancy dressage horse to do this? The answer is no. Any horse can do this! From quarter horses and Arabs to thoroughbreds, paints and cobs.

Shoulder-out (riding)

We have looked at how you can start this on the ground with your horse. Now it's time to repeat the same exercise in the saddle.

First we need your horse to have a little energy and to feel relaxed and confident. If your horse has zero energy this is going to be tricky because they will not have enough 'forward'. If your horse is worried or anxious, this is going to be tricky too. You are better off fixing those issues first, before you try shoulder-out.

- Ask your horse to walk along a fence line. You will be very aware that you are looking straight ahead, and not down at your horse's head. This is very important.
- Now walk along the fence line again. Ask your horse for a gentle neck bend to the outside.
- You will keep looking straight ahead (look where you're going!) and now you will also ask your horse to create a little bend in their body towards the fence, by lifting your weight a fraction from the seat bone that is closest to the inside of the arena, which will create a gentle bend in your horse's body.
- Make sure your leg which is closest to the inside of the arena is hardly touching your horse at all.
- Finally, move your leg which is closest to the fence line backwards just a fraction to encourage your horse to move

their hindquarters a little more towards the middle of the arena.
- Once you get even one step of a sideways movement stop asking your horse to go sideways and walk forwards normally, along the fence line.

Only ask for one step! Don't get greedy.

This is an athletic movement you are asking your horse to do, so just ask for a little when you begin.

Shoulder-in

Shoulder-in is the same exercise, but instead of the horse looking out of the arena, they are looking into the arena. If you used a fence line during shoulder-out, it helped to stop your horse pushing forwards. But with shoulder-in, you don't have the fence line to help you if your horse decides to push forwards! So make sure your backup and shoulder-out exercises are good, light and flowing before you try shoulder-in.

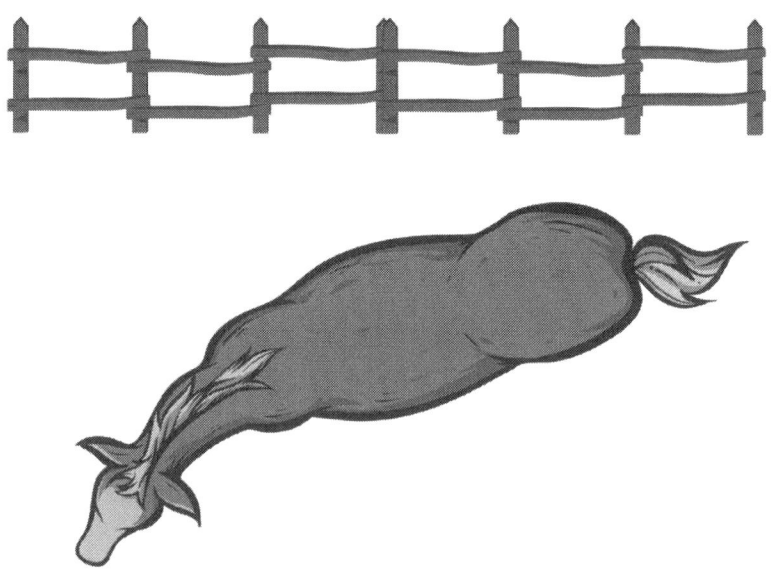

Sidepass

There are some exercises in this book that require your horse to move sideways over a pole on the ground. His two front hooves will be on one side of the pole, and his two hind hooves will be on the other side of the pole.

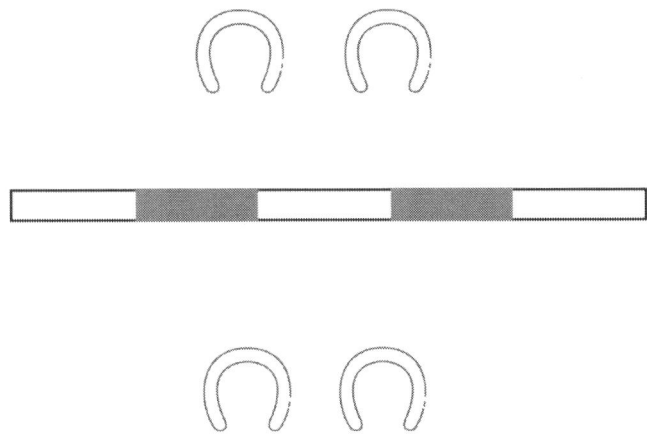

To teach it, I like to ask in two parts. First ask the horse to move one end to the side for 1 step (his two front legs), and after this is done, the second part is to ask the horse to move the other end to the side for 1 step (his two hind legs).

The good news is you have already done this! Earlier in this book you taught your horse the forequarter yield and hindquarter yield. Let's break it down into smaller parts first.

Sidepass in front of half a pole

This is a groundwork exercise. With a halter and lead rope, walk up to the middle of a pole on the ground with your horse. Your horse's front feet will be inches away from the pole. Stand at the side of your horse, and ask them to move their forequarters 1 step away from you – but not to walk over the pole! Take your time.

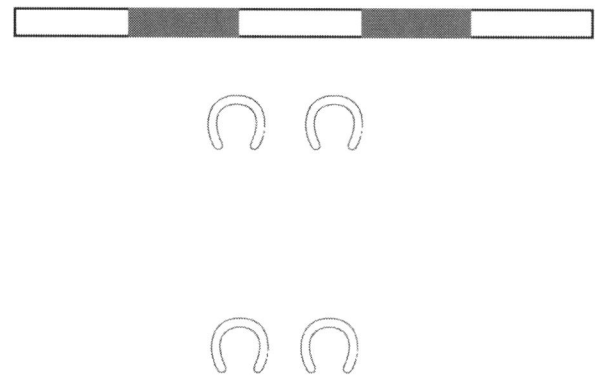

After this, ask them to move their hindquarters 1 step away from you – but not to walk over the pole! Take your time again. Then repeat this for another step, and then another step until your horse no longer has the pole in front of him. Give your horse a few minutes rest on a loose rope, praise them and let them yawn and lick and chew if they want to. Do this once or twice per session, for a few sessions. When it's good on one side, they start from scratch on the other side. Remember lots of rest and praise.

Sidepass over half a pole

This is a groundwork exercise. Make life easier for your horse and only do this when you've successful completed the previous exercise. Always set your horse up for success.

With a halter and lead rope, walk up to the middle of a pole on the ground with your horse, until your horse has 2 front feet on one side of the pole and 2 hind feet on the other side.

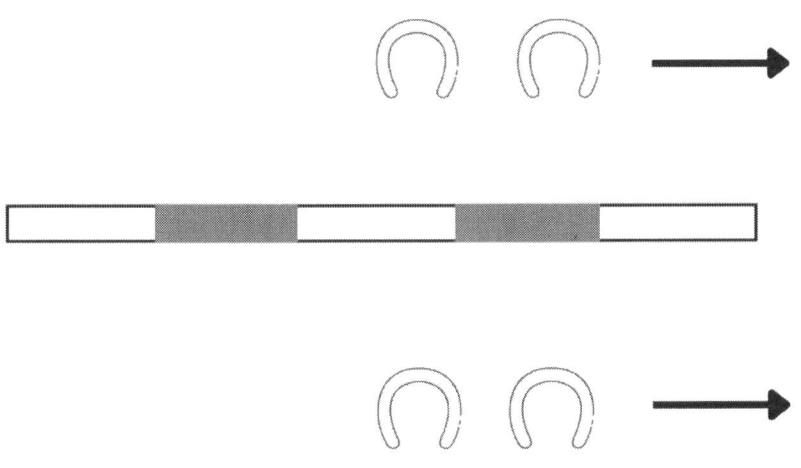

Stand at the side of your horse, and ask them to move their forequarters 1 step away from you – but not to walk over the pole! Take your time.

After this, ask them to move their hindquarters 1 step away from you – but not to walk over the pole! Take your time again.

Then repeat this for another step, and then another step until your horse no longer has the pole in front of him. Give your horse a few minutes rest on a loose rope, praise them and let them yawn and lick and chew if they want to. Do this once or twice per session, for a few sessions. When it's good on one side, they start from scratch on the other side. Remember lots of rest and praise.

Groundwork polework exercises

All of the polework exercises in this book can be done in hand or when riding. Doing them in hand can be useful when you are short on time, the weather is bad, the footing is not great or for many other reasons.

Groundwork polework exercises are a great way to connect and have fun with your horse, while improving their balance, agility, flexibility, muscle tone and suppleness. And they are useful for younger horses, retired horses and horses being rehabilitated (with the approval of your vet/physiotherapist) also.

1 Pole Challenge

Ask your horse to put their near feet on one side of the pole, and their off feet on the other side of the pole.

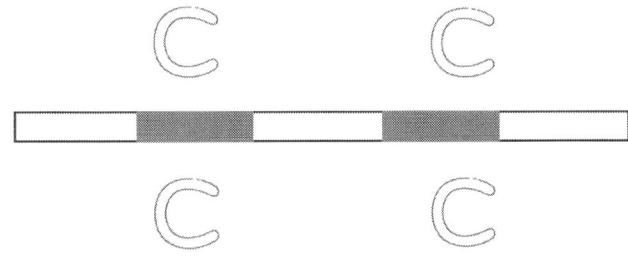

There is not one 'correct' way to do this. You can ask your horse to stand beside the pole, then step over it with two feet. Or you can walk up to the end pole and then ask your horse to get into position.

There is no time limit. This challenge will improve your feel & timing. It will also improve your horse's proprioception, awareness of where to put their feet & trust in you.

Some horses can do this in 3-5 minutes. Some horses can need 5 to 7 days to figure this out. And that's ok! The time required does not matter. Each horse is different. This is quite a challenging exercise, so be patient & reward your horse when they move in the right direction.

The Spider

Get four poles. Put them in a cross shape, with all four ends touching in the middle. Raise the four outer ends up a few inches. This is a great exercise both for groundwork and riding. For groundwork, you can walk over it with your horse, or you can have them on a longer lead rope and they walk over it by themselves. It looks odd, so allow your horse time to build their confidence and get used to it! Try it in lots of different directions.

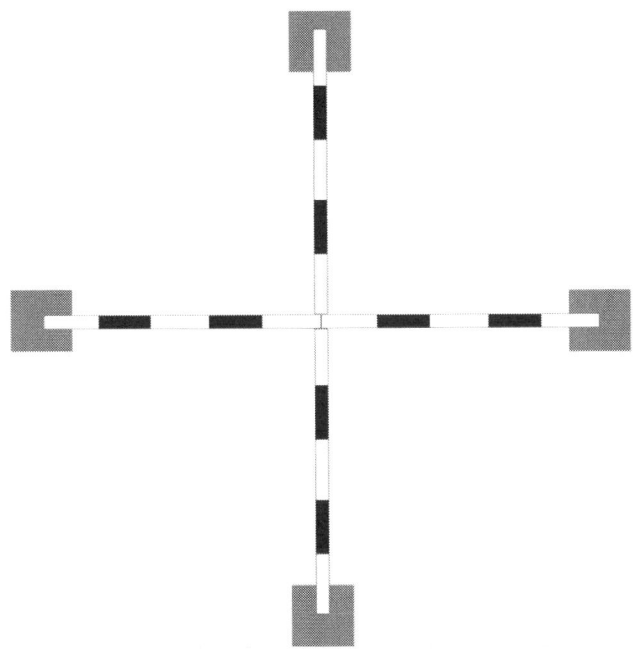

Polework exercises

Congratulations! All your prepartaion work is done. In the next section of this book you will find lots of polework exercises. They are arranged in order of how many poles you will need. Under each exercise is some useful information. You can check the level of difficulty, how many poles you will need, the benefits of each exercise, what gaits each exercise is suitable for and what lateral movements are needed.

Have fun with your horse!

Instructions

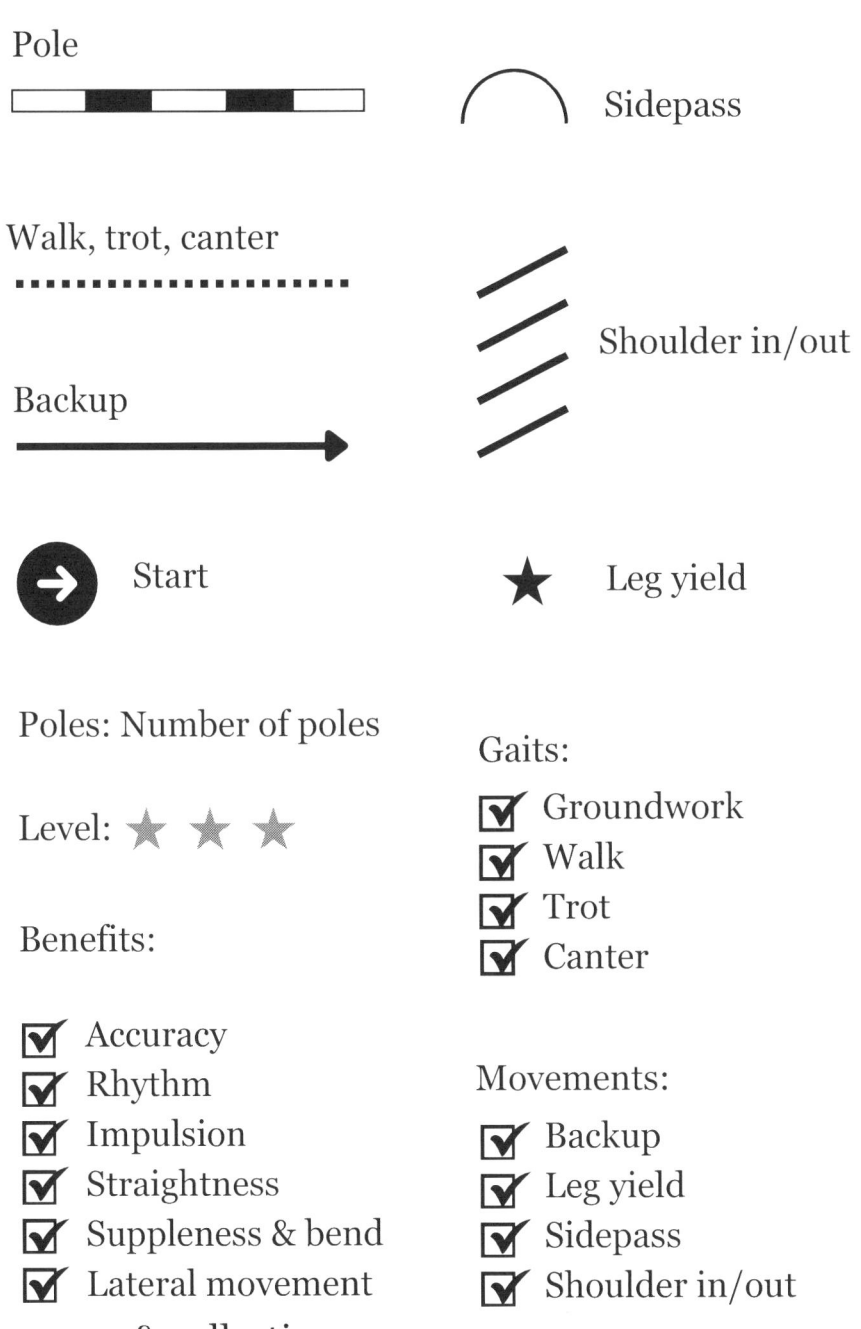

Pole

Sidepass

Walk, trot, canter

Shoulder in/out

Backup

Start

Leg yield

Poles: Number of poles

Level: ★ ★ ★

Benefits:

- ☑ Accuracy
- ☑ Rhythm
- ☑ Impulsion
- ☑ Straightness
- ☑ Suppleness & bend
- ☑ Lateral movement & collection

Gaits:

- ☑ Groundwork
- ☑ Walk
- ☑ Trot
- ☑ Canter

Movements:

- ☑ Backup
- ☑ Leg yield
- ☑ Sidepass
- ☑ Shoulder in/out

2 Poles

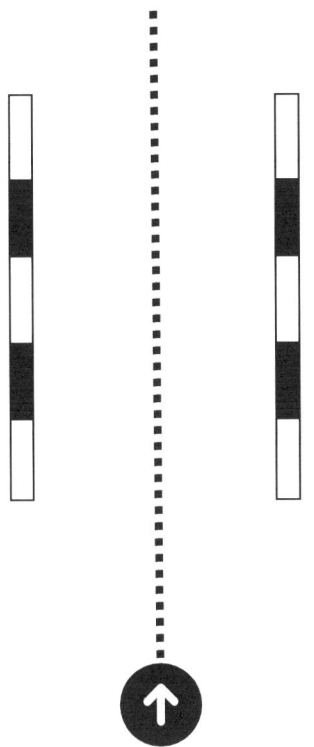

Poles: 4
Level: ★
Benefits:
- ☑ Accuracy
- ☑ Rhythm
- ☑ Impulsion
- ☑ Straightness
- ☐ Suppleness & bend
- ☐ Lateral movement & collection

Gaits:
- ☑ Groundwork
- ☑ Walk
- ☑ Trot
- ☑ Canter

Movements:
- ☐ Backup
- ☐ Leg yield
- ☐ Sidepass
- ☐ Shoulder in/out

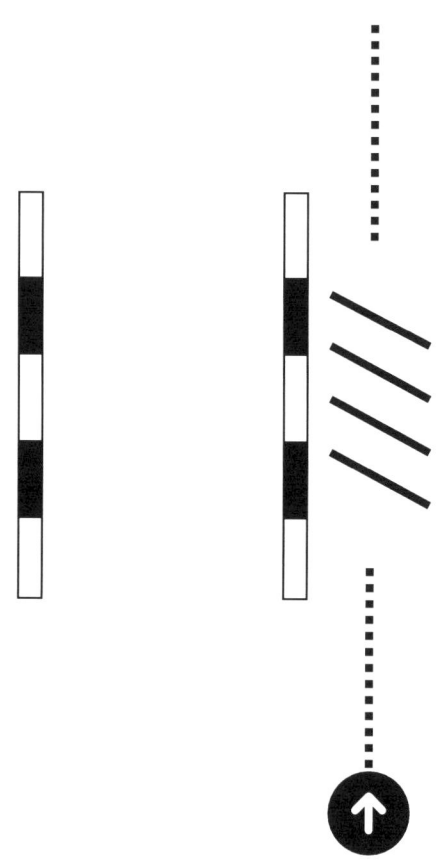

Poles: 4
Level: ★ ★
Benefits:
- ☑ Accuracy
- ☑ Rhythm
- ☑ Impulsion
- ☑ Straightness
- ☑ Suppleness & bend
- ☑ Lateral movement & collection

Gaits:
- ☑ Groundwork
- ☑ Walk
- ☑ Trot
- ☑ Canter

Movements:
- ☐ Backup
- ☐ Leg yield
- ☐ Sidepass
- ☑ Shoulder in

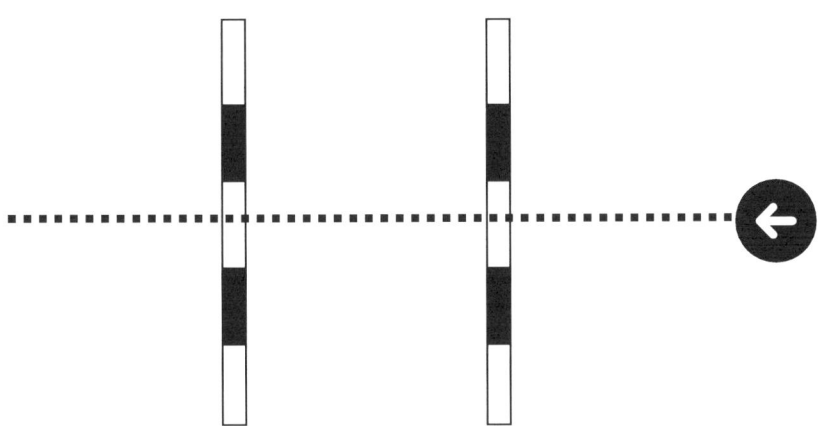

Poles: 4
Level: ★
Benefits:
- ☑ Accuracy
- ☑ Rhythm
- ☑ Impulsion
- ☑ Straightness
- ☐ Suppleness & bend
- ☐ Lateral movement & collection

Gaits:
- ☑ Groundwork
- ☑ Walk
- ☑ Trot
- ☑ Canter

Movements:
- ☐ Backup
- ☐ Leg yield
- ☐ Sidepass
- ☐ Shoulder in/out

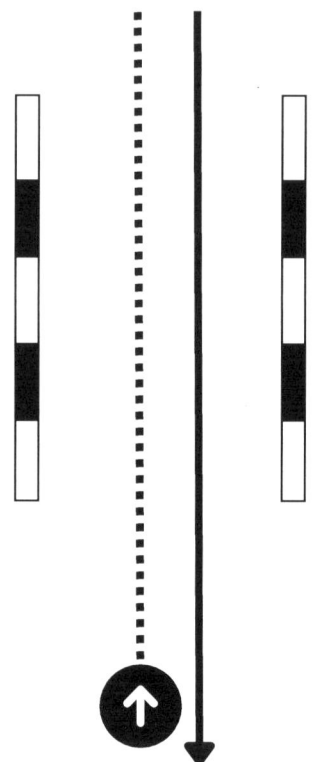

Poles: 4

Level: ★ ★

Benefits:
- ☑ Accuracy
- ☑ Rhythm
- ☑ Impulsion
- ☑ Straightness
- ☐ Suppleness & bend
- ☑ Lateral movement & collection

Gaits:
- ☑ Groundwork
- ☑ Walk
- ☑ Trot
- ☑ Canter

Movements:
- ☑ Backup
- ☐ Leg yield
- ☐ Sidepass
- ☐ Shoulder in/out

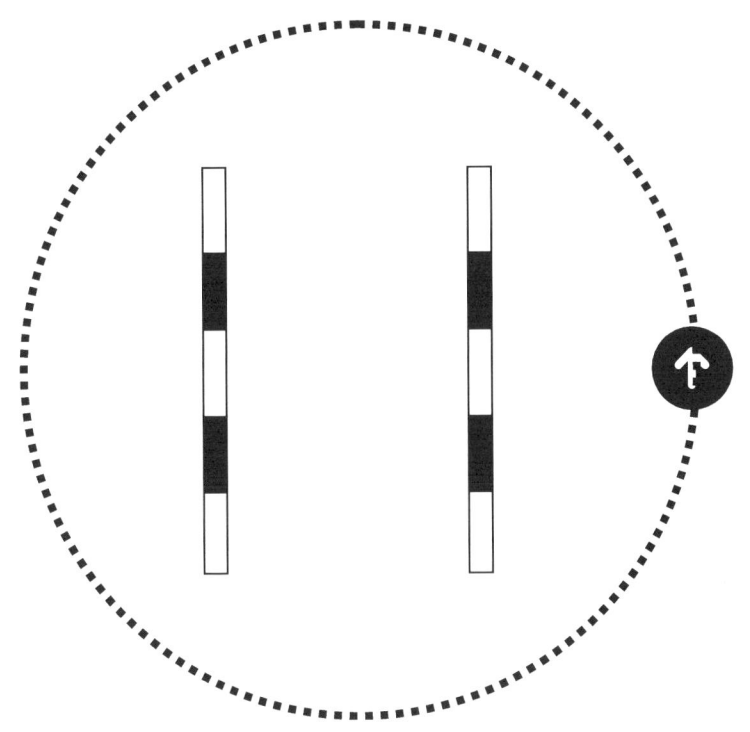

Poles: 4
Level: ★ ★ ★
Benefits:
- ☑ Accuracy
- ☑ Rhythm
- ☐ Impulsion
- ☐ Straightness
- ☑ Suppleness & bend
- ☑ Lateral movement
  & collection

Gaits:
- ☑ Groundwork
- ☑ Walk
- ☐ Trot
- ☐ Canter

Movements:
- ☑ Backup
- ☐ Leg yield
- ☐ Sidepass
- ☐ Shoulder in/out

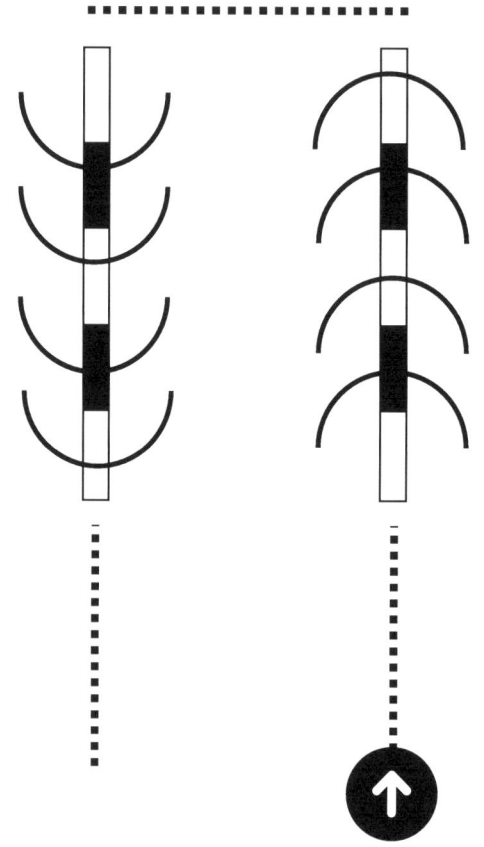

Poles: 4
Level: ★ ★
Benefits:
- ☑ Accuracy
- ☑ Rhythm
- ☑ Impulsion
- ☐ Straightness
- ☑ Suppleness & bend
- ☑ Lateral movement & collection

Gaits:
- ☑ Groundwork
- ☑ Walk
- ☑ Trot
- ☐ Canter

Movements:
- ☐ Backup
- ☐ Leg yield
- ☑ Sidepass
- ☐ Shoulder in/out

3 Poles

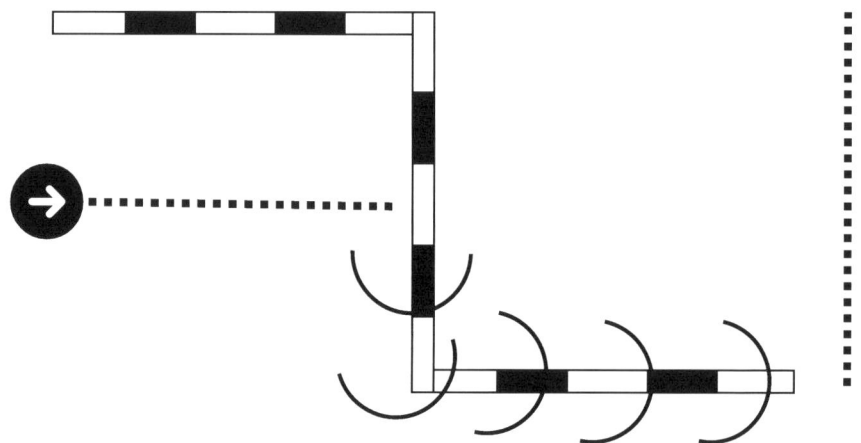

Poles: 4
Level: ★ ★ ★
Benefits:
- ☑ Accuracy
- ☑ Rhythm
- ☑ Impulsion
- ☐ Straightness
- ☐ Suppleness & bend
- ☑ Lateral movement & collection

Gaits:
- ☑ Groundwork
- ☑ Walk
- ☐ Trot
- ☐ Canter

Movements:
- ☐ Backup
- ☐ Leg yield
- ☑ Sidepass
- ☐ Shoulder in/out

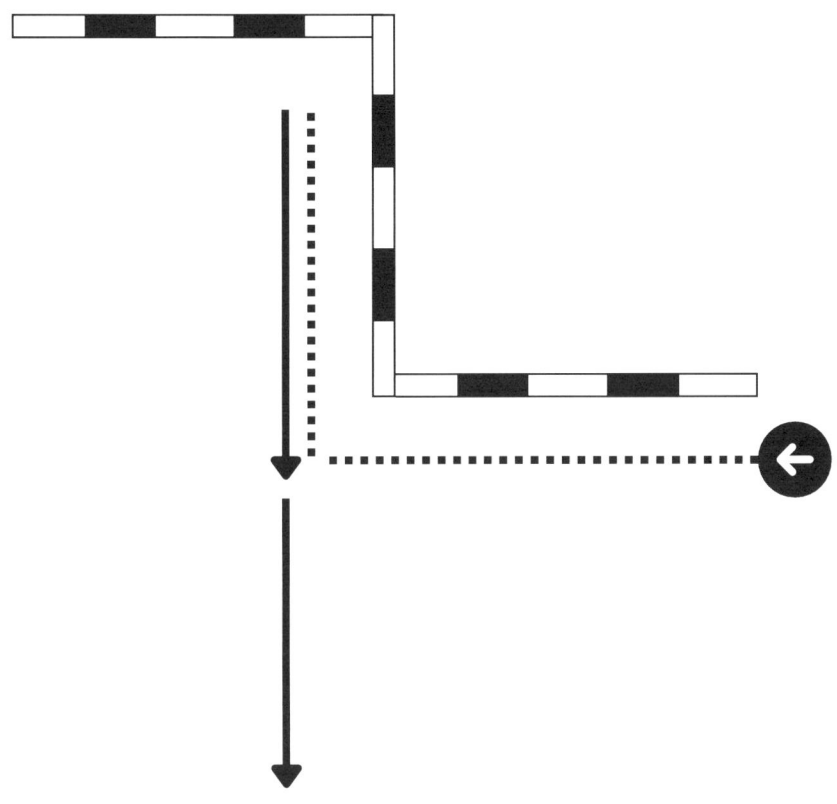

Poles: 4
Level: ★ ★
Benefits:
- ☑ Accuracy
- ☑ Rhythm
- ☑ Impulsion
- ☑ Straightness
- ☐ Suppleness & bend
- ☑ Lateral movement & collection

Gaits:
- ☑ Groundwork
- ☑ Walk
- ☐ Trot
- ☐ Canter

Movements:
- ☑ Backup
- ☐ Leg yield
- ☐ Sidepass
- ☐ Shoulder in/out

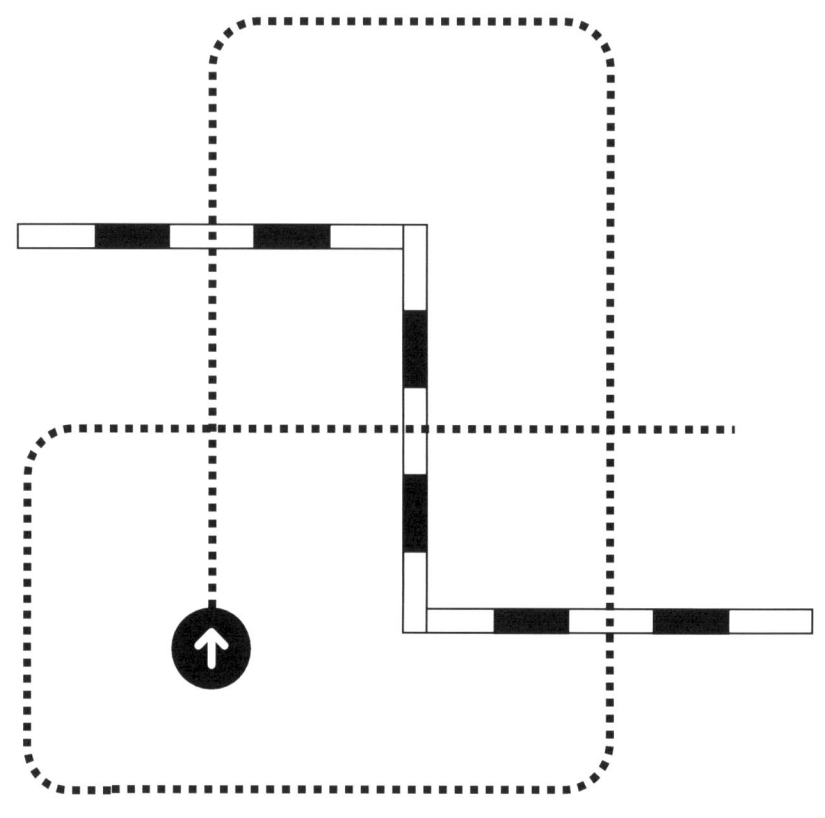

Poles: 4
Level: ⭐
Benefits:
- ☑ Accuracy
- ☑ Rhythm
- ☑ Impulsion
- ☑ Straightness
- ☑ Suppleness & bend
- ☐ Lateral movement & collection

Gaits:
- ☑ Groundwork
- ☑ Walk
- ☑ Trot
- ☐ Canter

Movements:
- ☐ Backup
- ☐ Leg yield
- ☐ Sidepass
- ☐ Shoulder in/out

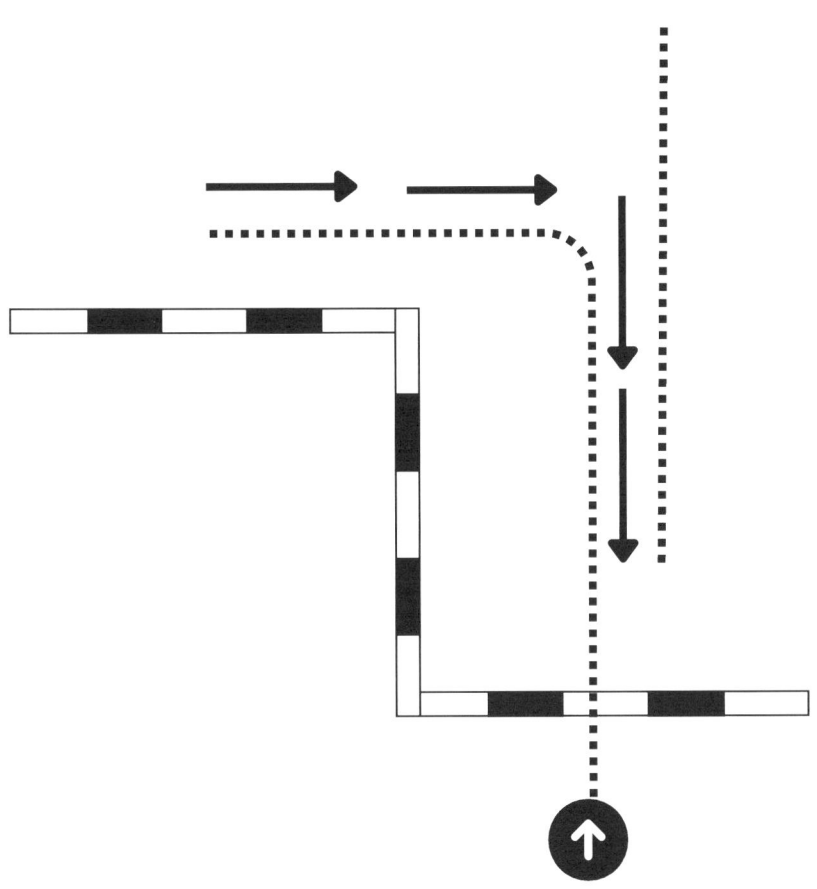

Poles: 4

Level: ★ ★

Benefits:
- ☑ Accuracy
- ☑ Rhythm
- ☑ Impulsion
- ☐ Straightness
- ☑ Suppleness & bend
- ☑ Lateral movement & collection

Gaits:
- ☑ Groundwork
- ☑ Walk
- ☐ Trot
- ☐ Canter

Movements:
- ☑ Backup
- ☐ Leg yield
- ☐ Sidepass
- ☐ Shoulder in/out

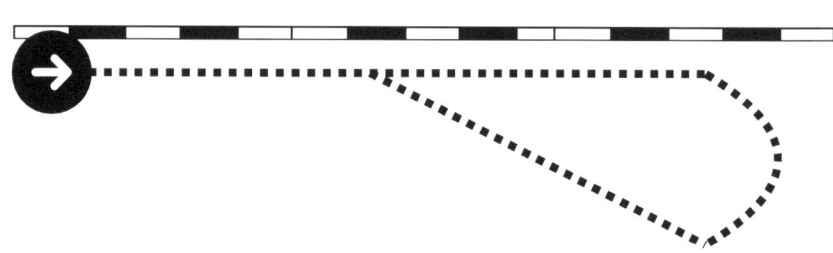

Poles: 4
Level: ★
Benefits:
- ☑ Accuracy
- ☑ Rhythm
- ☑ Impulsion
- ☑ Straightness
- ☑ Suppleness & bend
- ☐ Lateral movement & collection

Gaits:
- ☑ Groundwork
- ☑ Walk
- ☑ Trot
- ☑ Canter

Movements:
- ☐ Backup
- ☐ Leg yield
- ☐ Sidepass
- ☐ Shoulder in/out

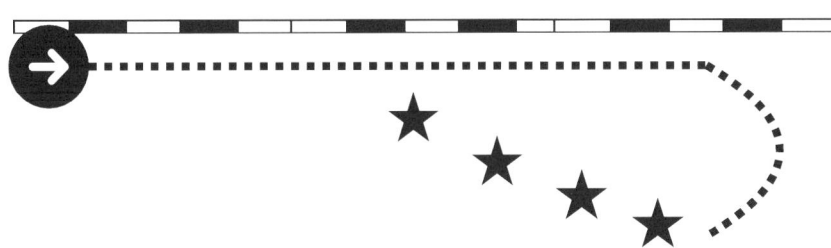

Poles: 4

Level: ★ ★

Benefits:
- ☑ Accuracy
- ☑ Rhythm
- ☑ Impulsion
- ☑ Straightness
- ☑ Suppleness & bend
- ☑ Lateral movement & collection

Gaits:
- ☑ Groundwork
- ☑ Walk
- ☑ Trot
- ☑ Canter

Movements:
- ☐ Backup
- ☑ Leg yield
- ☐ Sidepass
- ☐ Shoulder in/out

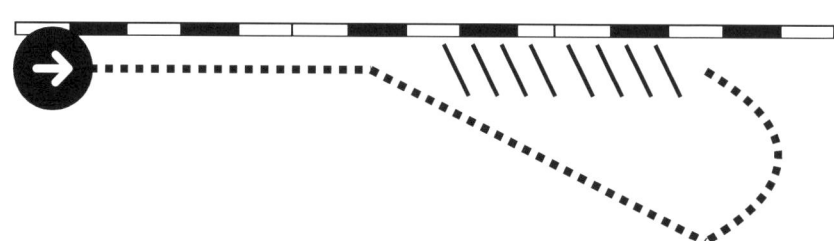

Poles: 4

Level: ★ ★

Benefits:

- ☑ Accuracy
- ☑ Rhythm
- ☑ Impulsion
- ☑ Straightness
- ☑ Suppleness & bend
- ☑ Lateral movement & collection

Gaits:

- ☑ Groundwork
- ☑ Walk
- ☑ Trot
- ☑ Canter

Movements:

- ☐ Backup
- ☐ Leg yield
- ☐ Sidepass
- ☑ Shoulder in

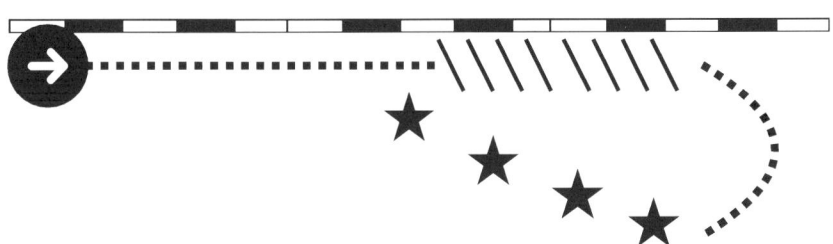

Poles: 4

Level: ★ ★ ★

Benefits:

- ☑ Accuracy
- ☑ Rhythm
- ☑ Impulsion
- ☑ Straightness
- ☑ Suppleness & bend
- ☑ Lateral movement & collection

Gaits:

- ☑ Groundwork
- ☑ Walk
- ☑ Trot
- ☑ Canter

Movements:

- ☐ Backup
- ☑ Leg yield
- ☐ Sidepass
- ☑ Shoulder in

4 Poles

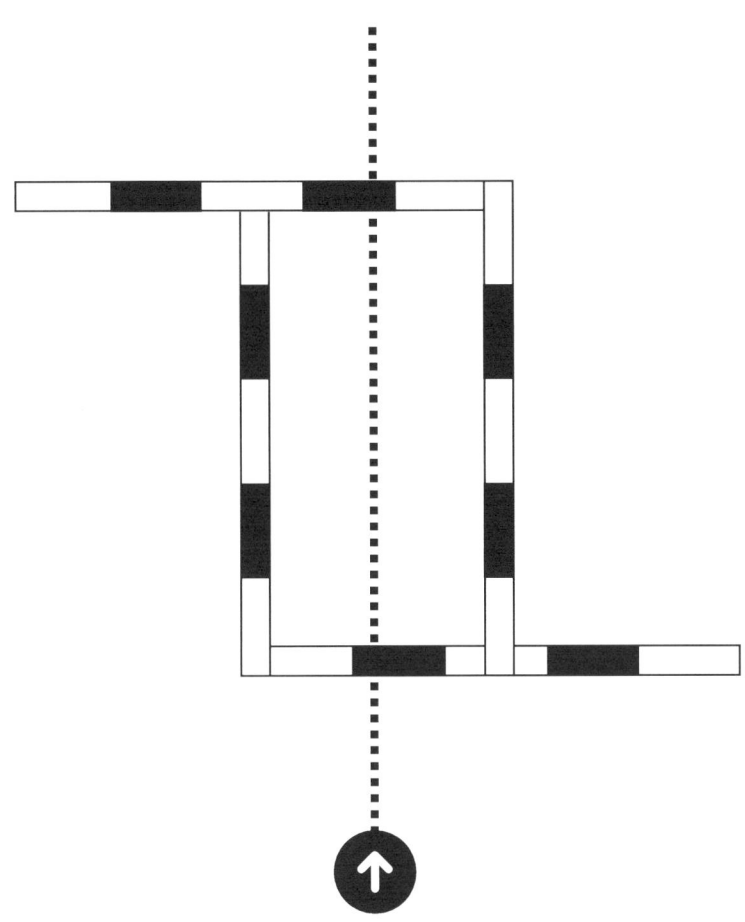

Poles: 4
Level: ★
Benefits:
- ☑ Accuracy
- ☑ Rhythm
- ☑ Impulsion
- ☑ Straightness
- ☐ Suppleness & bend
- ☐ Lateral movement
   & collection

Gaits:
- ☑ Groundwork
- ☑ Walk
- ☑ Trot
- ☑ Canter

Movements:
- ☐ Backup
- ☐ Leg yield
- ☐ Sidepass
- ☐ Shoulder in/out

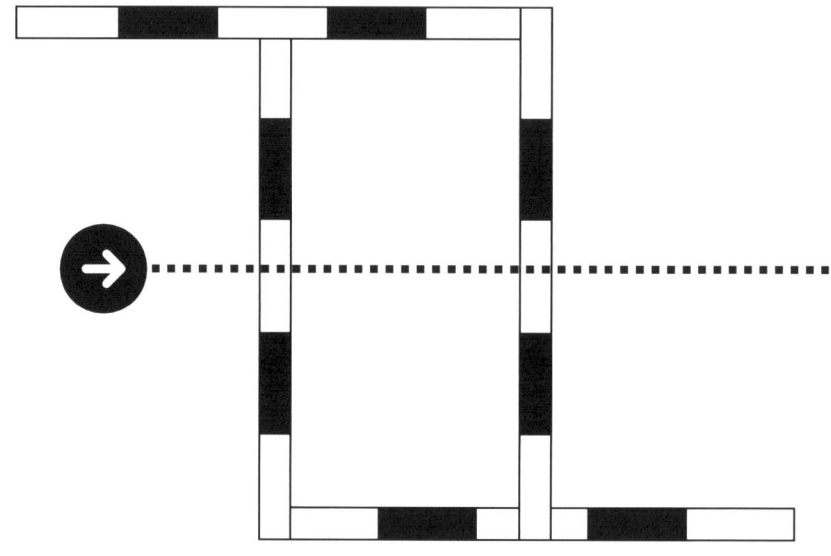

Poles: 4
Level: ★
Benefits:
- ☑ Accuracy
- ☑ Rhythm
- ☑ Impulsion
- ☑ Straightness
- ☐ Suppleness & bend
- ☐ Lateral movement
    & collection

Gaits:
- ☑ Groundwork
- ☑ Walk
- ☑ Trot
- ☐ Canter

Movements:
- ☐ Backup
- ☐ Leg yield
- ☐ Sidepass
- ☐ Shoulder in/out

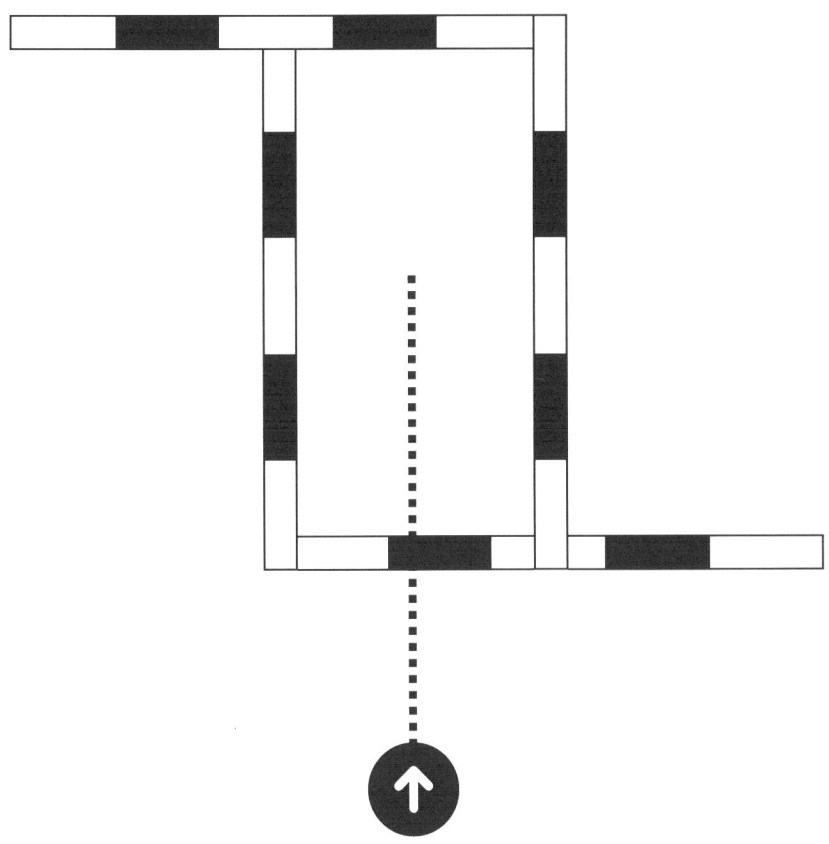

Poles: 4
Level: ★
Benefits:
- ☑ Accuracy
- ☑ Rhythm
- ☑ Impulsion
- ☑ Straightness
- ☐ Suppleness & bend
- ☐ Lateral movement & collection

Gaits:
- ☑ Groundwork
- ☑ Walk
- ☑ Trot
- ☑ Canter

Movements:
- ☐ Backup
- ☐ Leg yield
- ☐ Sidepass
- ☐ Shoulder in/out

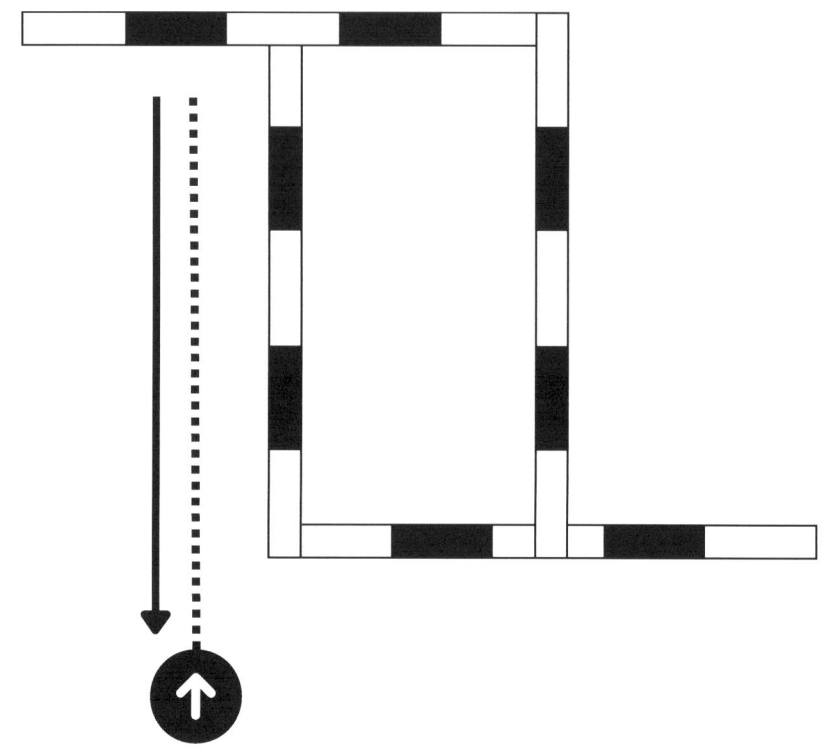

Poles: 4
Level: ★ ★
Benefits:
- ☑ Accuracy
- ☑ Rhythm
- ☑ Impulsion
- ☑ Straightness
- ☐ Suppleness & bend
- ☑ Lateral movement & collection

Gaits:
- ☑ Groundwork
- ☑ Walk
- ☑ Trot
- ☑ Canter

Movements:
- ☑ Backup
- ☐ Leg yield
- ☐ Sidepass
- ☐ Shoulder in/out

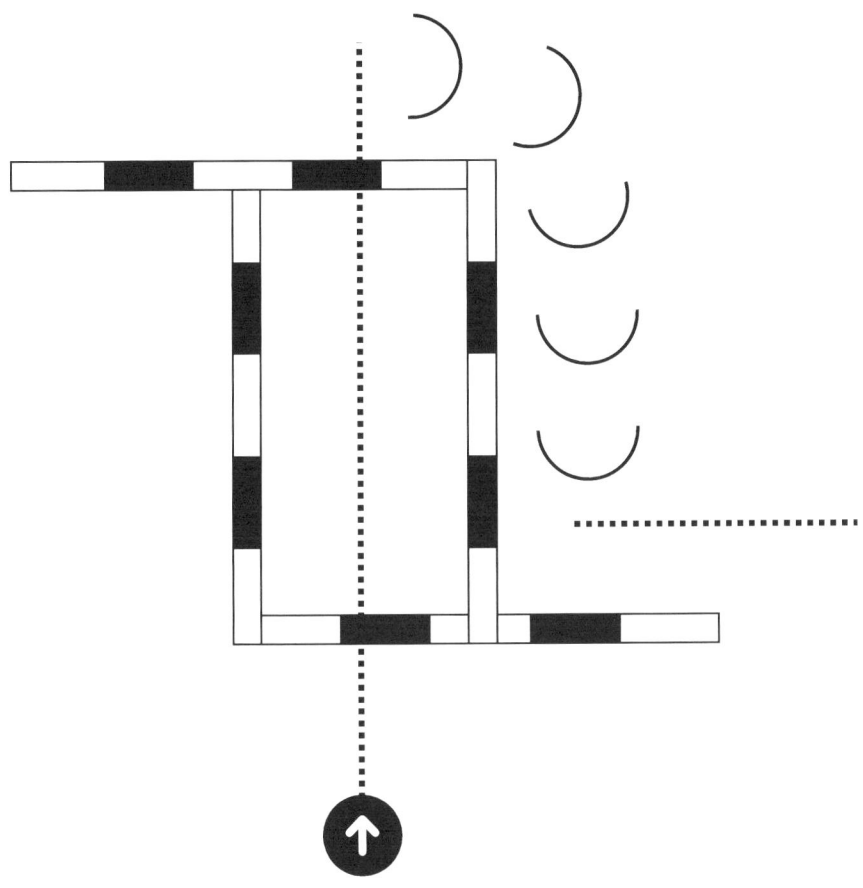

Poles: 4

Level: ★ ★

Benefits:
- ☑ Accuracy
- ☑ Rhythm
- ☑ Impulsion
- ☑ Straightness
- ☑ Suppleness & bend
- ☑ Lateral movement & collection

Gaits:
- ☑ Groundwork
- ☑ Walk
- ☑ Trot
- ☐ Canter

Movements:
- ☐ Backup
- ☐ Leg yield
- ☑ Sidepass
- ☐ Shoulder in/out

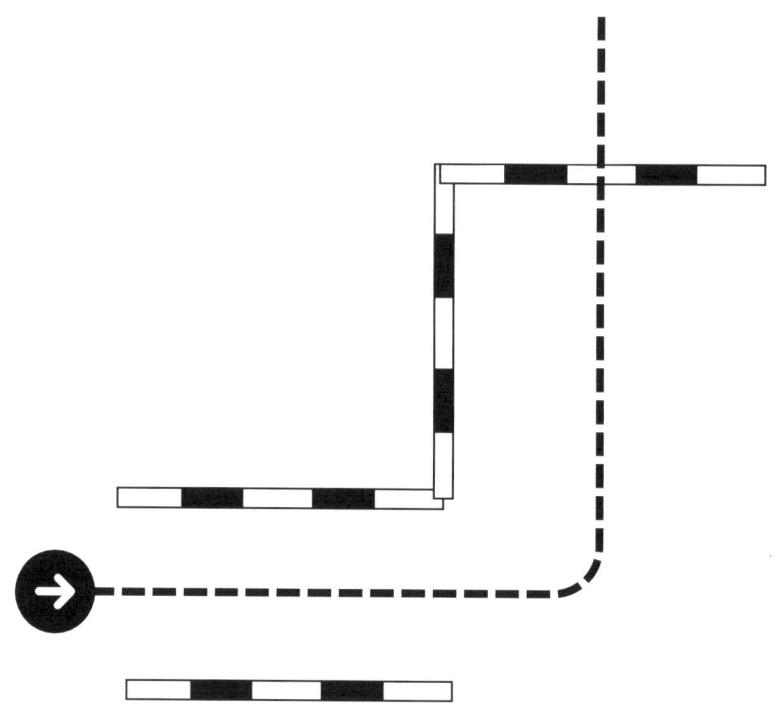

Poles: 4
Level: ★
Benefits:
- [x] Accuracy
- [x] Rhythm
- [x] Impulsion
- [x] Straightness
- [x] Suppleness & bend
- [ ] Lateral movement & collection

Gaits:
- [x] Groundwork
- [x] Walk
- [x] Trot
- [ ] Canter

Movements:
- [ ] Backup
- [ ] Leg yield
- [ ] Sidepass
- [ ] Shoulder in/out

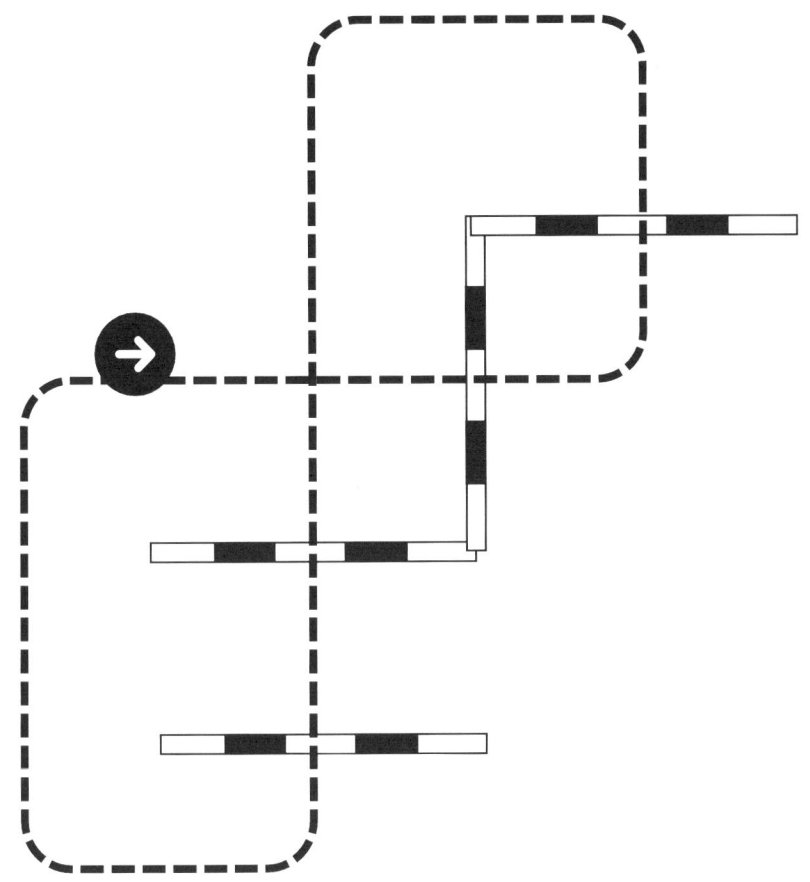

Poles: 4
Level: ★
Benefits:
- ☑ Accuracy
- ☑ Rhythm
- ☑ Impulsion
- ☑ Straightness
- ☑ Suppleness & bend
- ☐ Lateral movement & collection

Gaits:
- ☑ Groundwork
- ☑ Walk
- ☑ Trot
- ☐ Canter

Movements:
- ☐ Backup
- ☐ Leg yield
- ☐ Sidepass
- ☐ Shoulder in/out

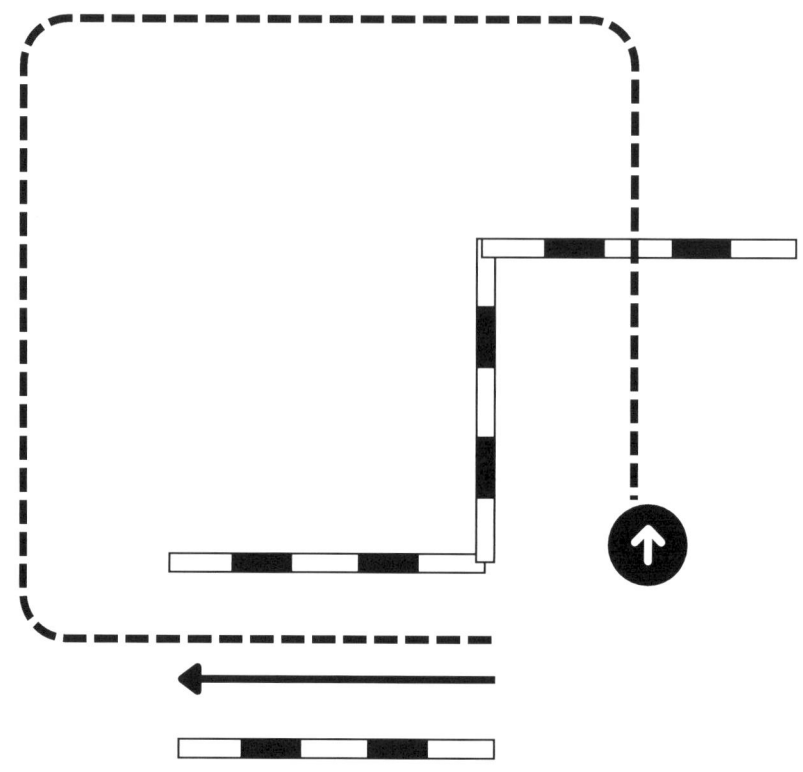

Poles: 4
Level: ★ ★
Benefits:
- ☑ Accuracy
- ☑ Rhythm
- ☑ Impulsion
- ☑ Straightness
- ☑ Suppleness & bend
- ☑ Lateral movement & collection

Gaits:
- ☑ Groundwork
- ☑ Walk
- ☑ Trot
- ☑ Canter

Movements:
- ☑ Backup
- ☐ Leg yield
- ☐ Sidepass
- ☐ Shoulder in/out

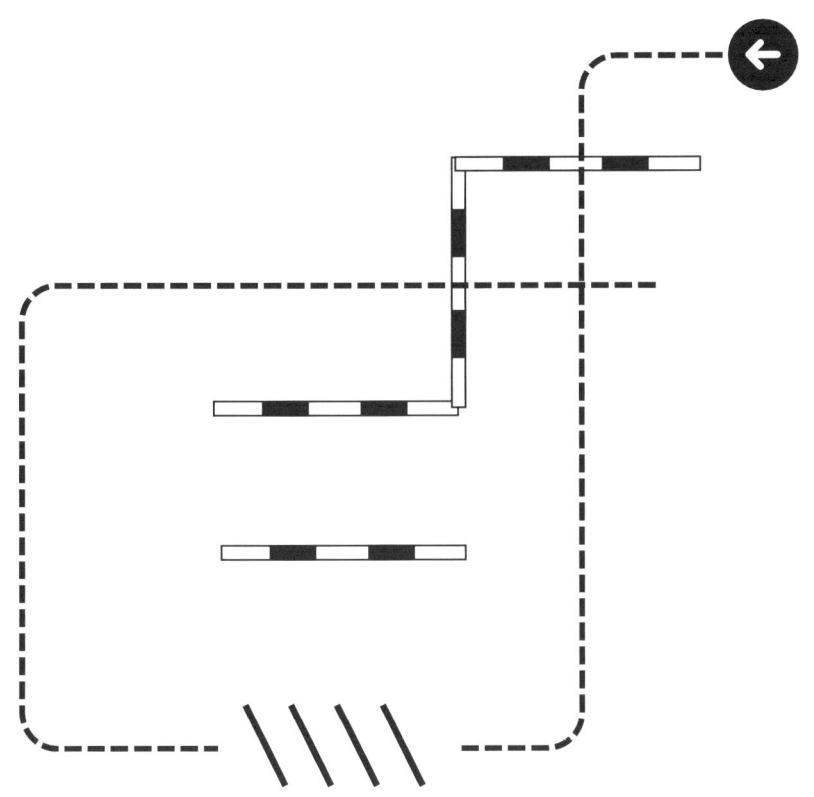

Poles: 4

Level: ★ ★

Benefits:

- ☑ Accuracy
- ☑ Rhythm
- ☑ Impulsion
- ☑ Straightness
- ☑ Suppleness & bend
- ☑ Lateral movement & collection

Gaits:

- ☑ Groundwork
- ☑ Walk
- ☑ Trot
- ☑ Canter

Movements:

- ☐ Backup
- ☐ Leg yield
- ☐ Sidepass
- ☑ Shoulder in/out

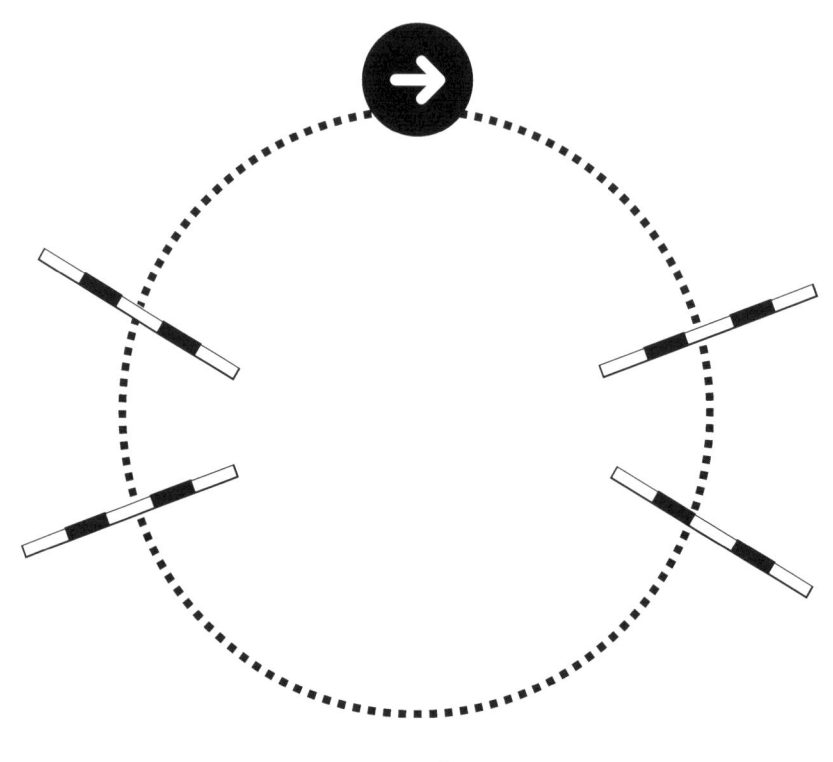

Poles: 4
Level: ★
Benefits:
- ☑ Accuracy
- ☑ Rhythm
- ☑ Impulsion
- ☐ Straightness
- ☑ Suppleness & bend
- ☐ Lateral movement & collection

Gaits:
- ☑ Groundwork
- ☑ Walk
- ☑ Trot
- ☐ Canter

Movements:
- ☐ Backup
- ☐ Leg yield
- ☐ Sidepass
- ☐ Shoulder in/out

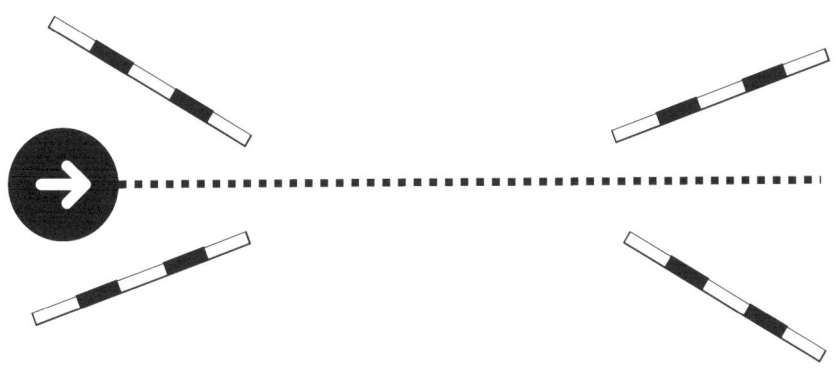

Poles: 4

Level: ★

Benefits:

- ☑ Accuracy
- ☑ Rhythm
- ☑ Impulsion
- ☑ Straightness
- ☑ Suppleness & bend
- ☐ Lateral movement & collection

Gaits:

- ☑ Groundwork
- ☑ Walk
- ☑ Trot
- ☑ Canter

Movements:

- ☐ Backup
- ☐ Leg yield
- ☐ Sidepass
- ☐ Shoulder in/out

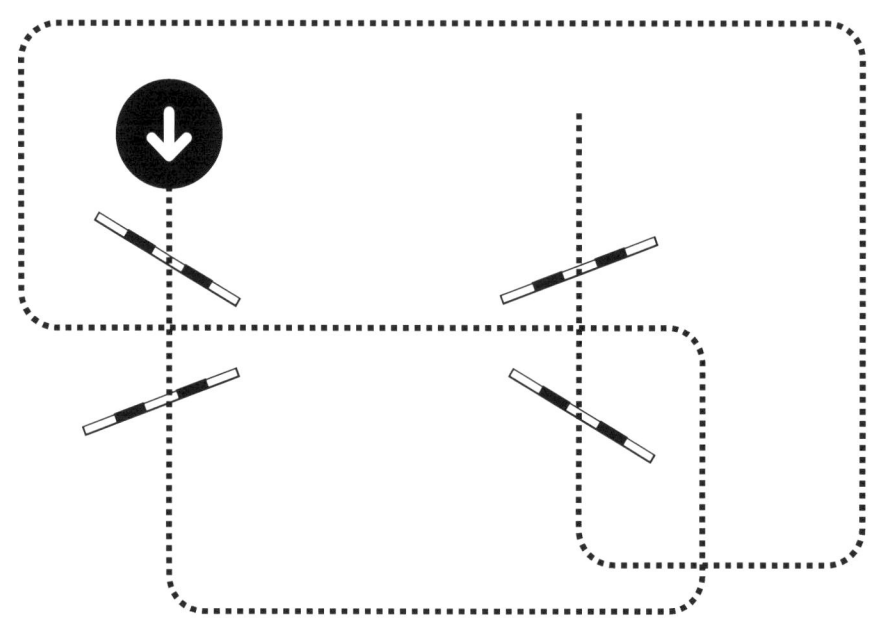

Poles: 4
Level: ★
Benefits:
- ☑ Accuracy
- ☑ Rhythm
- ☑ Impulsion
- ☑ Straightness
- ☑ Suppleness & bend
- ☐ Lateral movement & collection

Gaits:
- ☑ Groundwork
- ☑ Walk
- ☑ Trot
- ☑ Canter

Movements:
- ☐ Backup
- ☐ Leg yield
- ☐ Sidepass
- ☐ Shoulder in/out

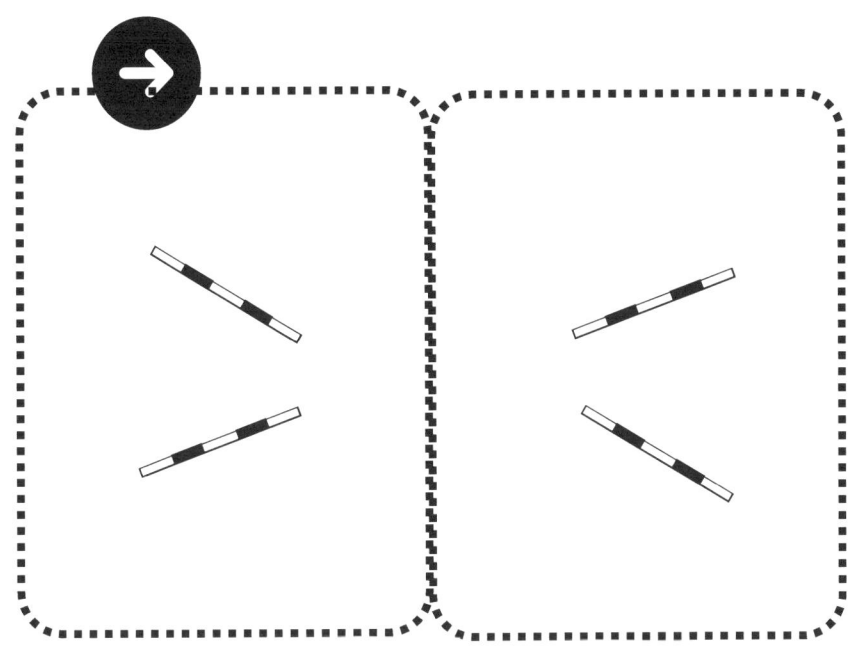

Poles: 4
Level: ★
Benefits:
- ☑ Accuracy
- ☑ Rhythm
- ☑ Impulsion
- ☐ Straightness
- ☑ Suppleness & bend
- ☐ Lateral movement & collection

Gaits:
- ☑ Groundwork
- ☑ Walk
- ☑ Trot
- ☑ Canter

Movements:
- ☐ Backup
- ☐ Leg yield
- ☐ Sidepass
- ☐ Shoulder in/out

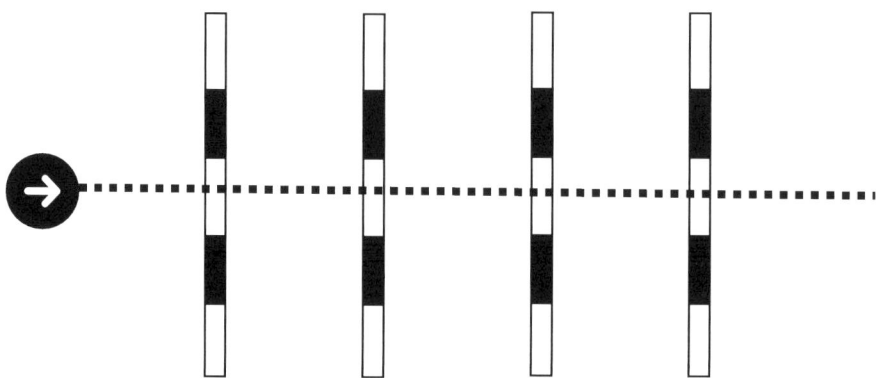

Poles: 4
Level: ★
Benefits:
- ☑ Accuracy
- ☑ Rhythm
- ☑ Impulsion
- ☑ Straightness
- ☐ Suppleness & bend
- ☐ Lateral movement & collection

Gaits:
- ☑ Groundwork
- ☑ Walk
- ☑ Trot
- ☐ Canter

Movements:
- ☐ Backup
- ☐ Leg yield
- ☐ Sidepass
- ☐ Shoulder in/out

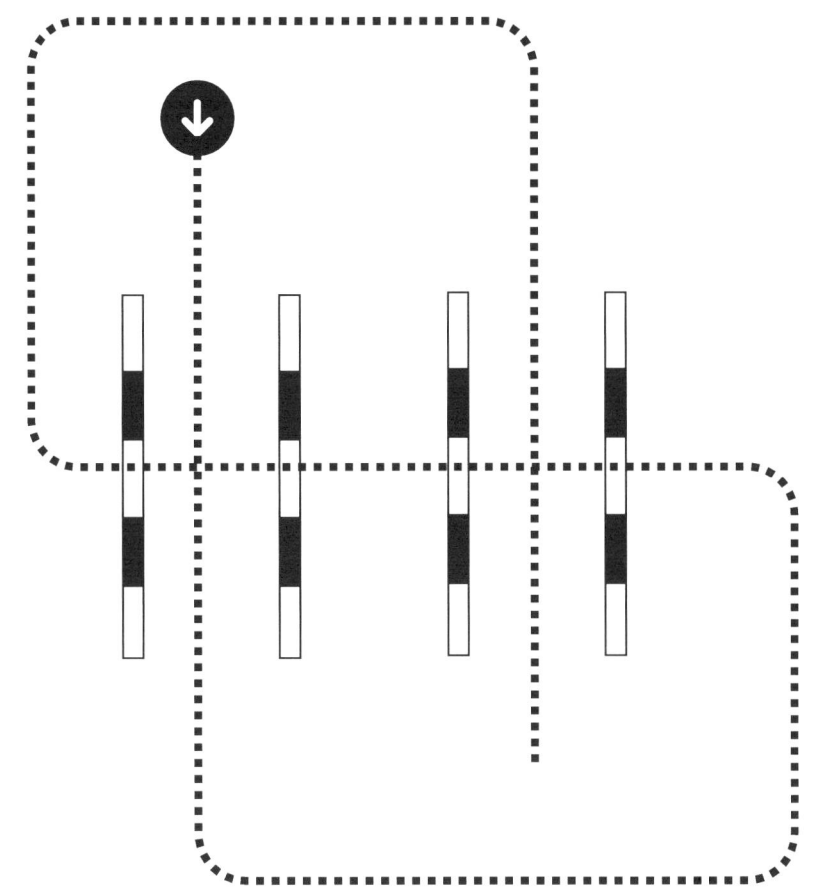

Poles: 4
Level: ★
Benefits:
- ☑ Accuracy
- ☑ Rhythm
- ☑ Impulsion
- ☑ Straightness
- ☑ Suppleness & bend
- ☐ Lateral movement & collection

Gaits:
- ☑ Groundwork
- ☑ Walk
- ☑ Trot
- ☐ Canter

Movements:
- ☐ Backup
- ☐ Leg yield
- ☐ Sidepass
- ☐ Shoulder in/out

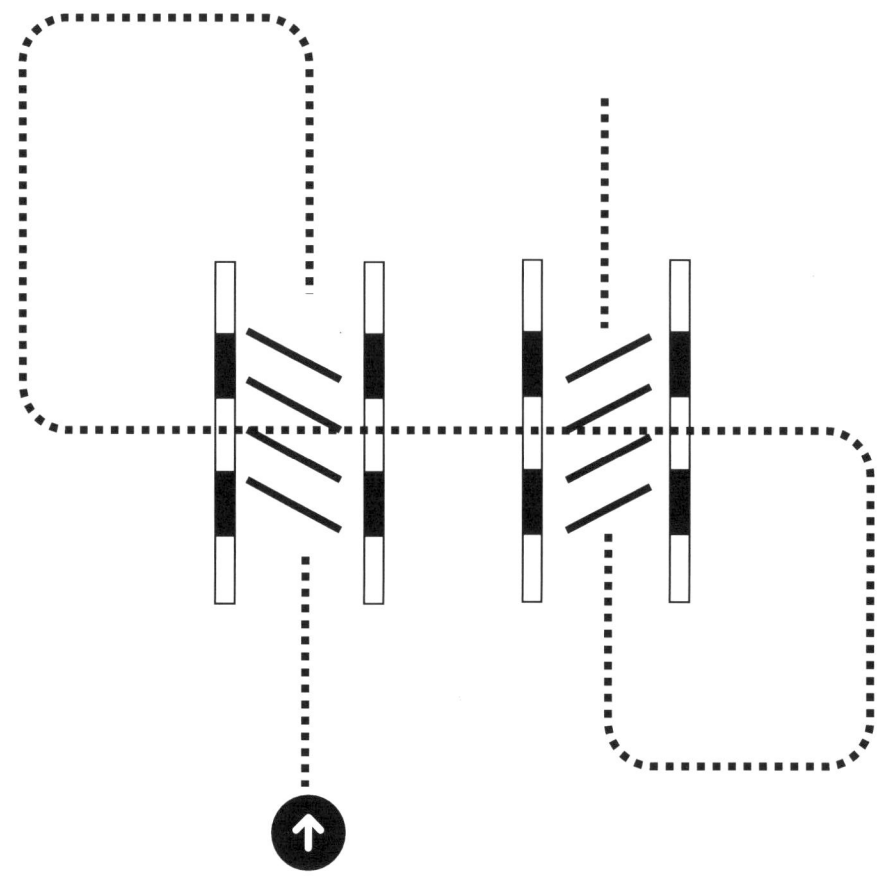

Poles: 4
Level: ★ ★
Benefits:
- ☑ Accuracy
- ☑ Rhythm
- ☑ Impulsion
- ☑ Straightness
- ☑ Suppleness & bend
- ☑ Lateral movement & collection

Gaits:
- ☑ Groundwork
- ☑ Walk
- ☑ Trot
- ☐ Canter

Movements:
- ☐ Backup
- ☐ Leg yield
- ☐ Sidepass
- ☑ Shoulder in/out

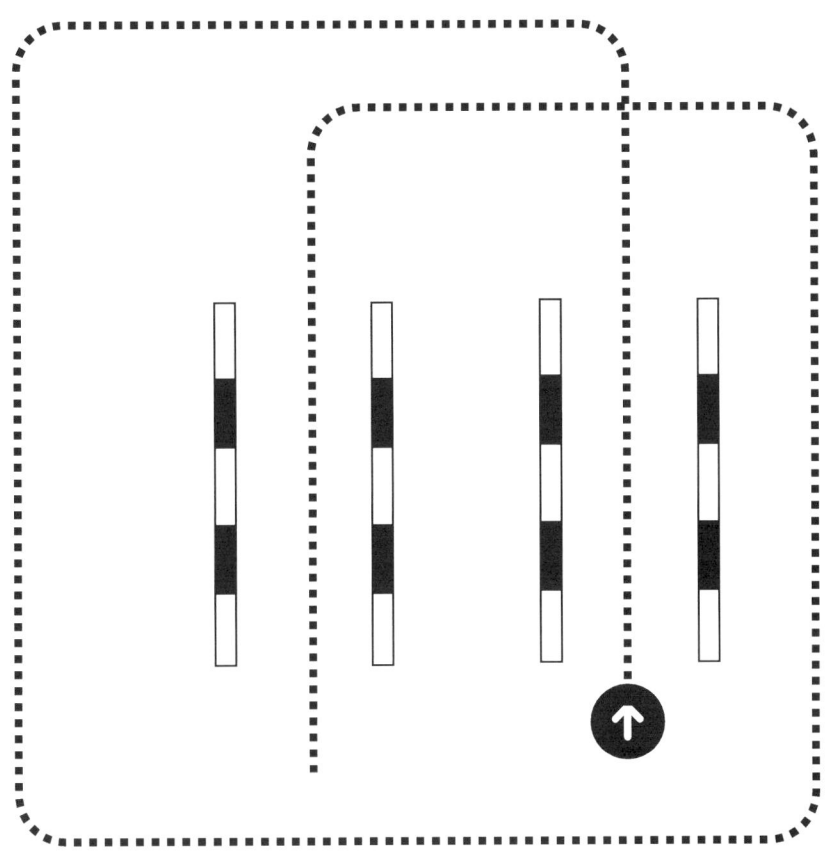

Poles: 4
Level: ★
Benefits:
- ☑ Accuracy
- ☑ Rhythm
- ☑ Impulsion
- ☑ Straightness
- ☑ Suppleness & bend
- ☐ Lateral movement & collection

Gaits:
- ☑ Groundwork
- ☑ Walk
- ☑ Trot
- ☑ Canter

Movements:
- ☐ Backup
- ☐ Leg yield
- ☐ Sidepass
- ☐ Shoulder in/out

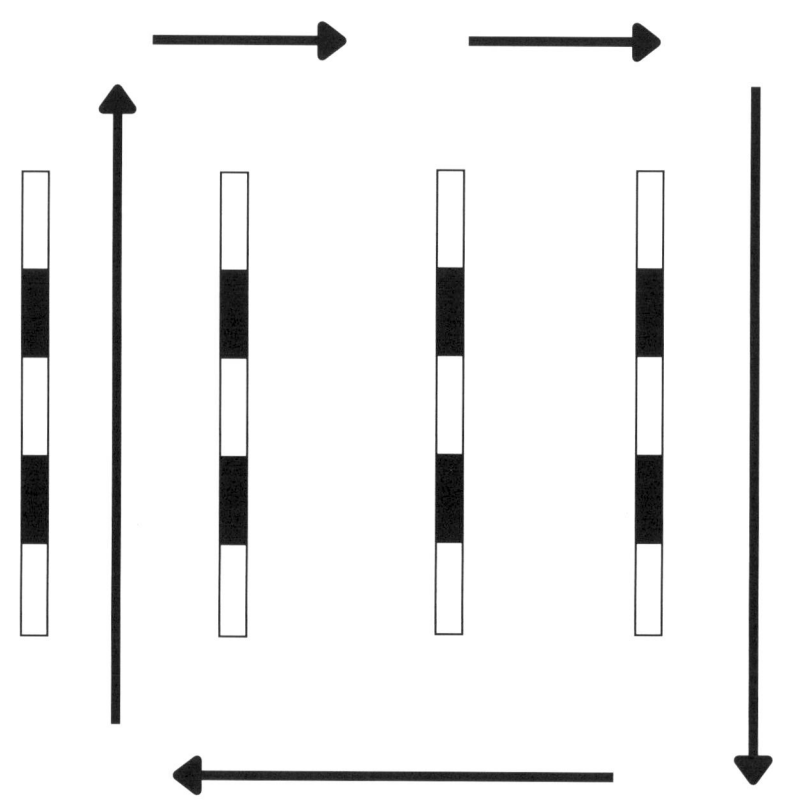

Poles: 4
Level: ★ ★ ★
Benefits:
- ☑ Accuracy
- ☑ Rhythm
- ☑ Impulsion
- ☑ Straightness
- ☑ Suppleness & bend
- ☑ Lateral movement & collection

Gaits:
- ☑ Groundwork
- ☑ Walk
- ☐ Trot
- ☐ Canter

Movements:
- ☑ Backup
- ☐ Leg yield
- ☐ Sidepass
- ☐ Shoulder in/out

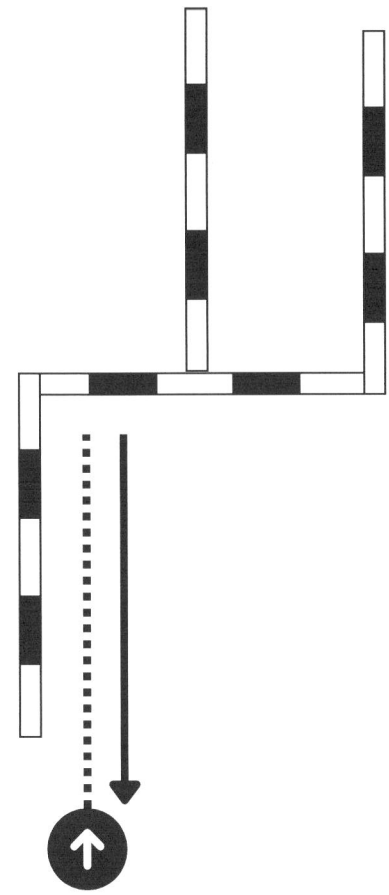

Poles: 4

Level: ★ ★

Benefits:

- ☑ Accuracy
- ☑ Rhythm
- ☑ Impulsion
- ☑ Straightness
- ☐ Suppleness & bend
- ☑ Lateral movement & collection

Gaits:

- ☑ Groundwork
- ☑ Walk
- ☑ Trot
- ☑ Canter

Movements:

- ☑ Backup
- ☐ Leg yield
- ☐ Sidepass
- ☐ Shoulder in/out

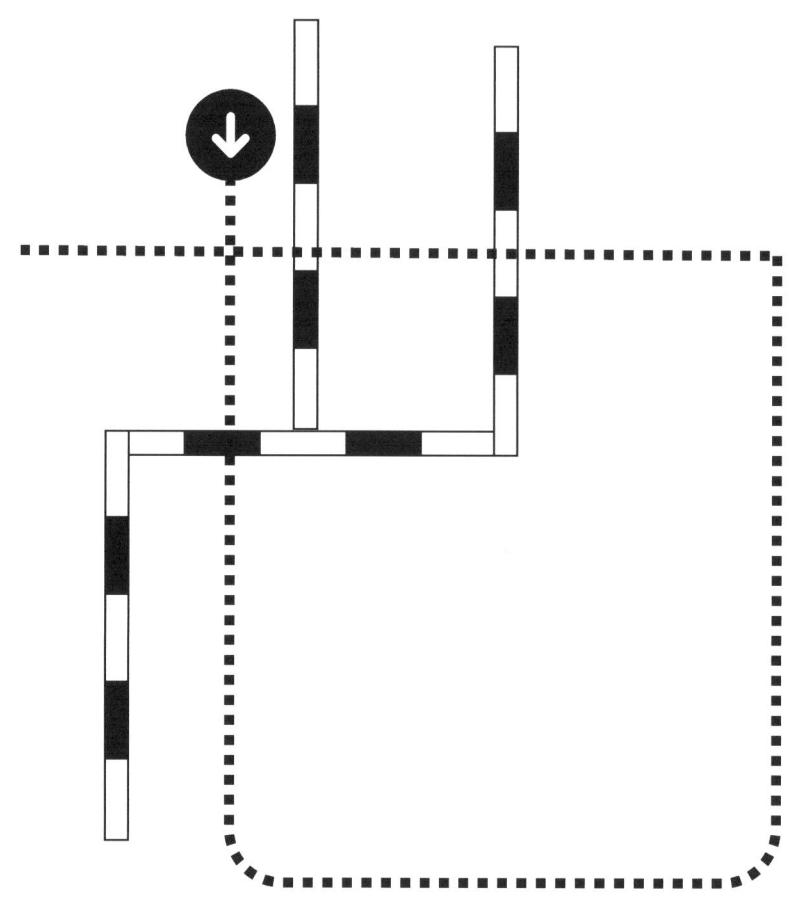

Poles: 4
Level: ★
Benefits:
- ☑ Accuracy
- ☑ Rhythm
- ☑ Impulsion
- ☑ Straightness
- ☑ Suppleness & bend
- ☐ Lateral movement & collection

Gaits:
- ☑ Groundwork
- ☑ Walk
- ☑ Trot
- ☐ Canter

Movements:
- ☐ Backup
- ☐ Leg yield
- ☐ Sidepass
- ☐ Shoulder in/out

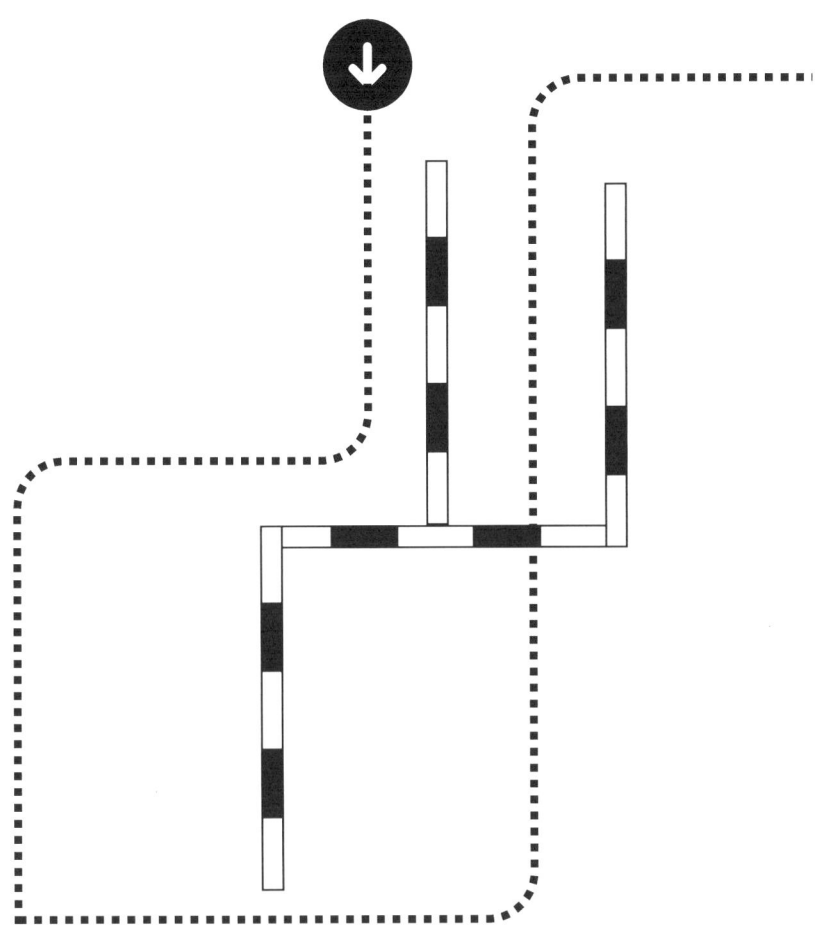

Poles: 4
Level: ★
Benefits:
- ☑ Accuracy
- ☑ Rhythm
- ☑ Impulsion
- ☑ Straightness
- ☑ Suppleness & bend
- ☐ Lateral movement & collection

Gaits:
- ☑ Groundwork
- ☑ Walk
- ☑ Trot
- ☐ Canter

Movements:
- ☐ Backup
- ☐ Leg yield
- ☐ Sidepass
- ☐ Shoulder in/out

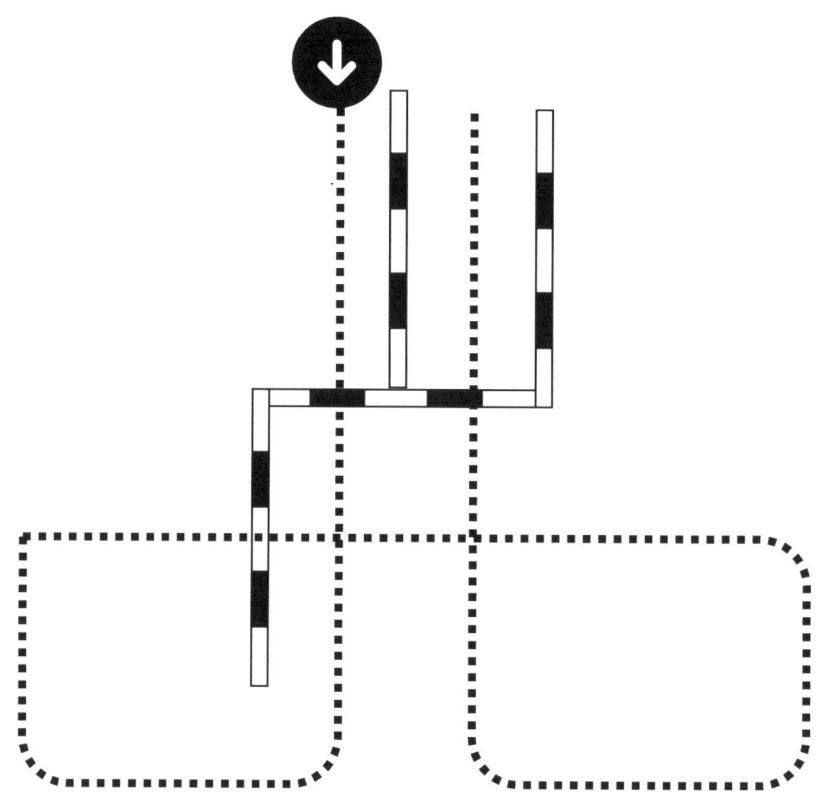

Poles: 4
Level: ★
Benefits:
- ☑ Accuracy
- ☑ Rhythm
- ☑ Impulsion
- ☑ Straightness
- ☑ Suppleness & bend
- ☐ Lateral movement & collection

Gaits:
- ☑ Groundwork
- ☑ Walk
- ☑ Trot
- ☑ Canter

Movements:
- ☐ Backup
- ☐ Leg yield
- ☐ Sidepass
- ☐ Shoulder in/out

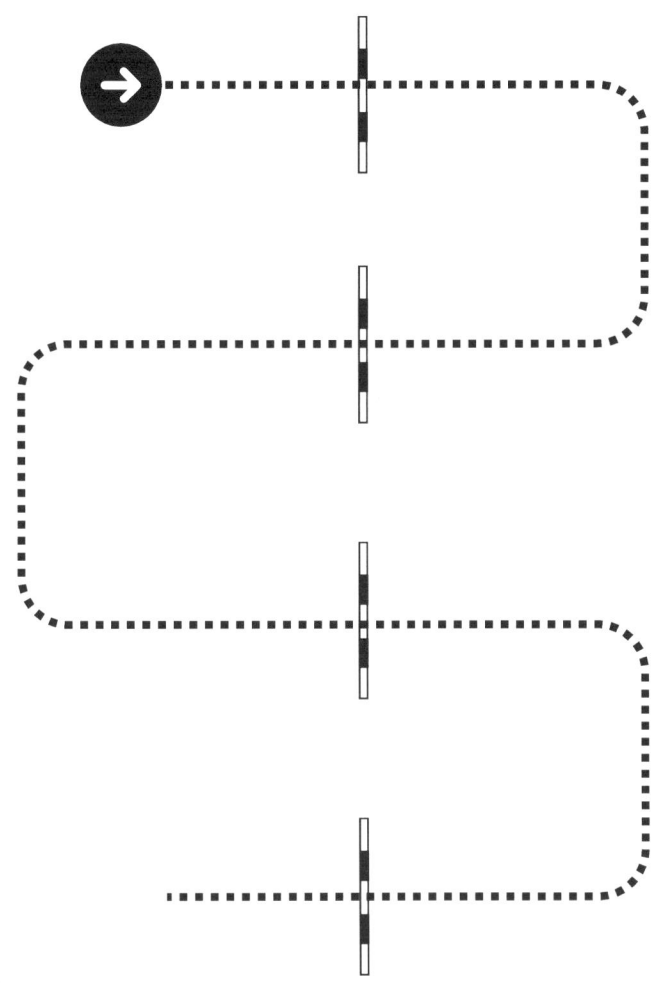

Poles: 4
Level: ★
Benefits:

- ☑ Accuracy
- ☑ Rhythm
- ☑ Impulsion
- ☑ Straightness
- ☑ Suppleness & bend
- ☐ Lateral movement & collection

Gaits:

- ☑ Groundwork
- ☑ Walk
- ☑ Trot
- ☑ Canter

Movements:

- ☐ Backup
- ☐ Leg yield
- ☐ Sidepass
- ☐ Shoulder in/out

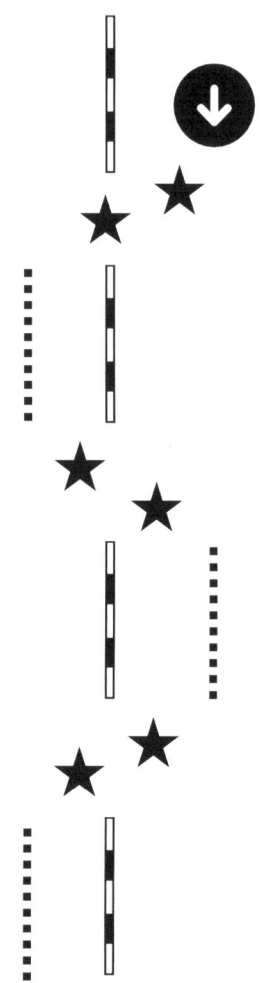

Poles: 4
Level: ★ ★
Benefits:
- ☑ Accuracy
- ☑ Rhythm
- ☑ Impulsion
- ☐ Straightness
- ☑ Suppleness & bend
- ☑ Lateral movement & collection

Gaits:
- ☑ Groundwork
- ☑ Walk
- ☐ Trot
- ☐ Canter

Movements:
- ☐ Backup
- ☑ Leg yield
- ☐ Sidepass
- ☐ Shoulder in/out

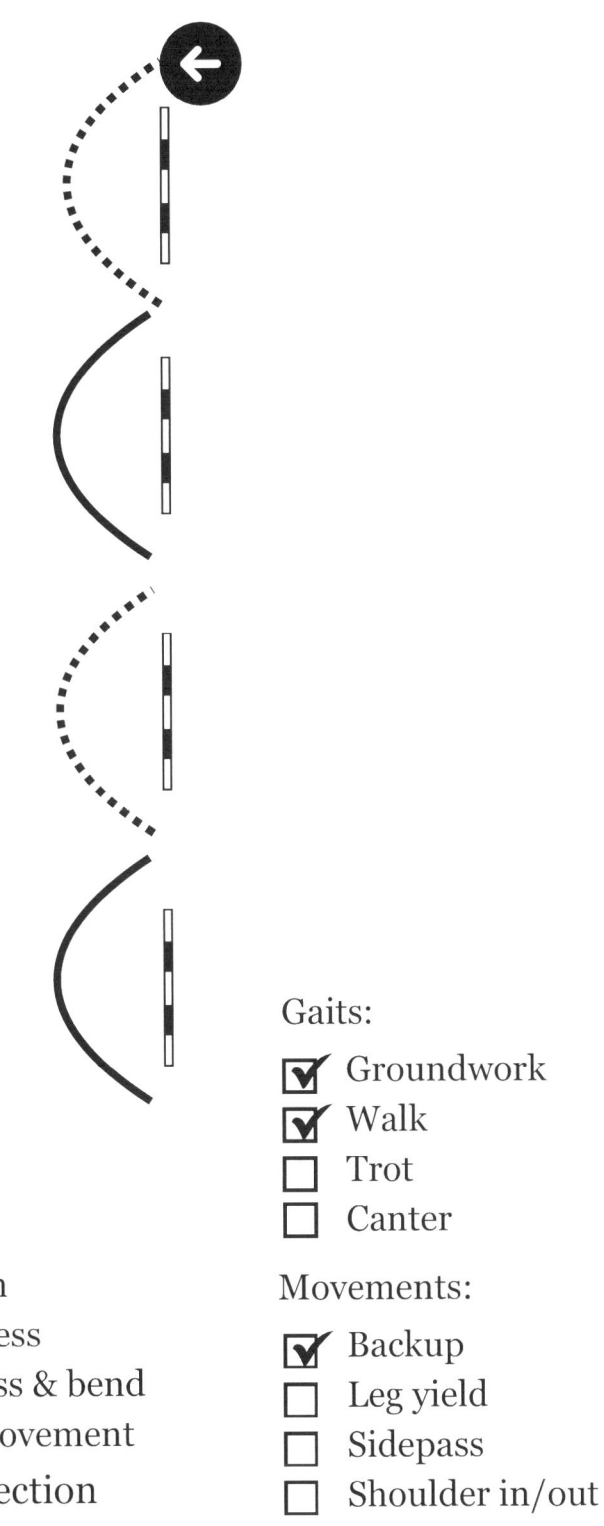

Poles: 4
Level: ★ ★
Benefits:
- ☑ Accuracy
- ☑ Rhythm
- ☑ Impulsion
- ☐ Straightness
- ☑ Suppleness & bend
- ☑ Lateral movement & collection

Gaits:
- ☑ Groundwork
- ☑ Walk
- ☐ Trot
- ☐ Canter

Movements:
- ☑ Backup
- ☐ Leg yield
- ☐ Sidepass
- ☐ Shoulder in/out

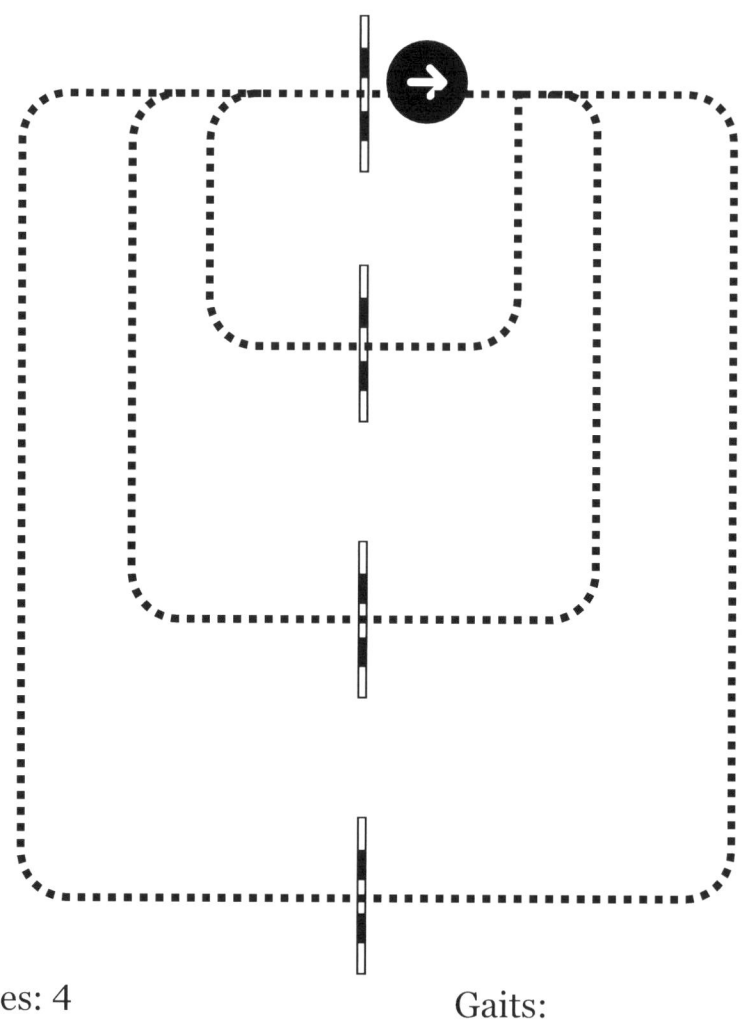

Poles: 4
Level: ⭐
Benefits:
- ☑ Accuracy
- ☑ Rhythm
- ☑ Impulsion
- ☑ Straightness
- ☑ Suppleness & bend
- ☐ Lateral movement & collection

Gaits:
- ☑ Groundwork
- ☑ Walk
- ☑ Trot
- ☐ Canter

Movements:
- ☐ Backup
- ☐ Leg yield
- ☐ Sidepass
- ☐ Shoulder in/out

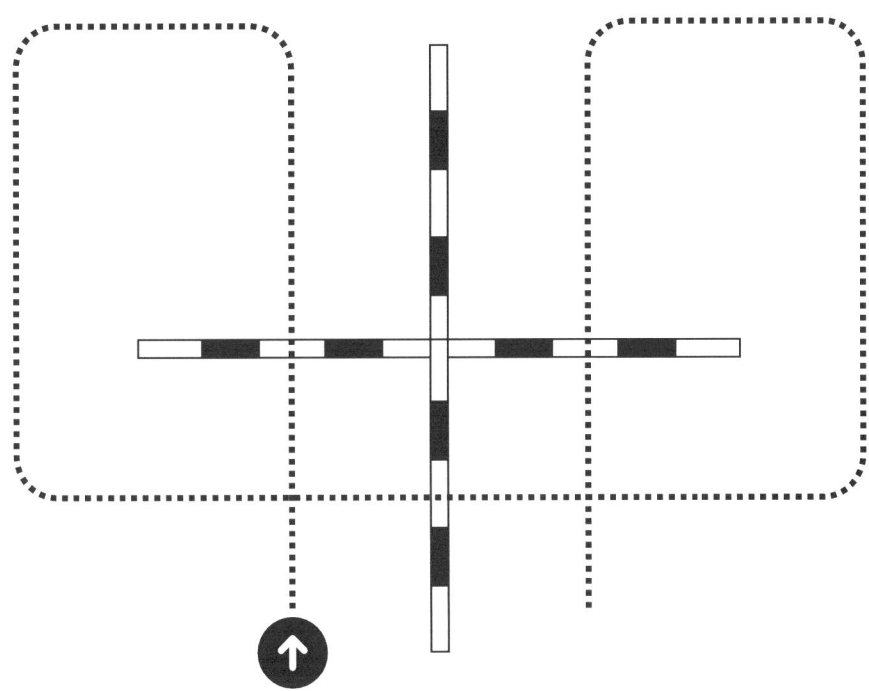

Poles: 4
Level: ⭐
Benefits:
- ☑ Accuracy
- ☑ Rhythm
- ☑ Impulsion
- ☑ Straightness
- ☑ Suppleness & bend
- ☐ Lateral movement & collection

Gaits:
- ☑ Groundwork
- ☑ Walk
- ☑ Trot
- ☑ Canter

Movements:
- ☐ Backup
- ☐ Leg yield
- ☐ Sidepass
- ☐ Shoulder in/out

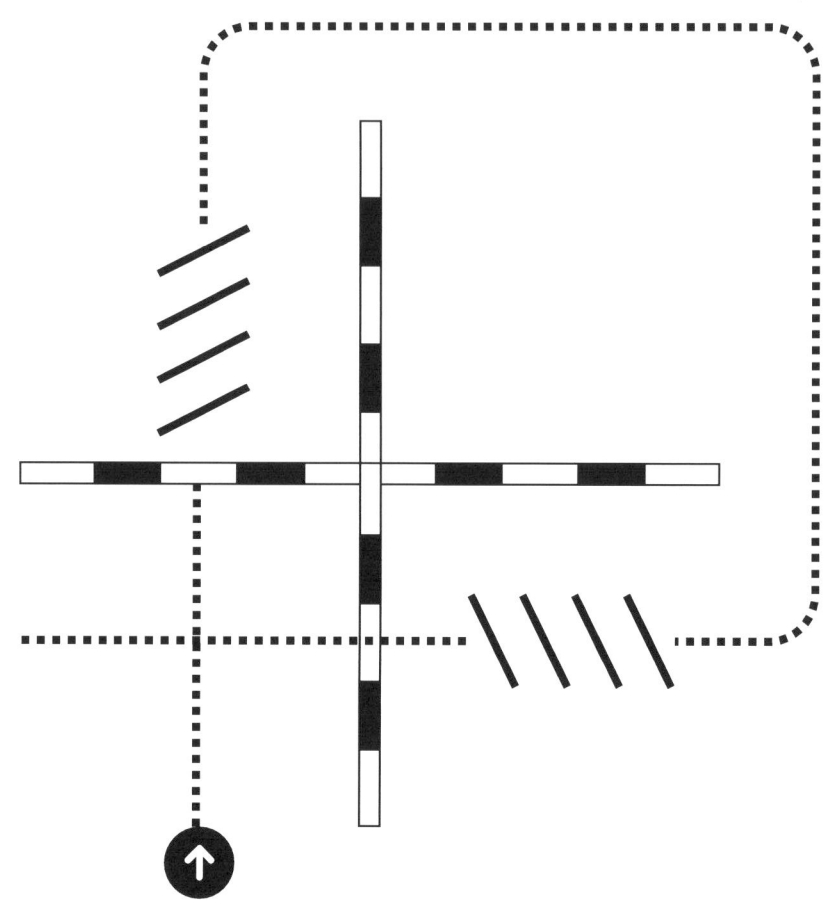

Poles: 4

Level: ★ ★

Benefits:

- ☑ Accuracy
- ☑ Rhythm
- ☑ Impulsion
- ☐ Straightness
- ☑ Suppleness & bend
- ☑ Lateral movement & collection

Gaits:

- ☑ Groundwork
- ☑ Walk
- ☑ Trot
- ☐ Canter

Movements:

- ☐ Backup
- ☐ Leg yield
- ☐ Sidepass
- ☑ Shoulder in

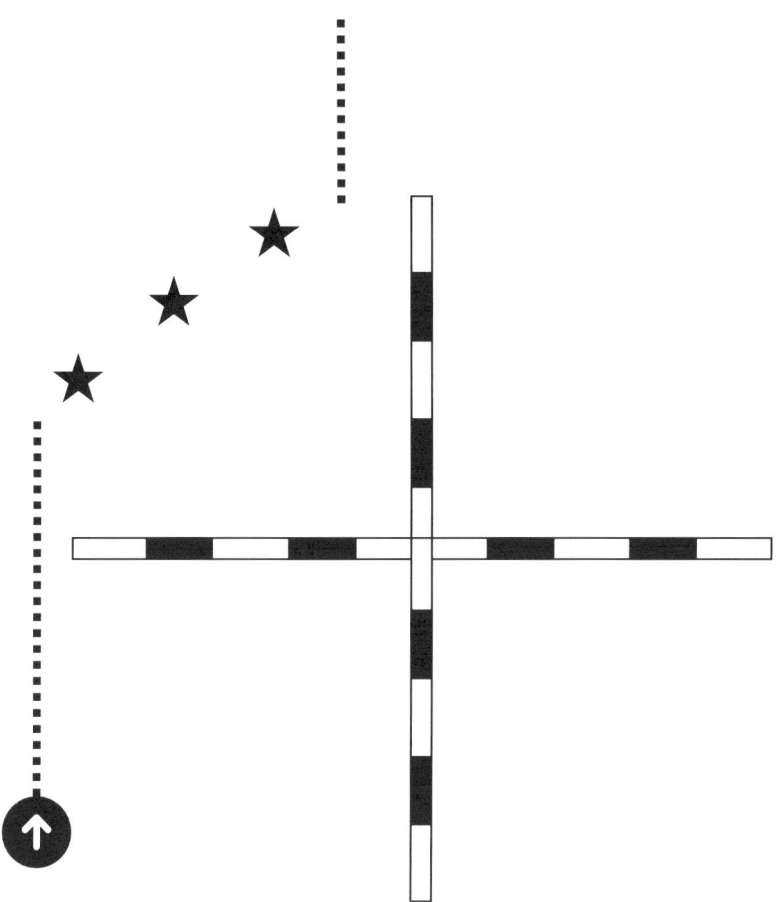

Poles: 4
Level: ★ ★
Benefits:
- ☑ Accuracy
- ☑ Rhythm
- ☑ Impulsion
- ☐ Straightness
- ☑ Suppleness & bend
- ☑ Lateral movement
    & collection

Gaits:
- ☑ Groundwork
- ☑ Walk
- ☑ Trot
- ☑ Canter

Movements:
- ☐ Backup
- ☑ Leg yield
- ☐ Sidepass
- ☐ Shoulder in

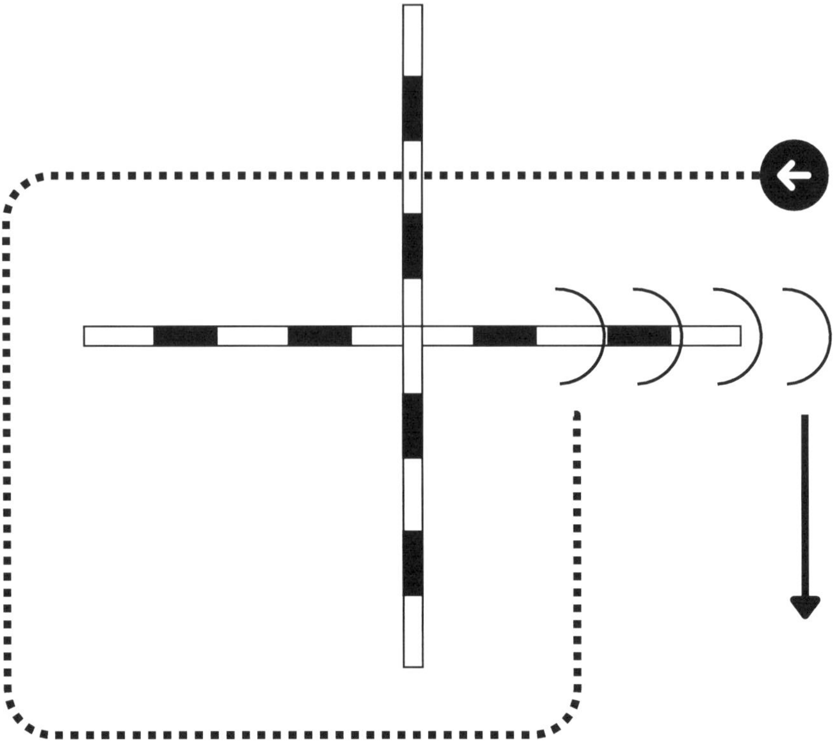

Poles: 4
Level: ★ ★ ★
Benefits:
- ☑ Accuracy
- ☑ Rhythm
- ☑ Impulsion
- ☐ Straightness
- ☑ Suppleness & bend
- ☑ Lateral movement & collection

Gaits:
- ☑ Groundwork
- ☑ Walk
- ☑ Trot
- ☑ Canter

Movements:
- ☑ Backup
- ☐ Leg yield
- ☑ Sidepass
- ☐ Shoulder in/out

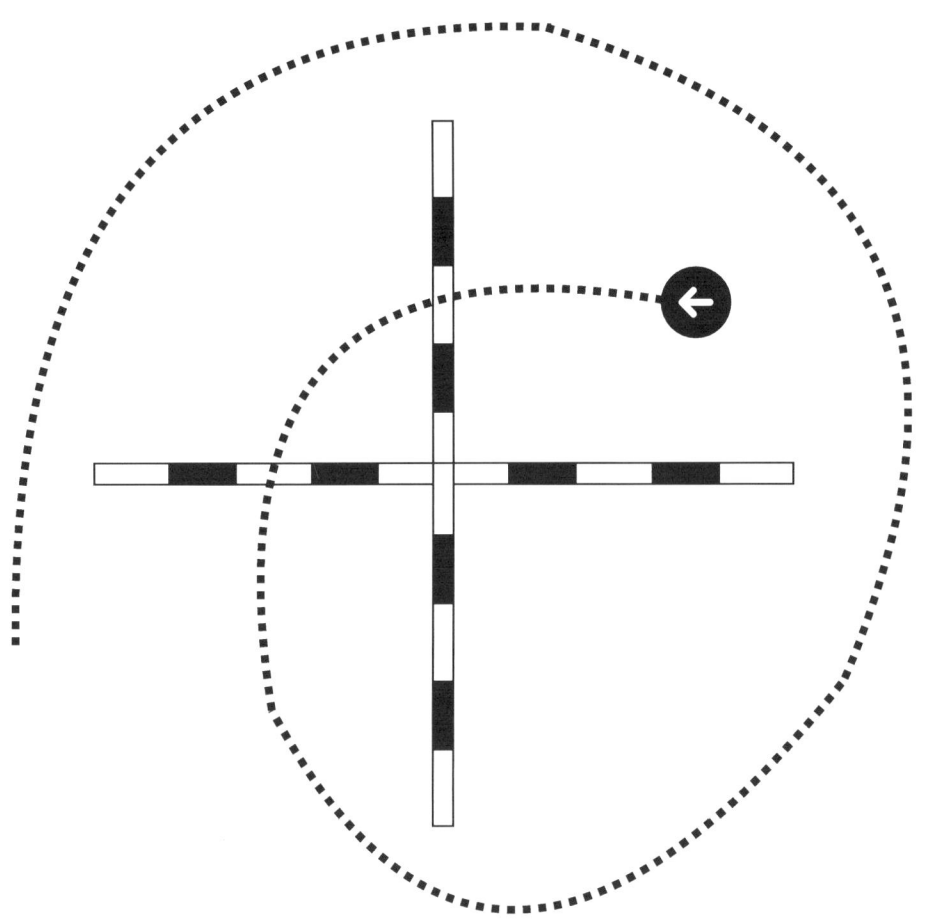

Poles: 4
Level: ★
Benefits:

- ☑ Accuracy
- ☑ Rhythm
- ☑ Impulsion
- ☐ Straightness
- ☑ Suppleness & bend
- ☐ Lateral movement & collection

Gaits:
- ☑ Groundwork
- ☑ Walk
- ☑ Trot
- ☑ Canter

Movements:
- ☐ Backup
- ☐ Leg yield
- ☐ Sidepass
- ☐ Shoulder in/out

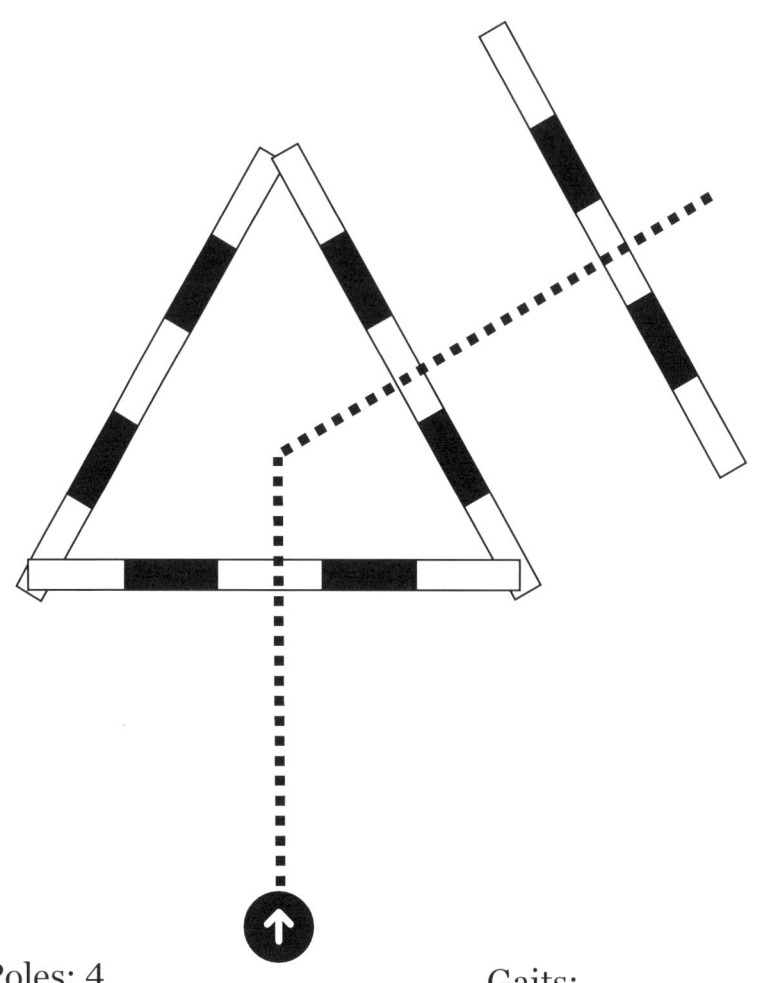

Poles: 4
Level: ★
Benefits:
- ☑ Accuracy
- ☑ Rhythm
- ☑ Impulsion
- ☑ Straightness
- ☑ Suppleness & bend
- ☐ Lateral movement & collection

Gaits:
- ☑ Groundwork
- ☑ Walk
- ☑ Trot
- ☐ Canter

Movements:
- ☐ Backup
- ☐ Leg yield
- ☐ Sidepass
- ☐ Shoulder in/out

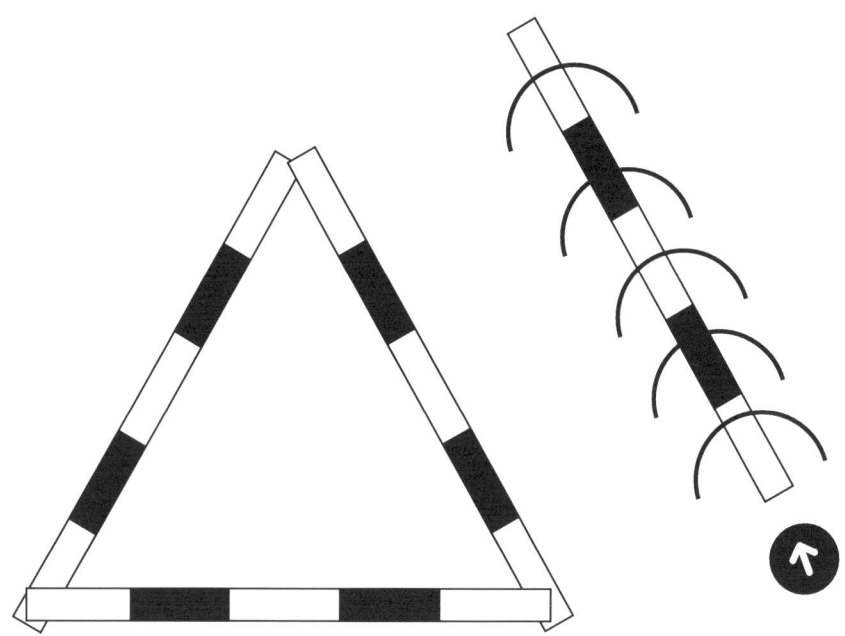

Poles: 4

Level: ★ ★ ★

Benefits:

- ☑ Accuracy
- ☑ Rhythm
- ☑ Impulsion
- ☑ Straightness
- ☑ Suppleness & bend
- ☑ Lateral movement & collection

Gaits:

- ☑ Groundwork
- ☑ Walk
- ☑ Trot
- ☑ Canter

Movements:

- ☐ Backup
- ☐ Leg yield
- ☑ Sidepass
- ☐ Shoulder in/out

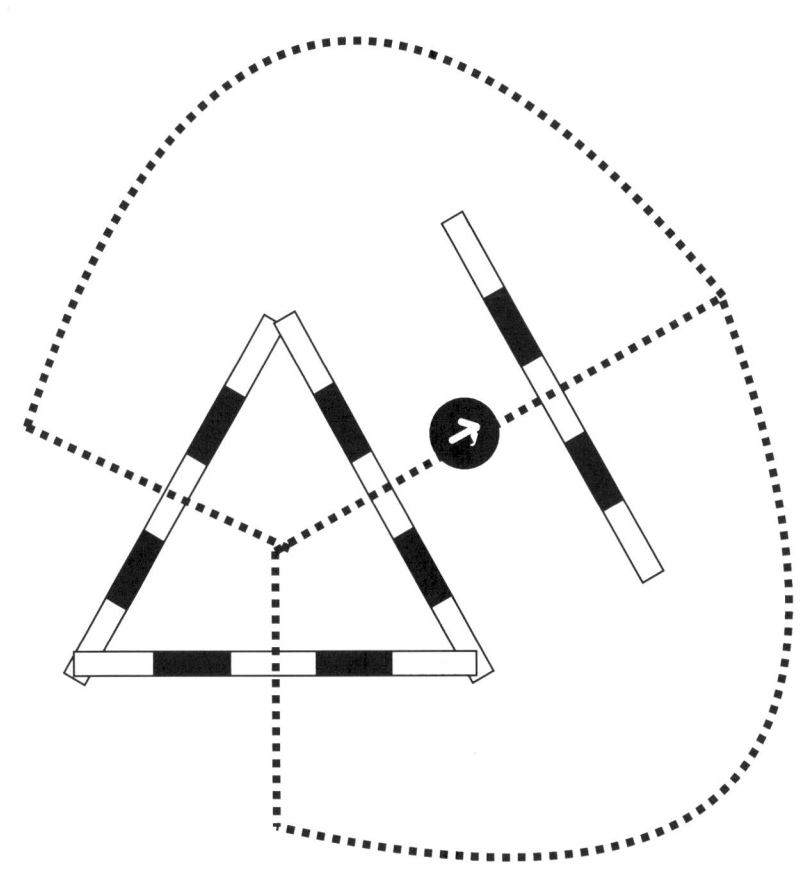

Poles: 4
Level: ★
Benefits:
- ☑ Accuracy
- ☑ Rhythm
- ☑ Impulsion
- ☑ Straightness
- ☑ Suppleness & bend
- ☐ Lateral movement & collection

Gaits:
- ☑ Groundwork
- ☑ Walk
- ☑ Trot
- ☐ Canter

Movements:
- ☐ Backup
- ☐ Leg yield
- ☐ Sidepass
- ☐ Shoulder in/out

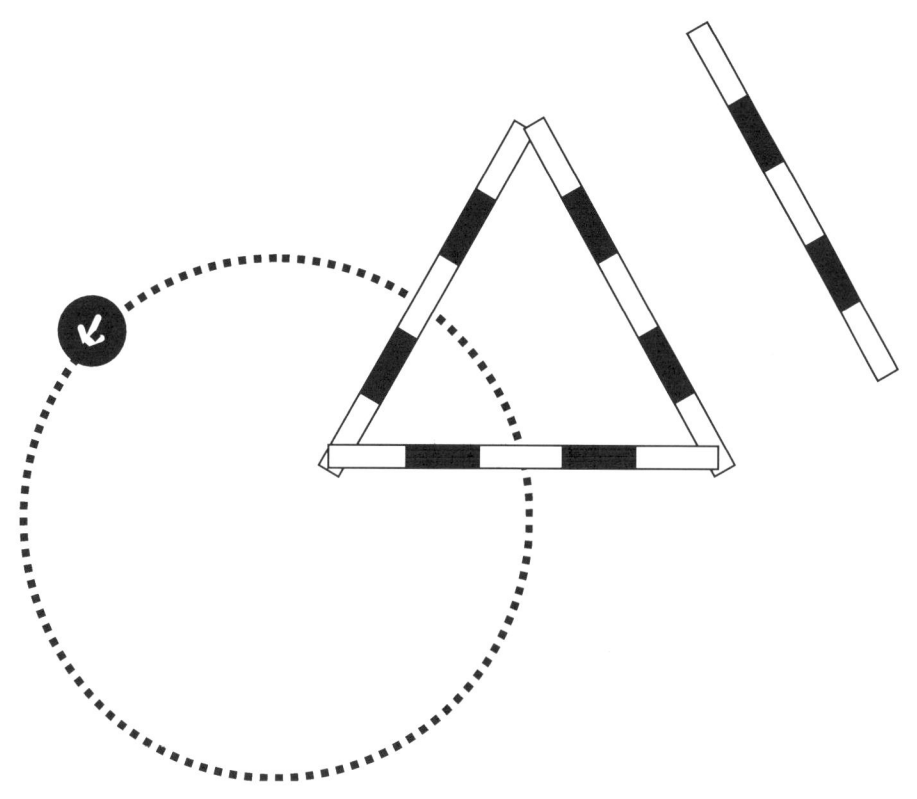

Poles: 4
Level: ★
Benefits:
- ☑ Accuracy
- ☑ Rhythm
- ☑ Impulsion
- ☑ Straightness
- ☑ Suppleness & bend
- ☐ Lateral movement & collection

Gaits:
- ☑ Groundwork
- ☑ Walk
- ☑ Trot
- ☑ Canter

Movements:
- ☐ Backup
- ☐ Leg yield
- ☐ Sidepass
- ☐ Shoulder in/out

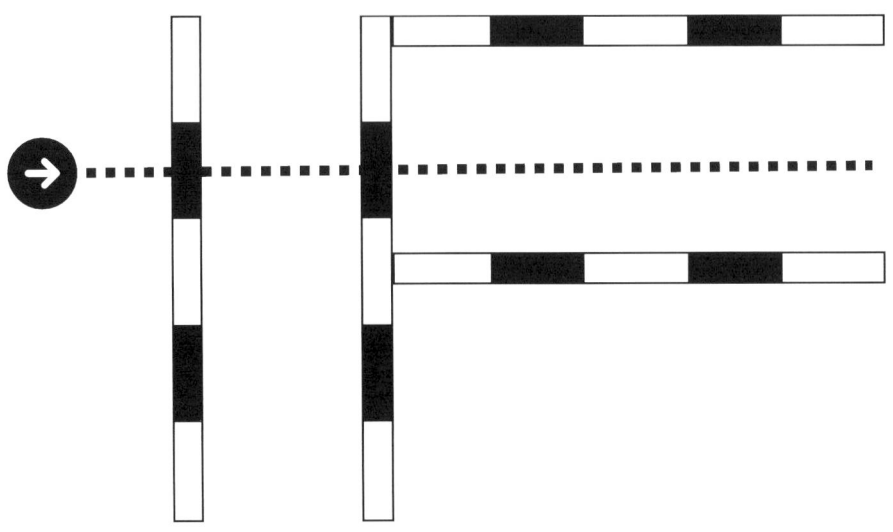

Poles: 4
Level: ★
Benefits:
- ☑ Accuracy
- ☑ Rhythm
- ☑ Impulsion
- ☑ Straightness
- ☐ Suppleness & bend
- ☐ Lateral movement & collection

Gaits:
- ☑ Groundwork
- ☑ Walk
- ☑ Trot
- ☐ Canter

Movements:
- ☐ Backup
- ☐ Leg yield
- ☐ Sidepass
- ☐ Shoulder in/out

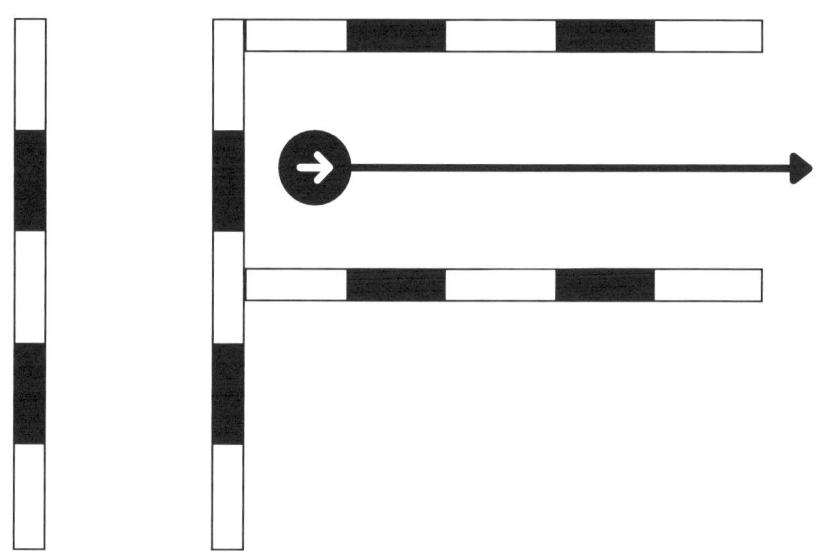

Poles: 4
Level: ★ ★
Benefits:
- ☑ Accuracy
- ☑ Rhythm
- ☑ Impulsion
- ☑ Straightness
- ☐ Suppleness & bend
- ☑ Lateral movement & collection

Gaits:
- ☑ Groundwork
- ☑ Walk
- ☐ Trot
- ☐ Canter

Movements:
- ☑ Backup
- ☐ Leg yield
- ☐ Sidepass
- ☐ Shoulder in/out

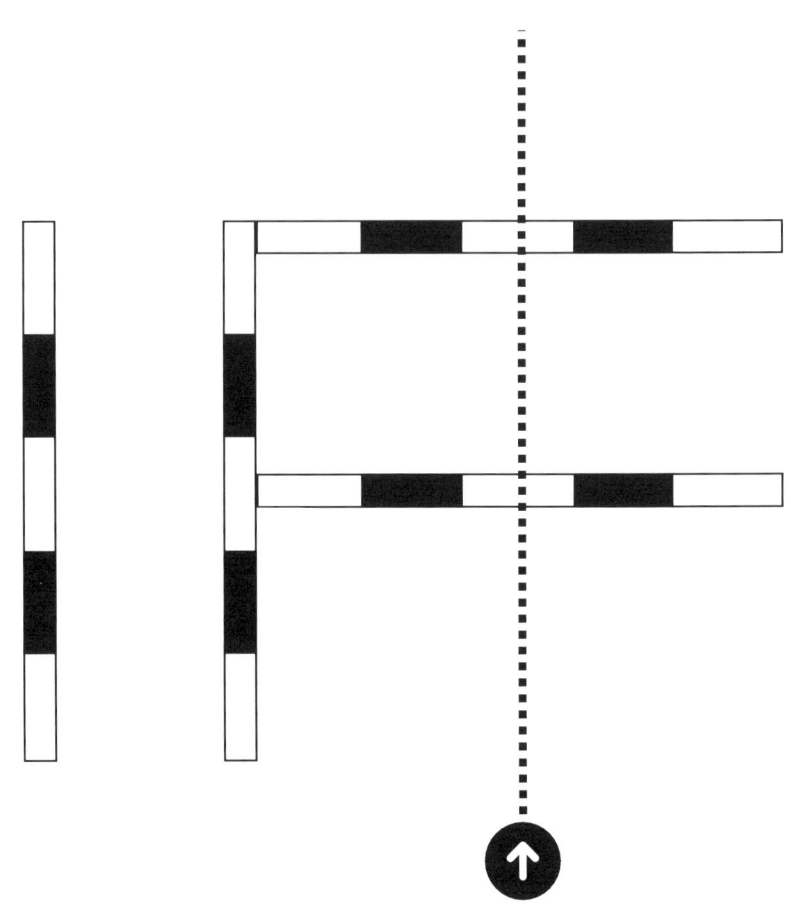

Poles: 4
Level: ★
Benefits:
- ☑ Accuracy
- ☑ Rhythm
- ☑ Impulsion
- ☑ Straightness
- ☐ Suppleness & bend
- ☐ Lateral movement & collection

Gaits:
- ☑ Groundwork
- ☑ Walk
- ☑ Trot
- ☐ Canter

Movements:
- ☐ Backup
- ☐ Leg yield
- ☐ Sidepass
- ☐ Shoulder in/out

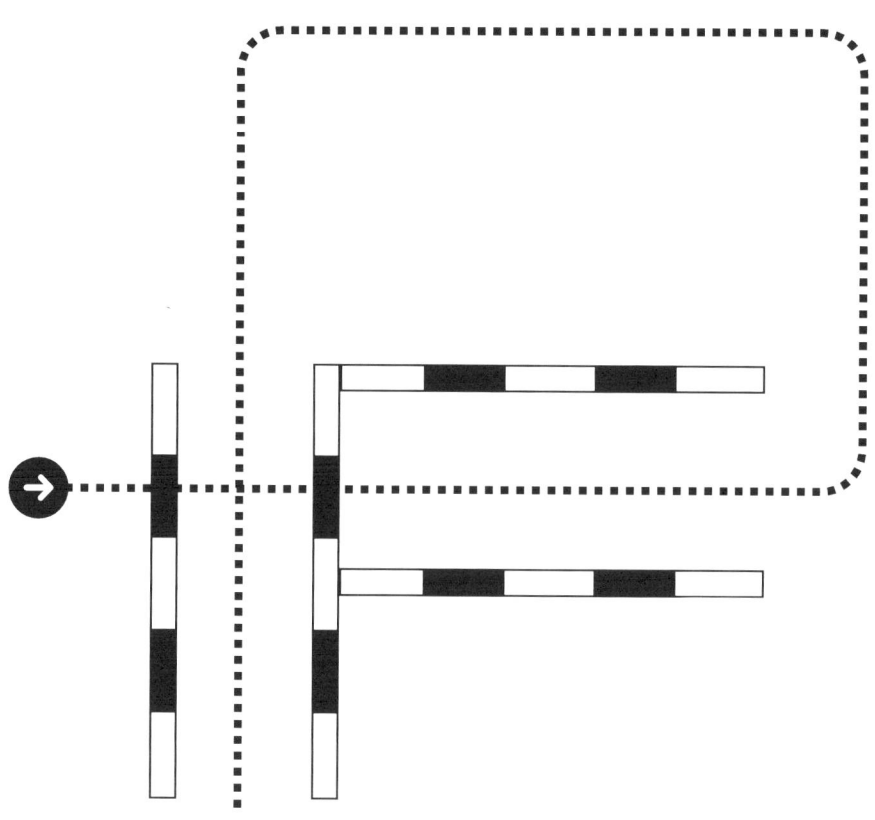

Poles: 4
Level: ⭐
Benefits:
- ☑ Accuracy
- ☑ Rhythm
- ☑ Impulsion
- ☑ Straightness
- ☑ Suppleness & bend
- ☐ Lateral movement & collection

Gaits:
- ☑ Groundwork
- ☑ Walk
- ☑ Trot
- ☐ Canter

Movements:
- ☐ Backup
- ☐ Leg yield
- ☐ Sidepass
- ☐ Shoulder in/out

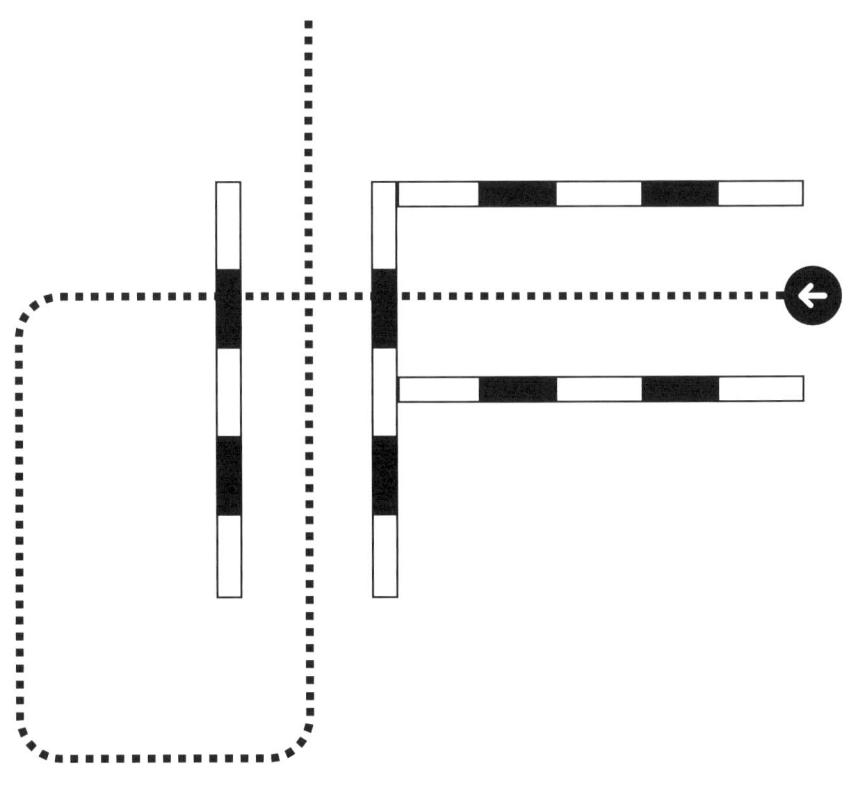

Poles: 4

Level: ★

Benefits:

- ☑ Accuracy
- ☑ Rhythm
- ☑ Impulsion
- ☑ Straightness
- ☑ Suppleness & bend
- ☐ Lateral movement & collection

Gaits:

- ☑ Groundwork
- ☑ Walk
- ☑ Trot
- ☐ Canter

Movements:

- ☐ Backup
- ☐ Leg yield
- ☐ Sidepass
- ☐ Shoulder in/out

5 Poles

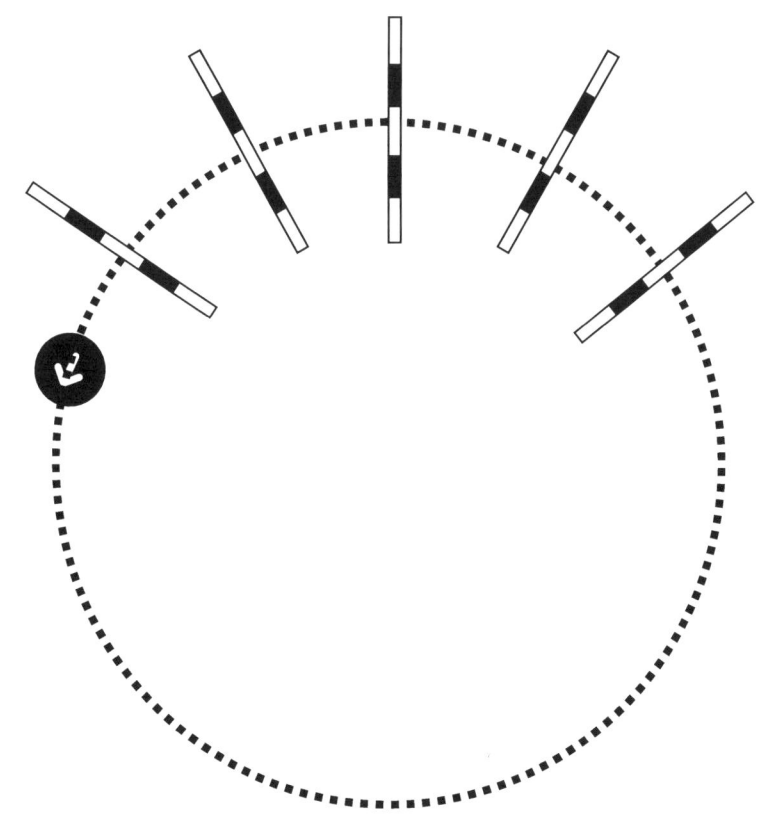

Poles: 5
Level: ⭐
Benefits:
- ☑ Accuracy
- ☑ Rhythm
- ☑ Impulsion
- ☐ Straightness
- ☑ Suppleness & bend
- ☐ Lateral movement & collection

Gaits:
- ☑ Groundwork
- ☑ Walk
- ☑ Trot
- ☐ Canter

Movements:
- ☐ Backup
- ☐ Leg yield
- ☐ Sidepass
- ☐ Shoulder in/out

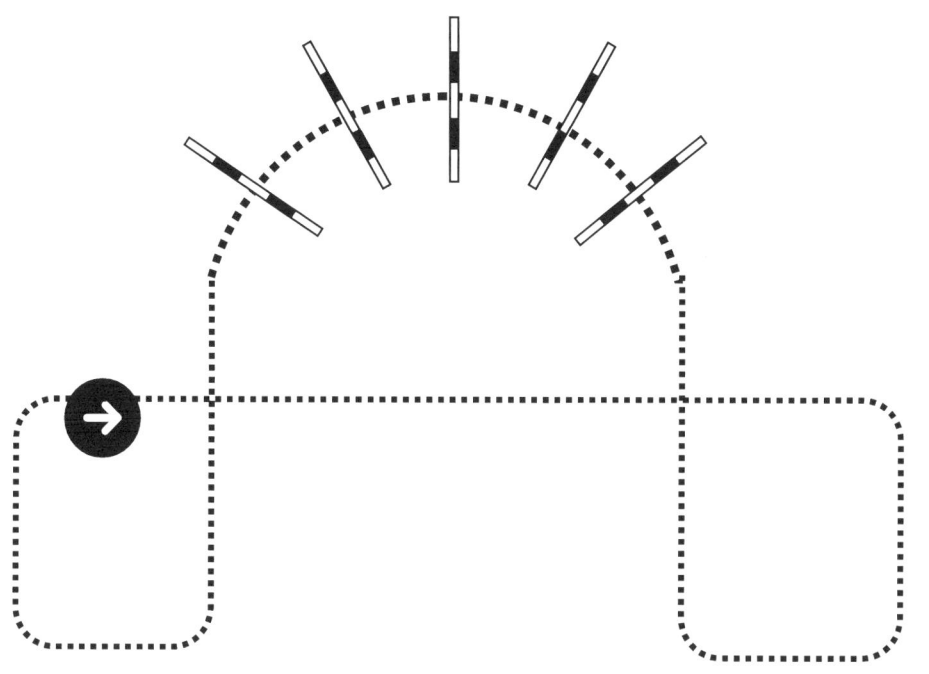

Poles: 5
Level: ★
Benefits:
- ☑ Accuracy
- ☑ Rhythm
- ☑ Impulsion
- ☐ Straightness
- ☑ Suppleness & bend
- ☐ Lateral movement & collection

Gaits:
- ☑ Groundwork
- ☑ Walk
- ☑ Trot
- ☐ Canter

Movements:
- ☐ Backup
- ☐ Leg yield
- ☐ Sidepass
- ☐ Shoulder in/out

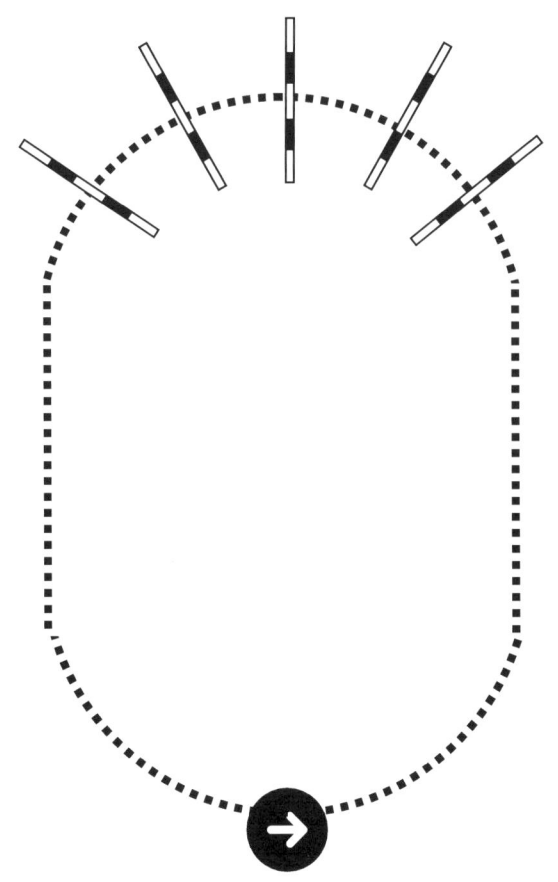

Poles: 5
Level: ★
Benefits:
- ☑ Accuracy
- ☑ Rhythm
- ☑ Impulsion
- ☐ Straightness
- ☑ Suppleness & bend
- ☐ Lateral movement & collection

Gaits:
- ☑ Groundwork
- ☑ Walk
- ☑ Trot
- ☐ Canter

Movements:
- ☐ Backup
- ☐ Leg yield
- ☐ Sidepass
- ☐ Shoulder in/out

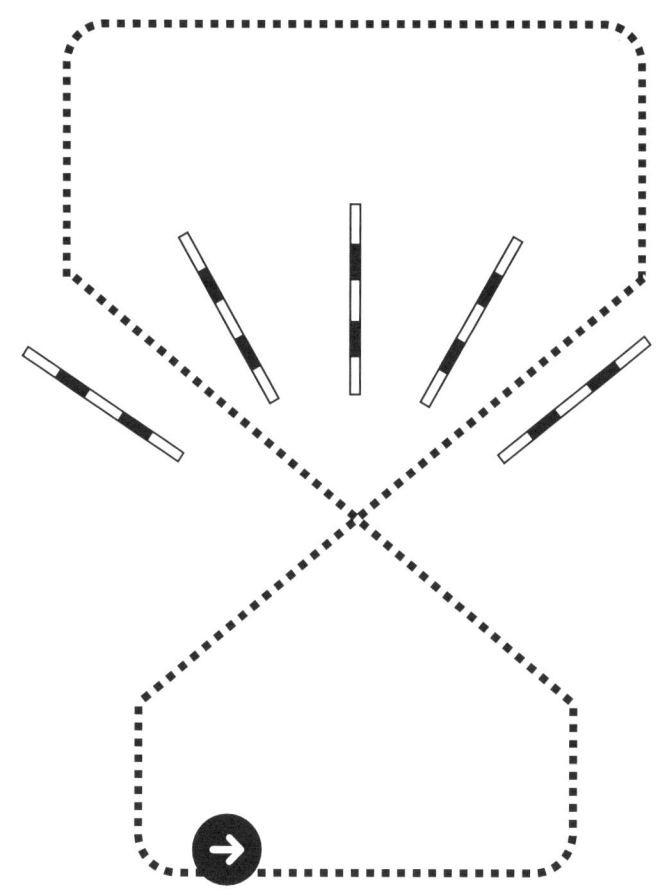

Poles: 5

Level: ★

Benefits:

- ☑ Accuracy
- ☑ Rhythm
- ☑ Impulsion
- ☑ Straightness
- ☑ Suppleness & bend
- ☐ Lateral movement & collection

Gaits:

- ☑ Groundwork
- ☑ Walk
- ☑ Trot
- ☑ Canter

Movements:

- ☐ Backup
- ☐ Leg yield
- ☐ Sidepass
- ☐ Shoulder in/out

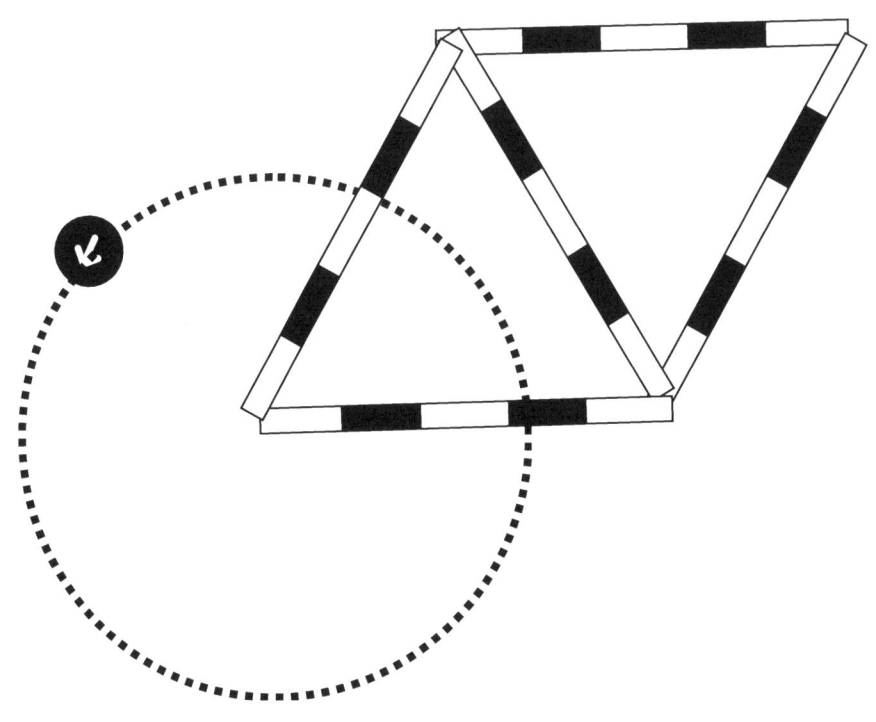

Poles: 5
Level: ★
Benefits:
- ☑ Accuracy
- ☑ Rhythm
- ☑ Impulsion
- ☐ Straightness
- ☑ Suppleness & bend
- ☐ Lateral movement & collection

Gaits:
- ☑ Groundwork
- ☑ Walk
- ☑ Trot
- ☑ Canter

Movements:
- ☐ Backup
- ☐ Leg yield
- ☐ Sidepass
- ☐ Shoulder in/out

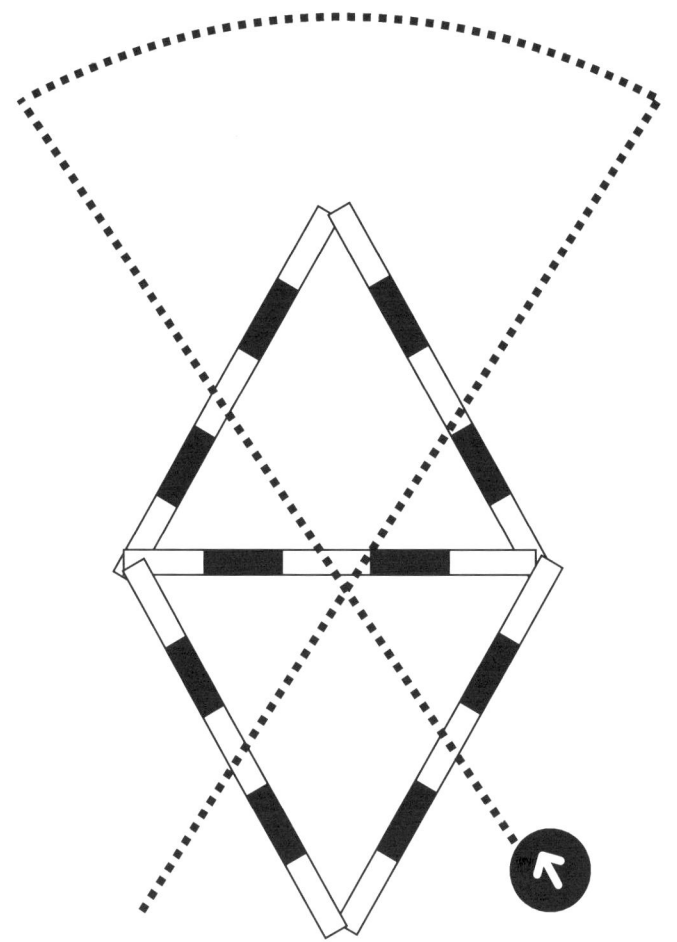

Poles: 5

Level: ★ ★

Benefits:

- ☑ Accuracy
- ☑ Rhythm
- ☑ Impulsion
- ☑ Straightness
- ☑ Suppleness & bend
- ☐ Lateral movement & collection

Gaits:

- ☑ Groundwork
- ☑ Walk
- ☑ Trot
- ☐ Canter

Movements:

- ☐ Backup
- ☐ Leg yield
- ☐ Sidepass
- ☐ Shoulder in/out

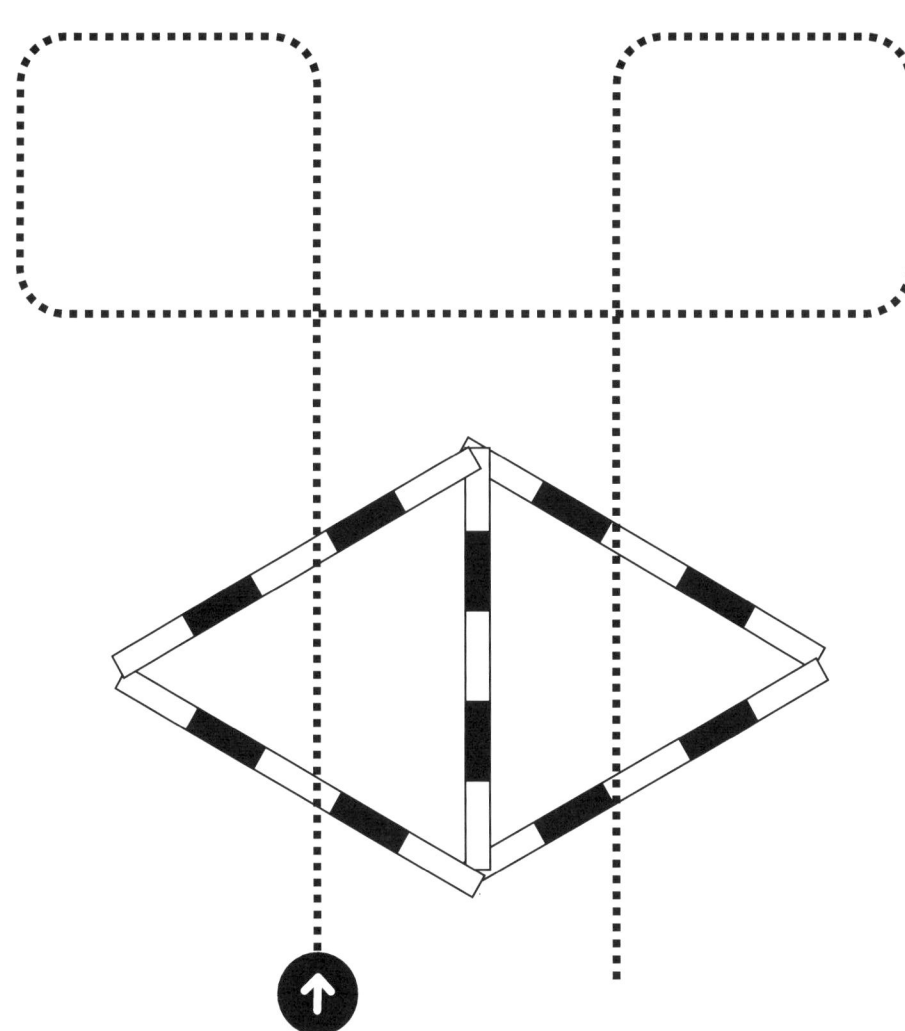

Poles: 5
Level: ⭐
Benefits:
- ☑ Accuracy
- ☑ Rhythm
- ☑ Impulsion
- ☑ Straightness
- ☑ Suppleness & bend
- ☐ Lateral movement & collection

Gaits:
- ☑ Groundwork
- ☑ Walk
- ☑ Trot
- ☐ Canter

Movements:
- ☐ Backup
- ☐ Leg yield
- ☐ Sidepass
- ☐ Shoulder in/out

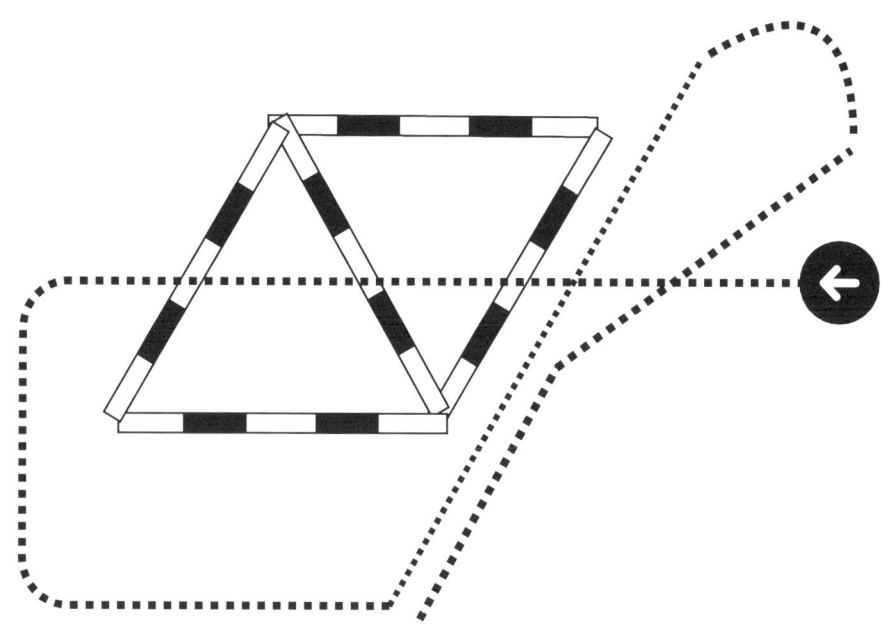

Poles: 5
Level: ★ ★
Benefits:
- ☑ Accuracy
- ☑ Rhythm
- ☑ Impulsion
- ☑ Straightness
- ☑ Suppleness & bend
- ☐ Lateral movement & collection

Gaits:
- ☑ Groundwork
- ☑ Walk
- ☑ Trot
- ☐ Canter

Movements:
- ☐ Backup
- ☐ Leg yield
- ☐ Sidepass
- ☐ Shoulder in/out

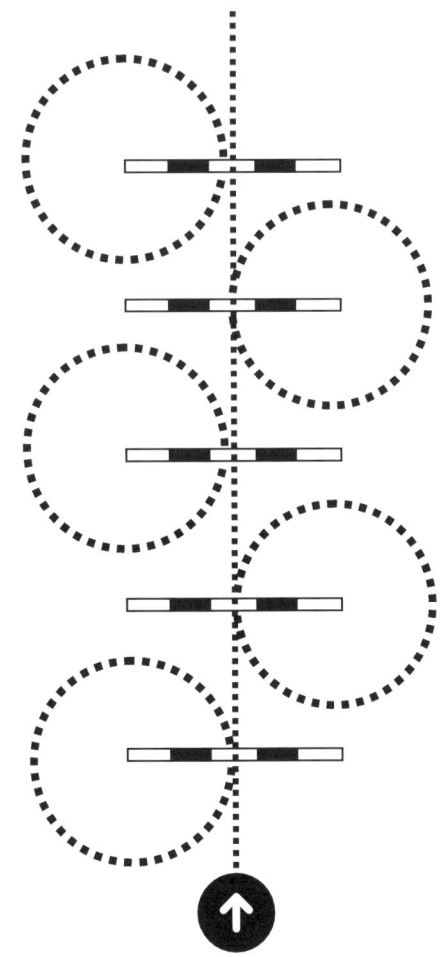

Poles: 5
Level: ★ ★
Benefits:
- ☑ Accuracy
- ☑ Rhythm
- ☑ Impulsion
- ☑ Straightness
- ☑ Suppleness & bend
- ☐ Lateral movement & collection

Gaits:
- ☑ Groundwork
- ☑ Walk
- ☑ Trot
- ☑ Canter

Movements:
- ☐ Backup
- ☐ Leg yield
- ☐ Sidepass
- ☐ Shoulder in/out

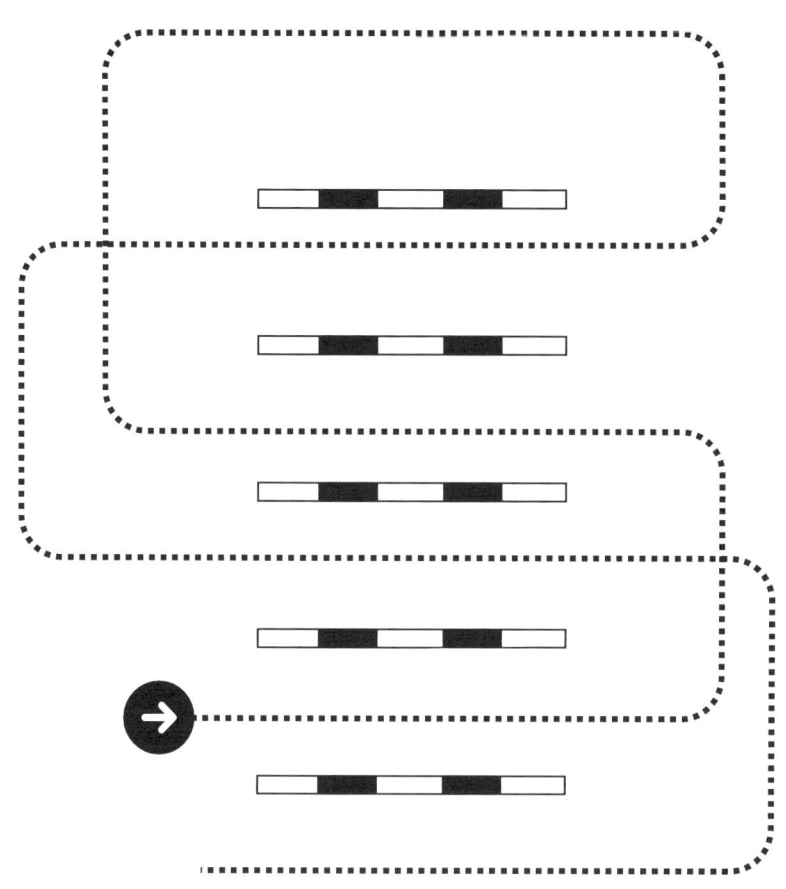

Poles: 5

Level: ⭐

Benefits:

- ☑ Accuracy
- ☑ Rhythm
- ☑ Impulsion
- ☑ Straightness
- ☑ Suppleness & bend
- ☐ Lateral movement & collection

Gaits:

- ☑ Groundwork
- ☑ Walk
- ☑ Trot
- ☑ Canter

Movements:

- ☐ Backup
- ☐ Leg yield
- ☐ Sidepass
- ☐ Shoulder in/out

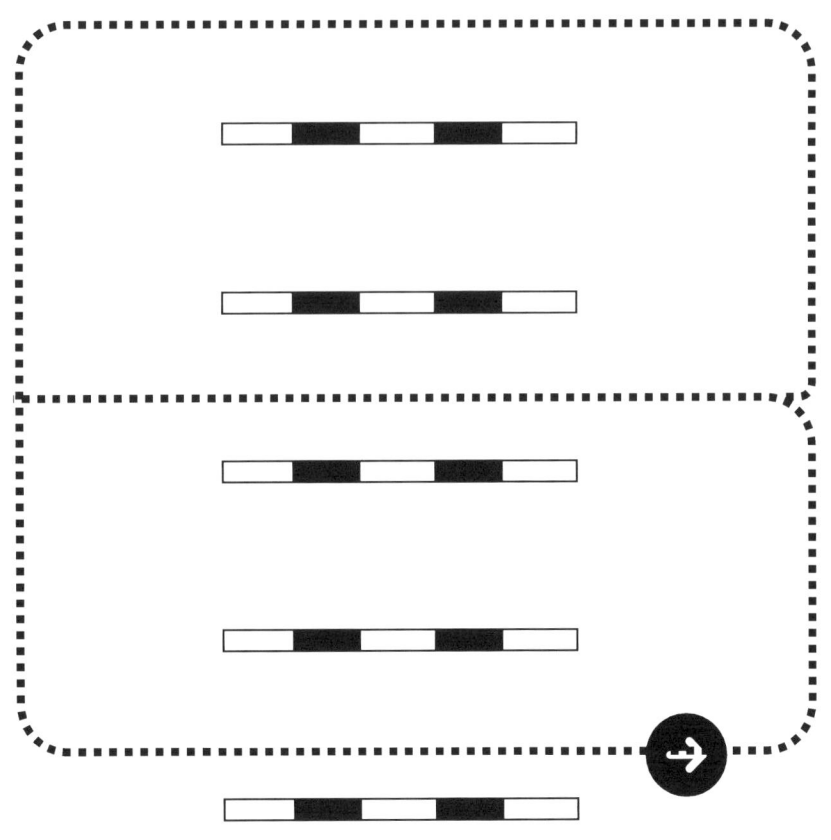

Poles: 5
Level: ★
Benefits:
☑ Accuracy
☑ Rhythm
☑ Impulsion
☑ Straightness
☑ Suppleness & bend
☐ Lateral movement
   & collection

Gaits:
☑ Groundwork
☑ Walk
☑ Trot
☑ Canter

Movements:
☐ Backup
☐ Leg yield
☐ Sidepass
☐ Shoulder in/out

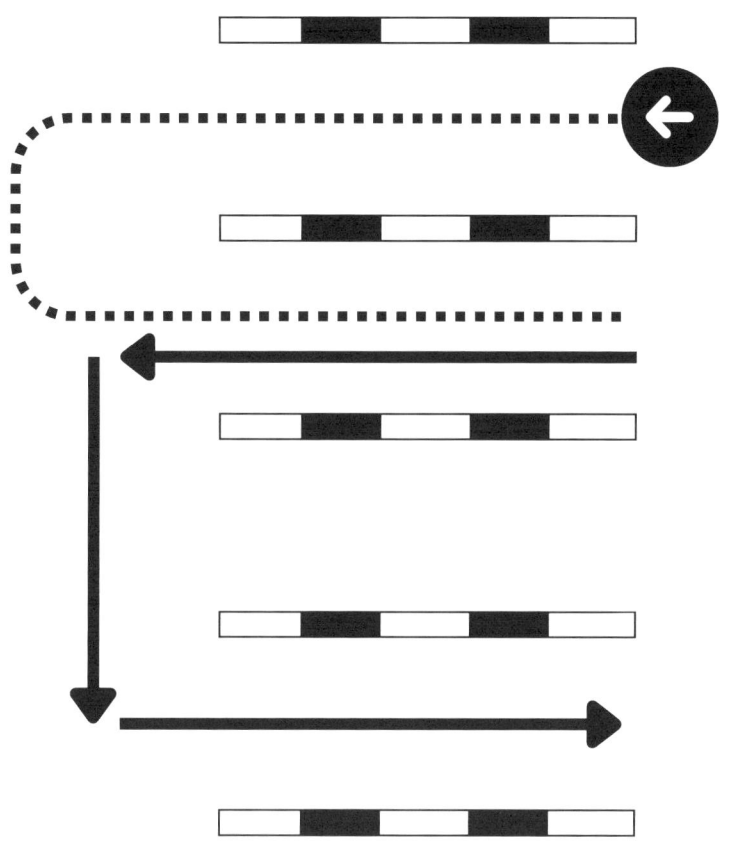

Poles: 5

Level: ★ ★ ★

Benefits:
- ☑ Accuracy
- ☑ Rhythm
- ☑ Impulsion
- ☑ Straightness
- ☑ Suppleness & bend
- ☑ Lateral movement & collection

Gaits:
- ☑ Groundwork
- ☑ Walk
- ☑ Trot
- ☑ Canter

Movements:
- ☑ Backup
- ☐ Leg yield
- ☐ Sidepass
- ☐ Shoulder in/out

6 Poles

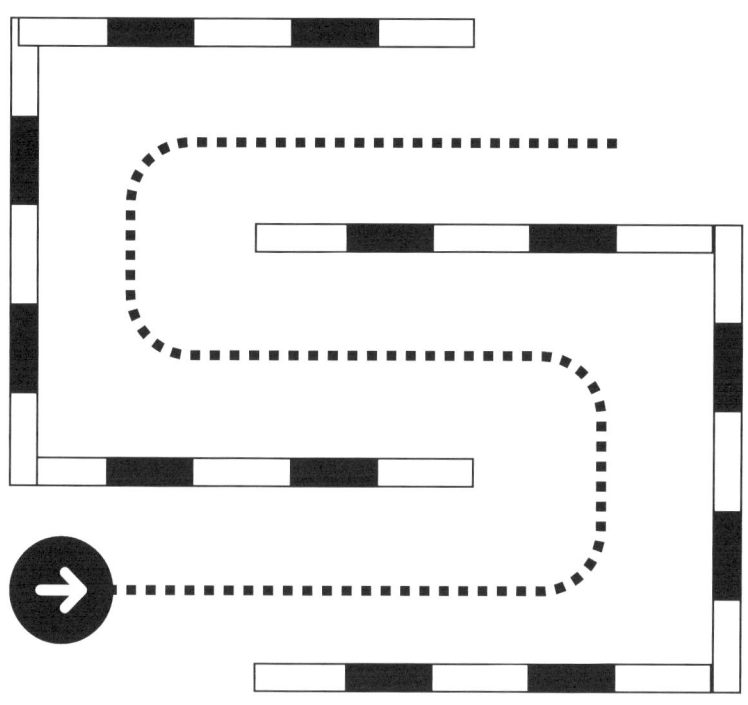

Poles: 6

Level: ★

Benefits:

- ☑ Accuracy
- ☑ Rhythm
- ☑ Impulsion
- ☐ Straightness
- ☑ Suppleness & bend
- ☐ Lateral movement & collection

Gaits:

- ☑ Groundwork
- ☑ Walk
- ☐ Trot
- ☐ Canter

Movements:

- ☐ Backup
- ☐ Leg yield
- ☐ Sidepass
- ☐ Shoulder in/out

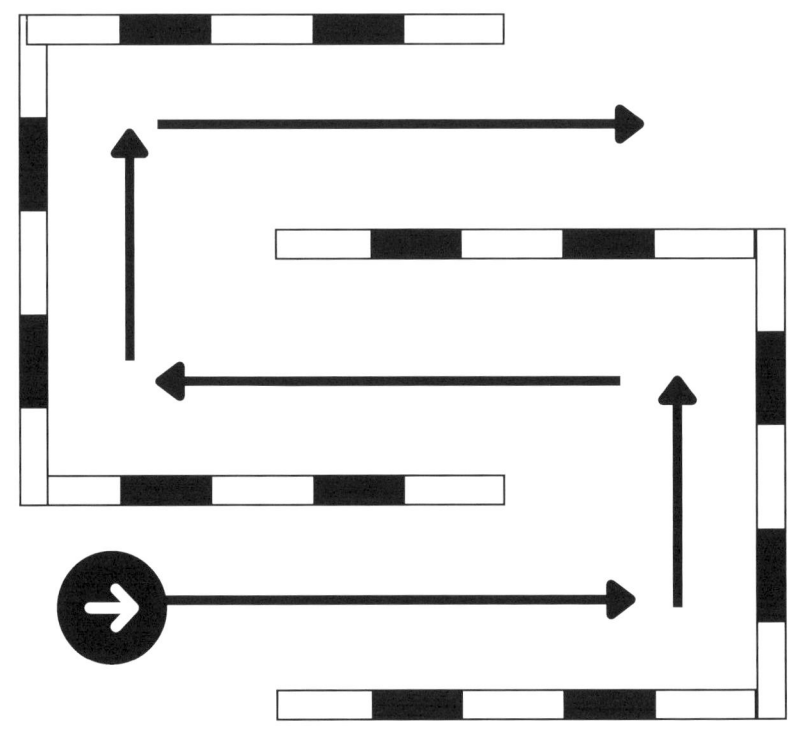

Poles: 6

Level: ★ ★ ★

Benefits:
- ☑ Accuracy
- ☑ Rhythm
- ☑ Impulsion
- ☐ Straightness
- ☐ Suppleness & bend
- ☑ Lateral movement & collection

Gaits:
- ☑ Groundwork
- ☑ Walk
- ☐ Trot
- ☐ Canter

Movements:
- ☑ Backup
- ☐ Leg yield
- ☐ Sidepass
- ☐ Shoulder in/out

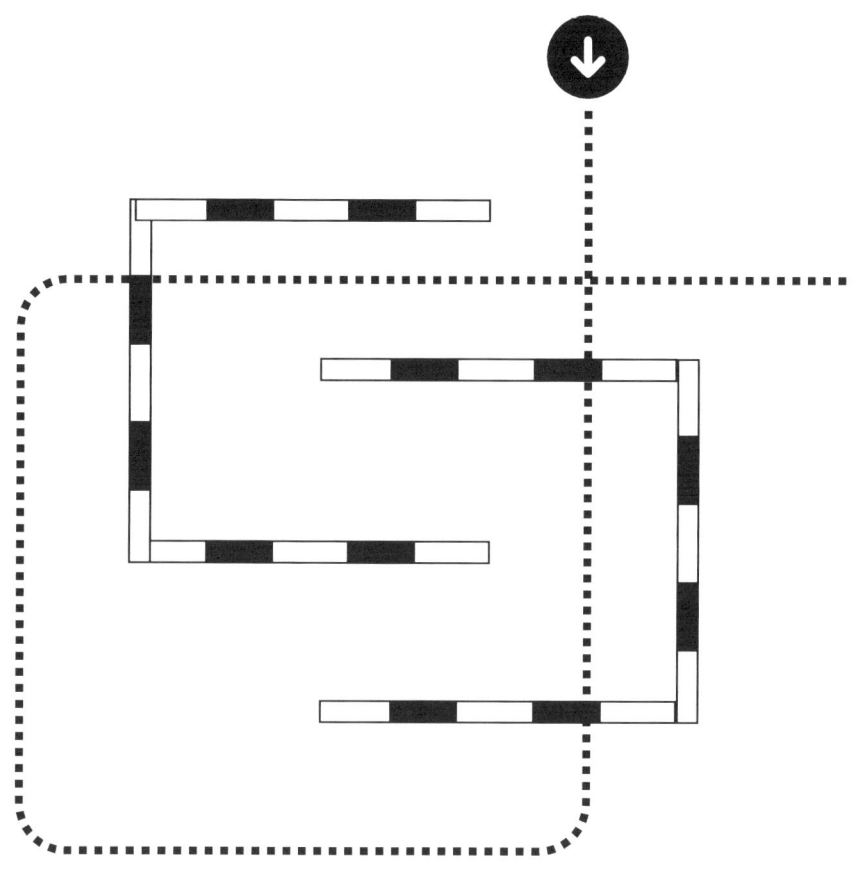

Poles: 6
Level: ★
Benefits:
- ☑ Accuracy
- ☑ Rhythm
- ☑ Impulsion
- ☑ Straightness
- ☑ Suppleness & bend
- ☐ Lateral movement & collection

Gaits:
- ☑ Groundwork
- ☑ Walk
- ☑ Trot
- ☑ Canter

Movements:
- ☐ Backup
- ☐ Leg yield
- ☐ Sidepass
- ☐ Shoulder in/out

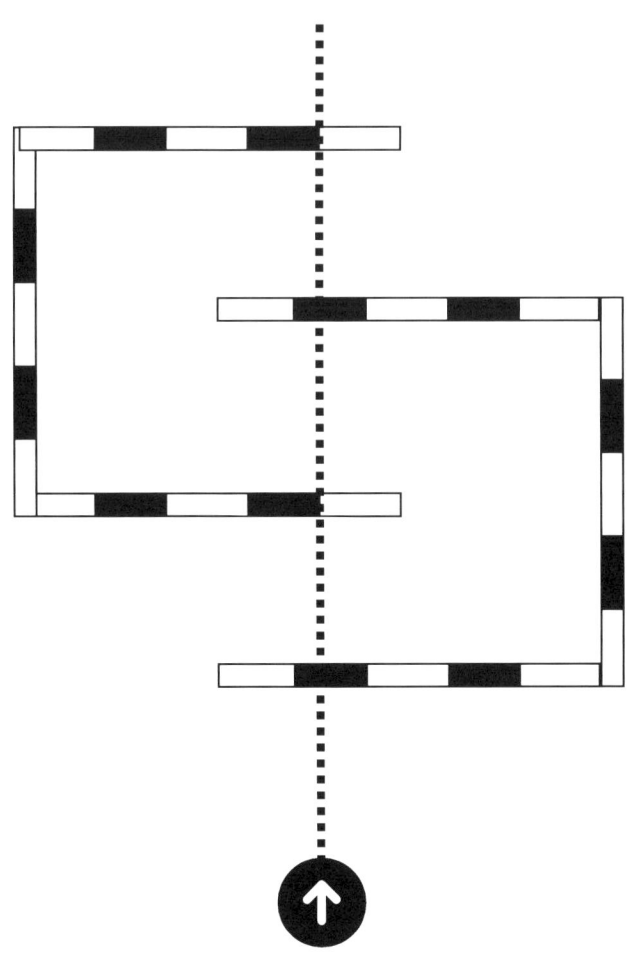

Poles: 6
Level: ★
Benefits:
- ☑ Accuracy
- ☑ Rhythm
- ☑ Impulsion
- ☑ Straightness
- ☐ Suppleness & bend
- ☐ Lateral movement & collection

Gaits:
- ☑ Groundwork
- ☑ Walk
- ☑ Trot
- ☐ Canter

Movements:
- ☐ Backup
- ☐ Leg yield
- ☐ Sidepass
- ☐ Shoulder in/out

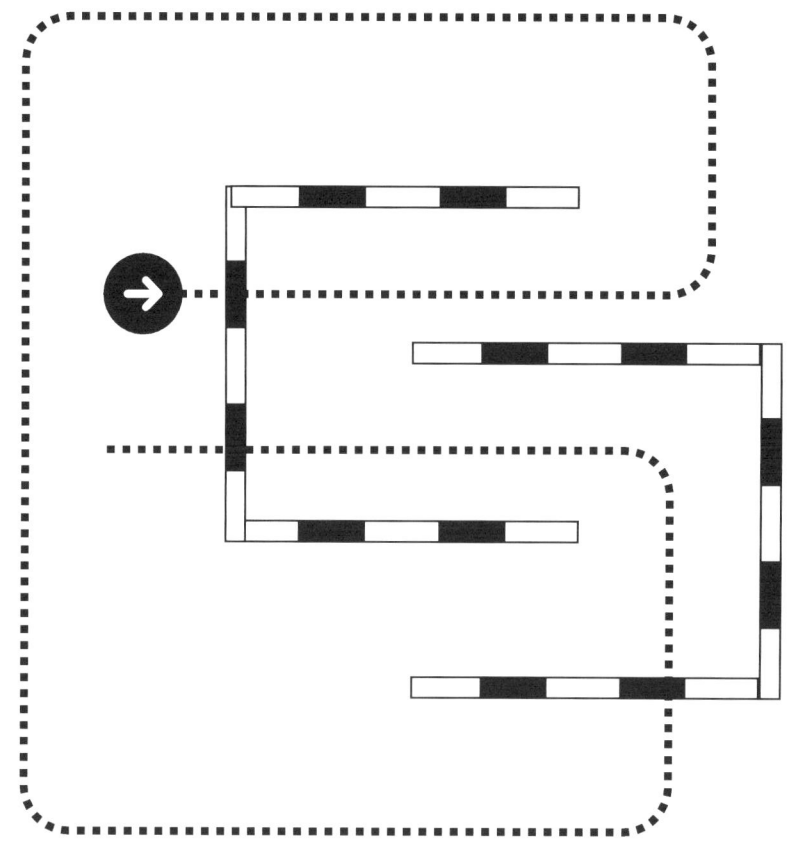

Poles: 6
Level: ★
Benefits:
- ☑ Accuracy
- ☑ Rhythm
- ☑ Impulsion
- ☑ Straightness
- ☑ Suppleness & bend
- ☐ Lateral movement & collection

Gaits:
- ☑ Groundwork
- ☑ Walk
- ☑ Trot
- ☐ Canter

Movements:
- ☐ Backup
- ☐ Leg yield
- ☐ Sidepass
- ☐ Shoulder in/out

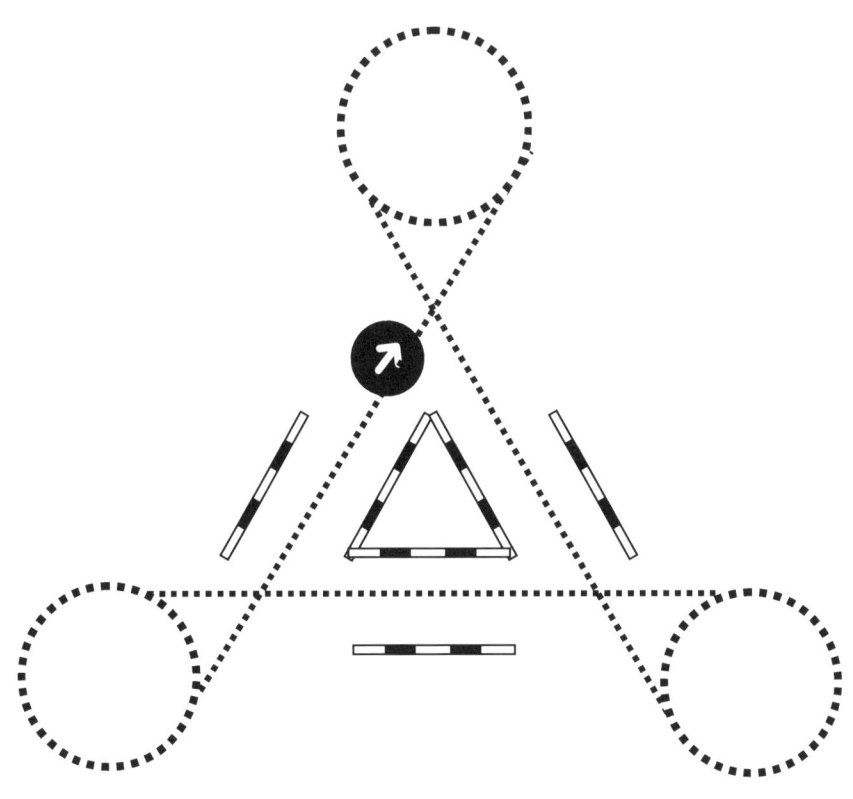

Poles: 6
Level: ★
Benefits:
- ☑ Accuracy
- ☑ Rhythm
- ☑ Impulsion
- ☑ Straightness
- ☑ Suppleness & bend
- ☐ Lateral movement & collection

Gaits:
- ☑ Groundwork
- ☑ Walk
- ☑ Trot
- ☑ Canter

Movements:
- ☐ Backup
- ☐ Leg yield
- ☐ Sidepass
- ☐ Shoulder in/out

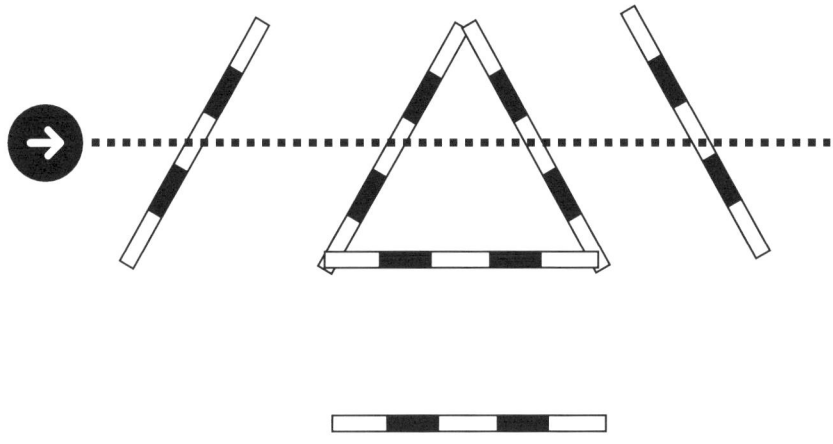

Poles: 6
Level: ★
Benefits:
- ☑ Accuracy
- ☑ Rhythm
- ☑ Impulsion
- ☑ Straightness
- ☐ Suppleness & bend
- ☐ Lateral movement
   & collection

Gaits:
- ☑ Groundwork
- ☑ Walk
- ☑ Trot
- ☐ Canter

Movements:
- ☐ Backup
- ☐ Leg yield
- ☐ Sidepass
- ☐ Shoulder in/out

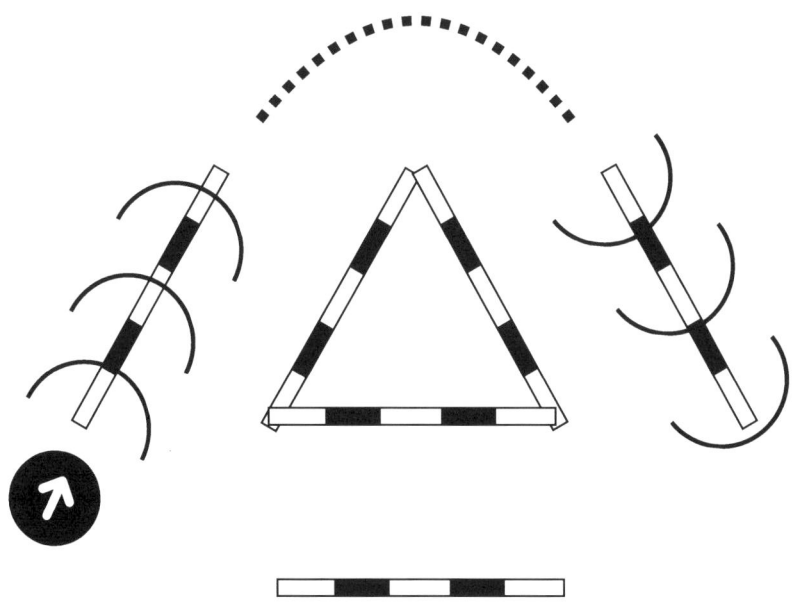

Poles: 6

Level: ★ ★

Benefits:
- ☑ Accuracy
- ☑ Rhythm
- ☑ Impulsion
- ☐ Straightness
- ☑ Suppleness & bend
- ☑ Lateral movement & collection

Gaits:
- ☑ Groundwork
- ☑ Walk
- ☐ Trot
- ☐ Canter

Movements:
- ☐ Backup
- ☐ Leg yield
- ☑ Sidepass
- ☐ Shoulder in/out

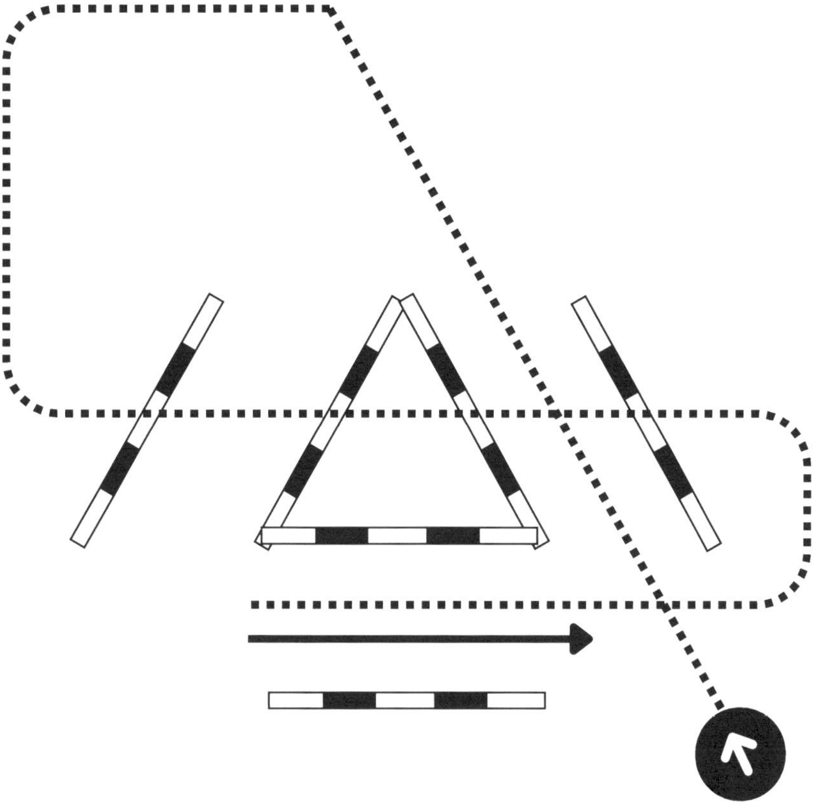

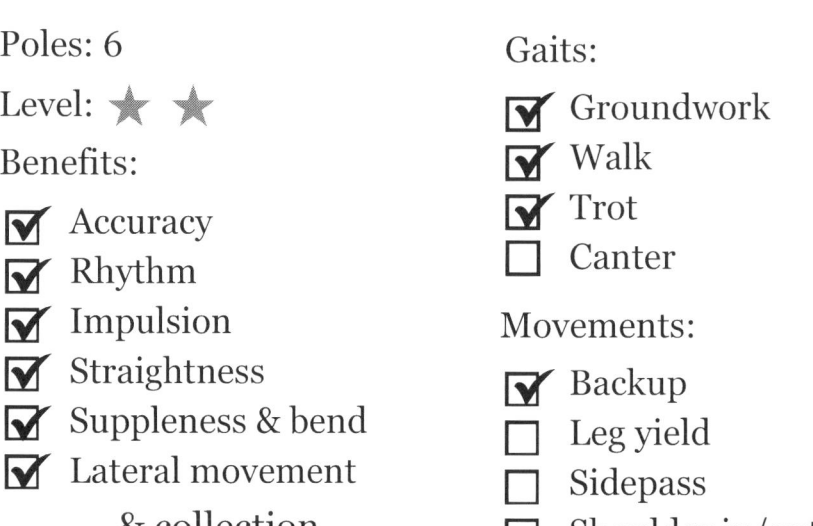

Poles: 6
Level: ★ ★
Benefits:
- ☑ Accuracy
- ☑ Rhythm
- ☑ Impulsion
- ☑ Straightness
- ☑ Suppleness & bend
- ☑ Lateral movement & collection

Gaits:
- ☑ Groundwork
- ☑ Walk
- ☑ Trot
- ☐ Canter

Movements:
- ☑ Backup
- ☐ Leg yield
- ☐ Sidepass
- ☐ Shoulder in/out

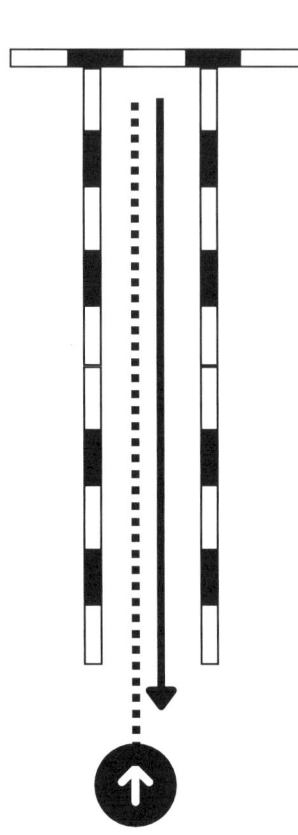

Poles: 6
Level: ★ ★
Benefits:
- ☑ Accuracy
- ☑ Rhythm
- ☑ Impulsion
- ☑ Straightness
- ☐ Suppleness & bend
- ☑ Lateral movement & collection

Gaits:
- ☑ Groundwork
- ☑ Walk
- ☑ Trot
- ☑ Canter

Movements:
- ☑ Backup
- ☐ Leg yield
- ☐ Sidepass
- ☐ Shoulder in/out

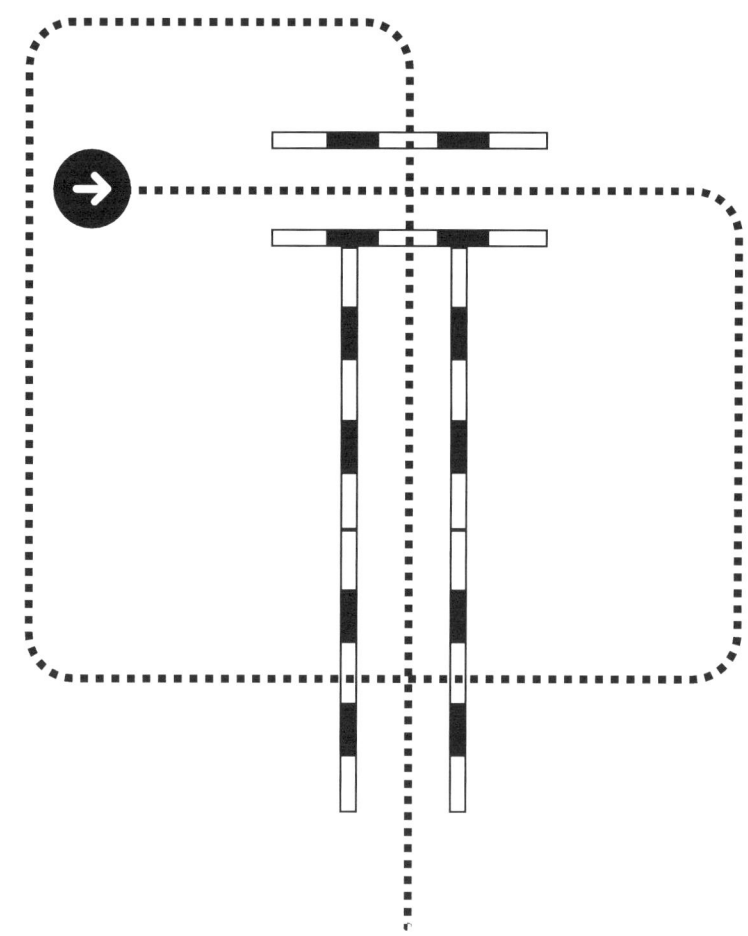

Poles: 6
Level: ★
Benefits:
- ☑ Accuracy
- ☑ Rhythm
- ☑ Impulsion
- ☑ Straightness
- ☑ Suppleness & bend
- ☐ Lateral movement & collection

Gaits:
- ☑ Groundwork
- ☑ Walk
- ☑ Trot
- ☐ Canter

Movements:
- ☐ Backup
- ☐ Leg yield
- ☐ Sidepass
- ☐ Shoulder in/out

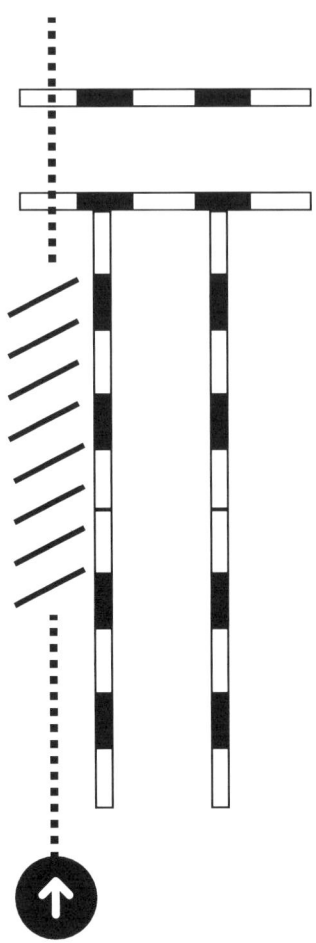

Poles: 6
Level: ★ ★
Benefits:
- ☑ Accuracy
- ☑ Rhythm
- ☑ Impulsion
- ☑ Straightness
- ☐ Suppleness & bend
- ☑ Lateral movement & collection

Gaits:
- ☑ Groundwork
- ☑ Walk
- ☐ Trot
- ☐ Canter

Movements:
- ☐ Backup
- ☐ Leg yield
- ☐ Sidepass
- ☑ Shoulder in

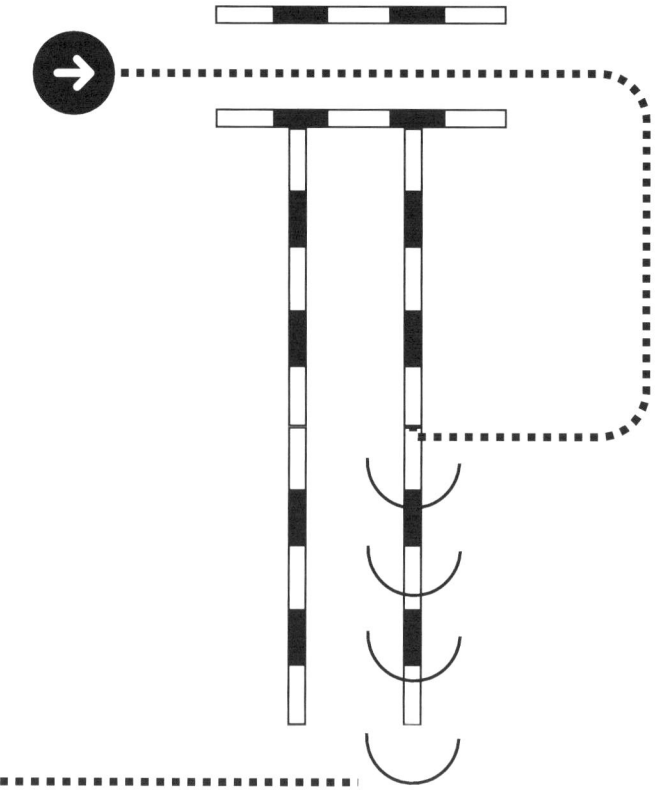

Poles: 6
Level: ★ ★
Benefits:
- ☑ Accuracy
- ☑ Rhythm
- ☑ Impulsion
- ☑ Straightness
- ☑ Suppleness & bend
- ☑ Lateral movement & collection

Gaits:
- ☑ Groundwork
- ☑ Walk
- ☑ Trot
- ☐ Canter

Movements:
- ☐ Backup
- ☐ Leg yield
- ☑ Sidepass
- ☐ Shoulder in/out

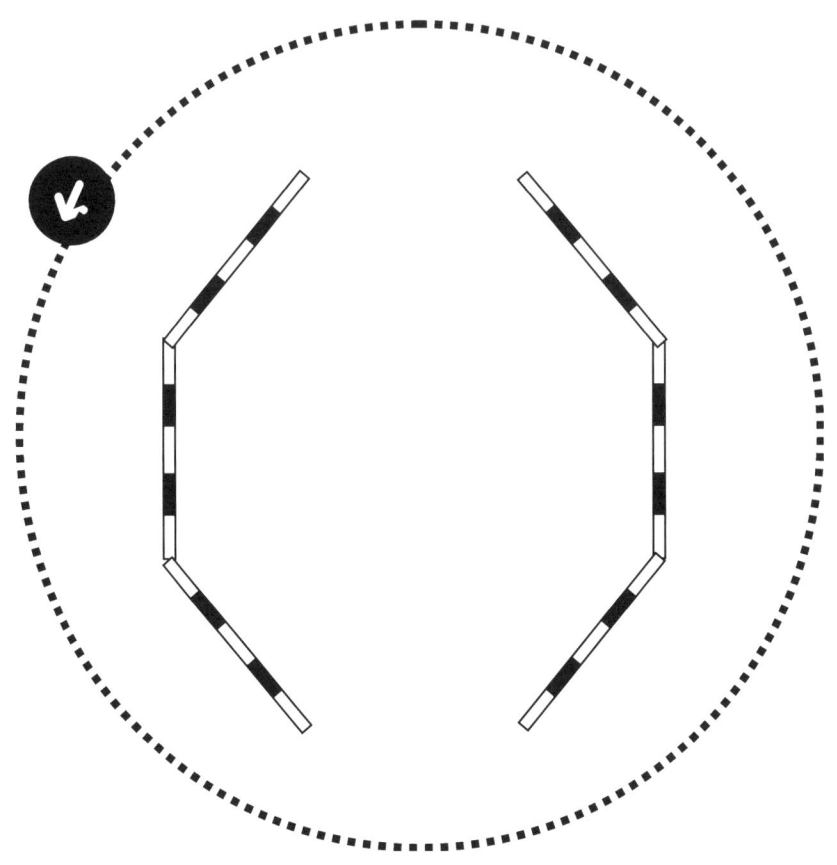

Poles: 6
Level: ★
Benefits:
- ☑ Accuracy
- ☑ Rhythm
- ☑ Impulsion
- ☐ Straightness
- ☑ Suppleness & bend
- ☐ Lateral movement & collection

Gaits:
- ☑ Groundwork
- ☑ Walk
- ☑ Trot
- ☑ Canter

Movements:
- ☐ Backup
- ☐ Leg yield
- ☐ Sidepass
- ☐ Shoulder in/out

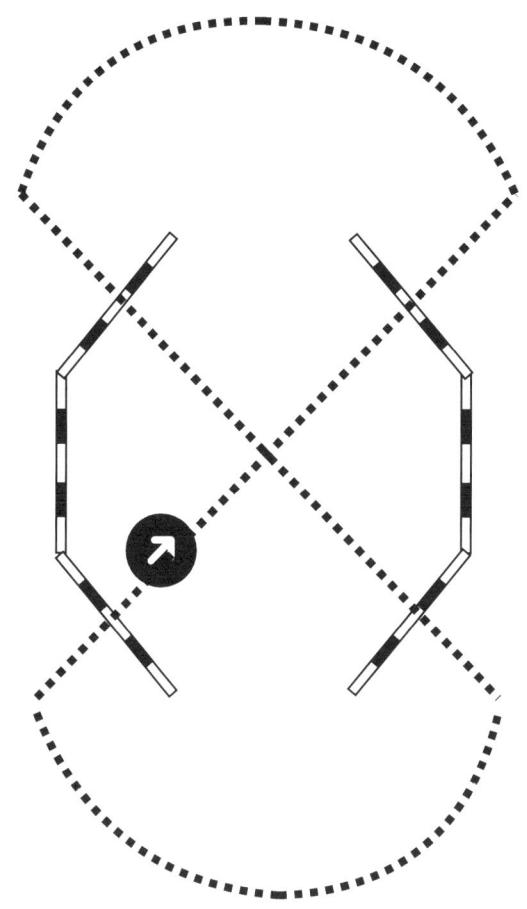

Poles: 6
Level: ★
Benefits:
- ☑ Accuracy
- ☑ Rhythm
- ☑ Impulsion
- ☑ Straightness
- ☑ Suppleness & bend
- ☐ Lateral movement & collection

Gaits:
- ☑ Groundwork
- ☑ Walk
- ☑ Trot
- ☑ Canter

Movements:
- ☐ Backup
- ☐ Leg yield
- ☐ Sidepass
- ☐ Shoulder in/out

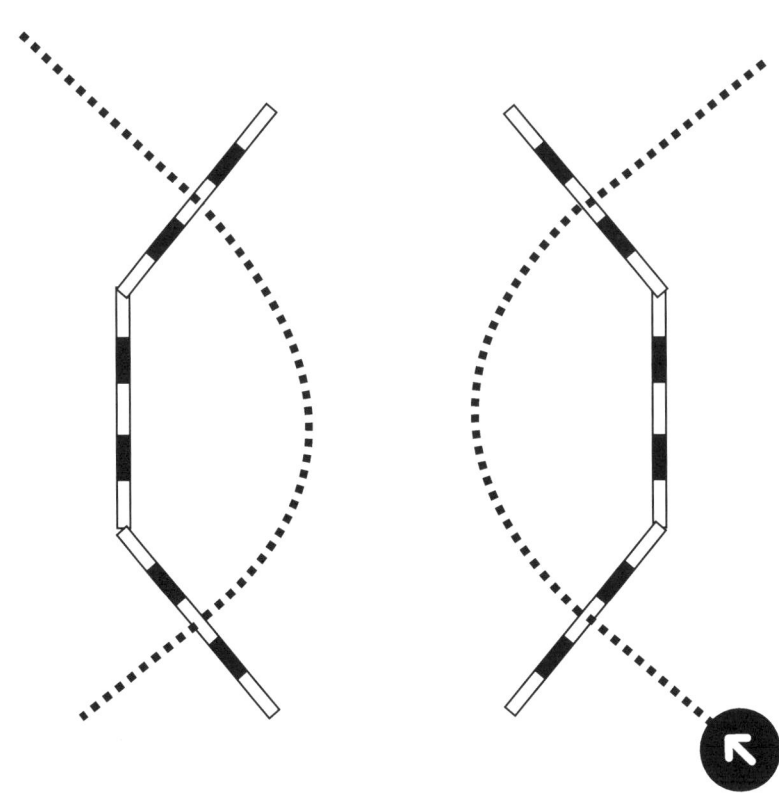

Poles: 6
Level: ★
Benefits:
- ☑ Accuracy
- ☑ Rhythm
- ☑ Impulsion
- ☐ Straightness
- ☑ Suppleness & bend
- ☐ Lateral movement
  & collection

Gaits:
- ☑ Groundwork
- ☑ Walk
- ☑ Trot
- ☑ Canter

Movements:
- ☐ Backup
- ☐ Leg yield
- ☐ Sidepass
- ☐ Shoulder in/out

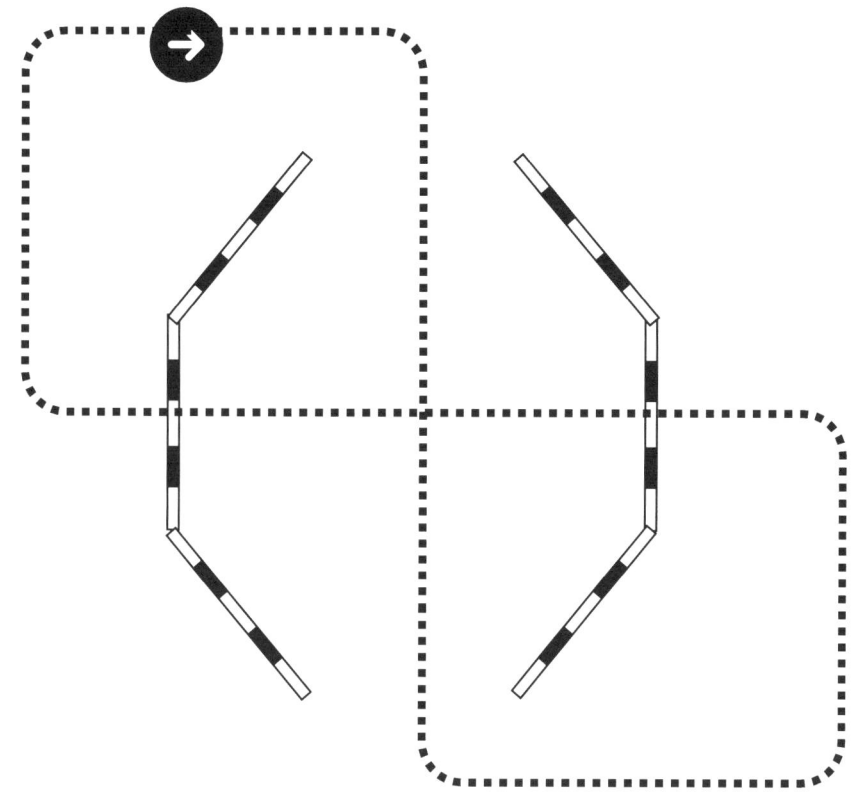

Poles: 6
Level: ★
Benefits:
- ☑ Accuracy
- ☑ Rhythm
- ☑ Impulsion
- ☑ Straightness
- ☑ Suppleness & bend
- ☐ Lateral movement & collection

Gaits:
- ☑ Groundwork
- ☑ Walk
- ☑ Trot
- ☑ Canter

Movements:
- ☐ Backup
- ☐ Leg yield
- ☐ Sidepass
- ☐ Shoulder in/out

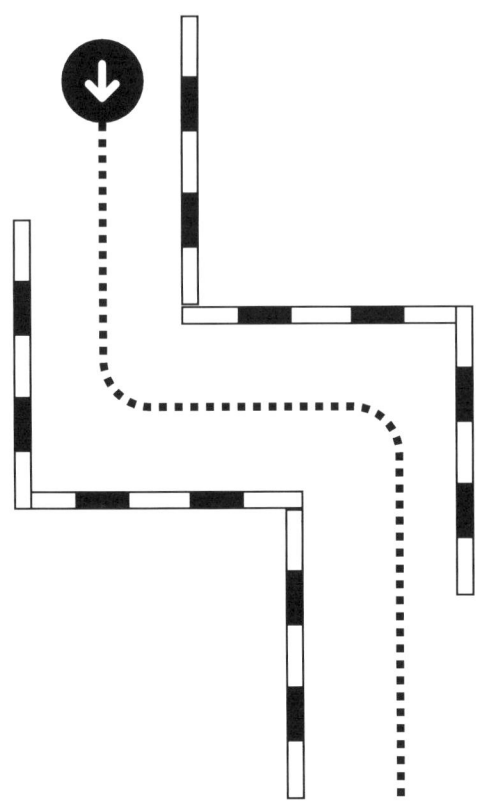

Poles: 6
Level: ★
Benefits:
- ☑ Accuracy
- ☑ Rhythm
- ☑ Impulsion
- ☑ Straightness
- ☑ Suppleness & bend
- ☐ Lateral movement & collection

Gaits:
- ☑ Groundwork
- ☑ Walk
- ☐ Trot
- ☐ Canter

Movements:
- ☐ Backup
- ☐ Leg yield
- ☐ Sidepass
- ☐ Shoulder in/out

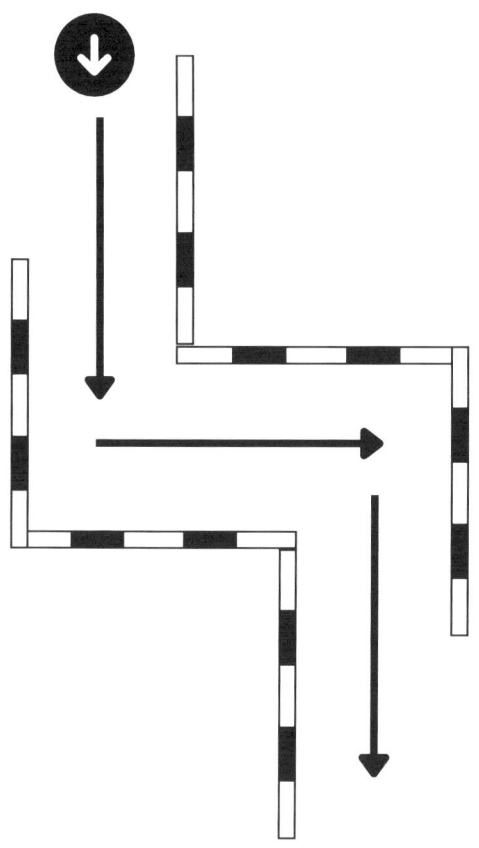

Poles: 6
Level: ★ ★
Benefits:
- ☑ Accuracy
- ☑ Rhythm
- ☑ Impulsion
- ☑ Straightness
- ☑ Suppleness & bend
- ☑ Lateral movement & collection

Gaits:
- ☑ Groundwork
- ☑ Walk
- ☐ Trot
- ☐ Canter

Movements:
- ☑ Backup
- ☐ Leg yield
- ☐ Sidepass
- ☐ Shoulder in/out

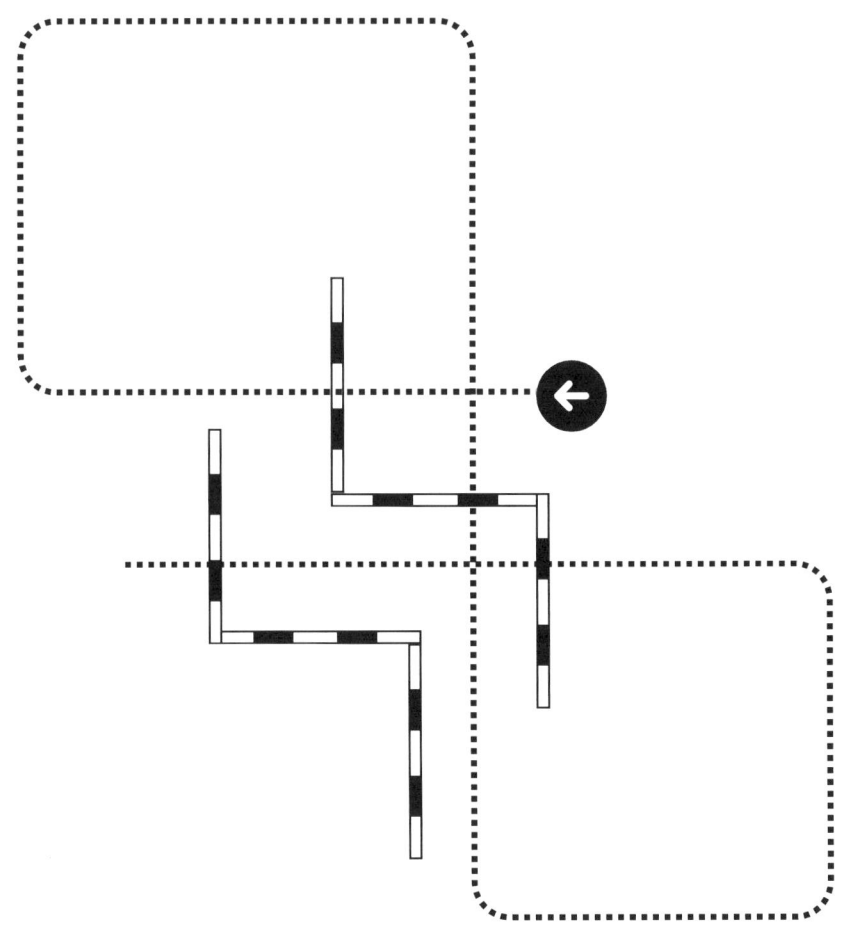

Poles: 6
Level: ★
Benefits:
- ☑ Accuracy
- ☑ Rhythm
- ☑ Impulsion
- ☑ Straightness
- ☑ Suppleness & bend
- ☐ Lateral movement & collection

Gaits:
- ☑ Groundwork
- ☑ Walk
- ☑ Trot
- ☑ Canter

Movements:
- ☐ Backup
- ☐ Leg yield
- ☐ Sidepass
- ☐ Shoulder in/out

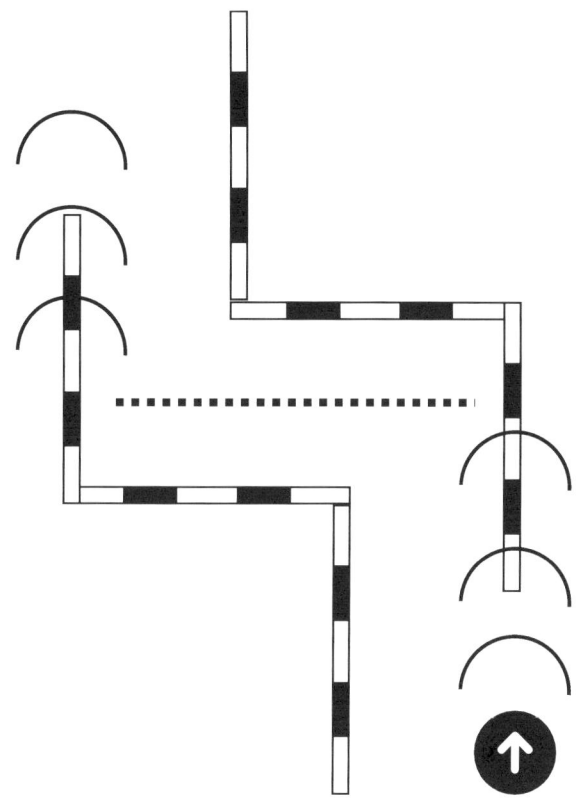

Poles: 6
Level: ★ ★
Benefits:
- ☑ Accuracy
- ☑ Rhythm
- ☑ Impulsion
- ☑ Straightness
- ☑ Suppleness & bend
- ☑ Lateral movement & collection

Gaits:
- ☑ Groundwork
- ☑ Walk
- ☐ Trot
- ☐ Canter

Movements:
- ☐ Backup
- ☐ Leg yield
- ☑ Sidepass
- ☐ Shoulder in/out

7 Poles

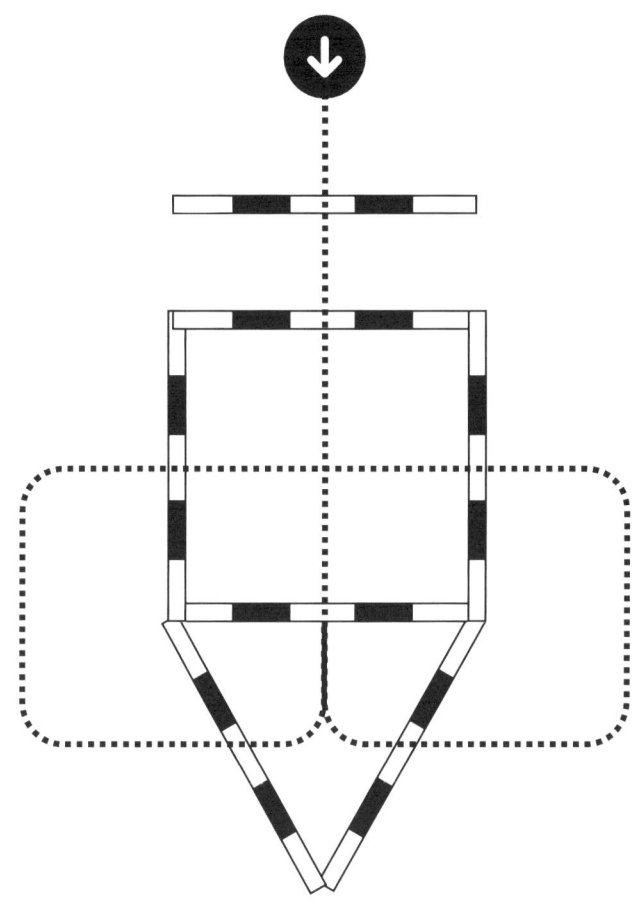

Poles: 7
Level: ⭐
Benefits:
- ☑ Accuracy
- ☑ Rhythm
- ☑ Impulsion
- ☑ Straightness
- ☑ Suppleness & bend
- ☐ Lateral movement & collection

Gaits:
- ☑ Groundwork
- ☑ Walk
- ☑ Trot
- ☐ Canter

Movements:
- ☐ Backup
- ☐ Leg yield
- ☐ Sidepass
- ☐ Shoulder in/out

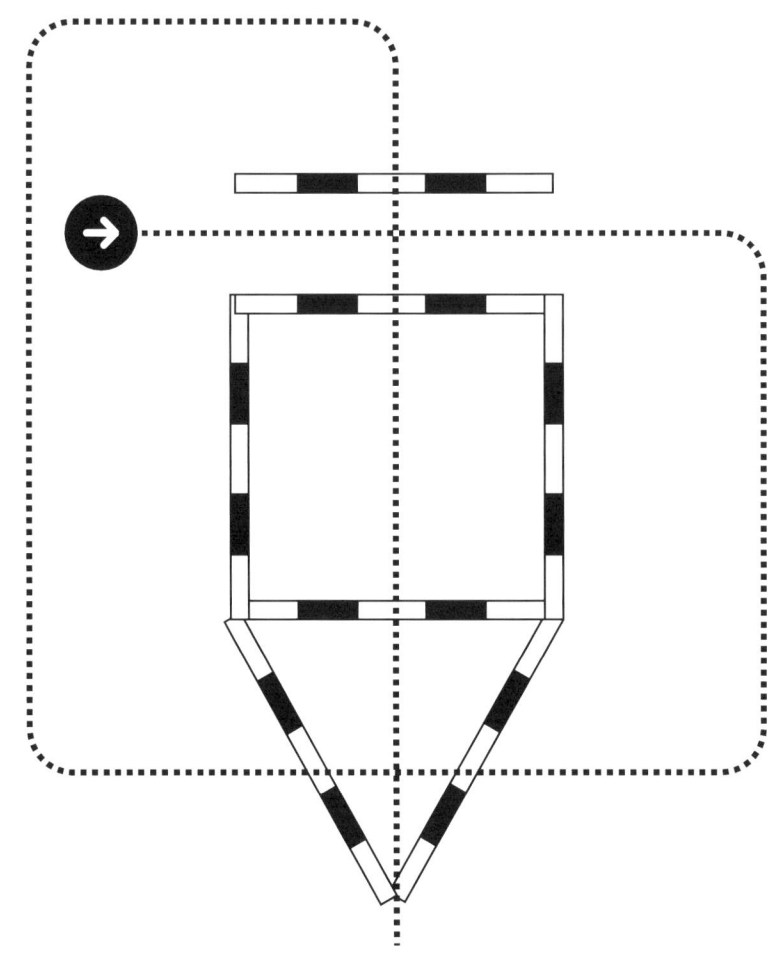

Poles: 7
Level: ★
Benefits:
- ☑ Accuracy
- ☑ Rhythm
- ☑ Impulsion
- ☑ Straightness
- ☑ Suppleness & bend
- ☐ Lateral movement & collection

Gaits:
- ☑ Groundwork
- ☑ Walk
- ☑ Trot
- ☐ Canter

Movements:
- ☐ Backup
- ☐ Leg yield
- ☐ Sidepass
- ☐ Shoulder in/out

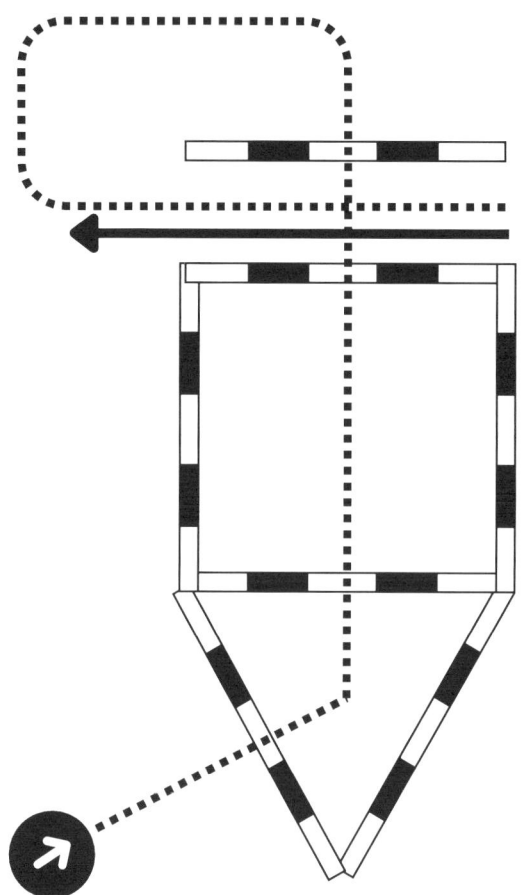

Poles: 7

Level: ★ ★

Benefits:
- ☑ Accuracy
- ☑ Rhythm
- ☑ Impulsion
- ☑ Straightness
- ☑ Suppleness & bend
- ☑ Lateral movement & collection

Gaits:
- ☑ Groundwork
- ☑ Walk
- ☑ Trot
- ☐ Canter

Movements:
- ☑ Backup
- ☐ Leg yield
- ☐ Sidepass
- ☐ Shoulder in/out

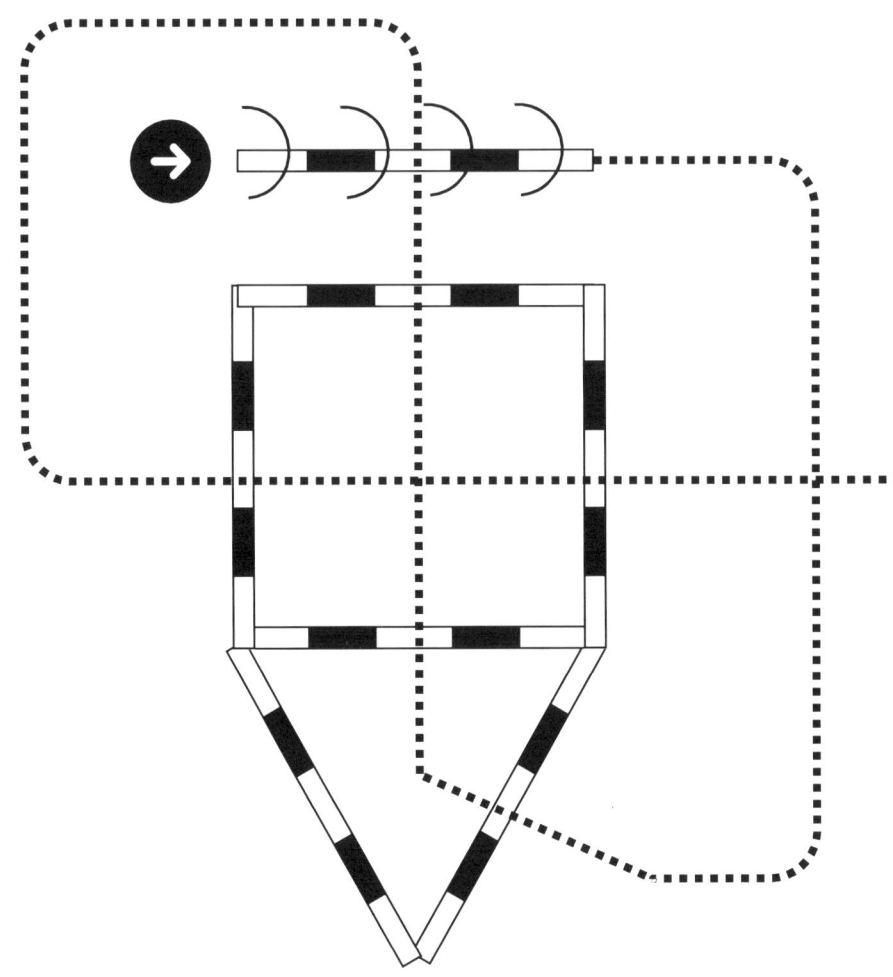

Poles: 7

Level: ★ ★

Benefits:

- ☑ Accuracy
- ☑ Rhythm
- ☑ Impulsion
- ☑ Straightness
- ☑ Suppleness & bend
- ☑ Lateral movement & collection

Gaits:

- ☑ Groundwork
- ☑ Walk
- ☑ Trot
- ☐ Canter

Movements:

- ☐ Backup
- ☐ Leg yield
- ☑ Sidepass
- ☐ Shoulder in/out

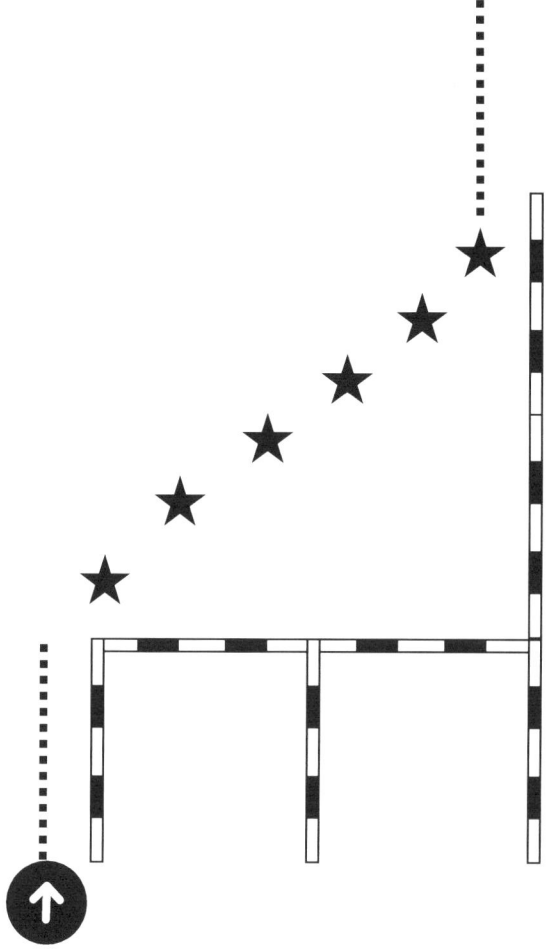

Poles: 7
Level: ★ ★
Benefits:
- ☑ Accuracy
- ☑ Rhythm
- ☑ Impulsion
- ☑ Straightness
- ☑ Suppleness & bend
- ☑ Lateral movement & collection

Gaits:
- ☑ Groundwork
- ☑ Walk
- ☑ Trot
- ☑ Canter

Movements:
- ☐ Backup
- ☑ Leg yield
- ☐ Sidepass
- ☐ Shoulder in/out

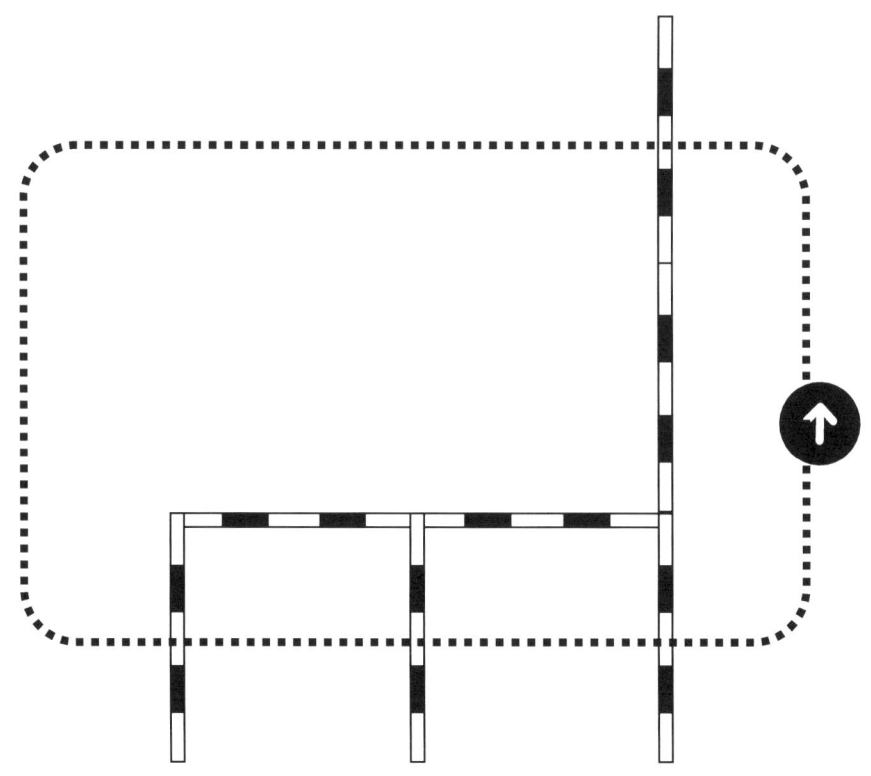

Poles: 7
Level: ★
Benefits:
- ☑ Accuracy
- ☑ Rhythm
- ☑ Impulsion
- ☑ Straightness
- ☑ Suppleness & bend
- ☐ Lateral movement & collection

Gaits:
- ☑ Groundwork
- ☑ Walk
- ☑ Trot
- ☐ Canter

Movements:
- ☐ Backup
- ☐ Leg yield
- ☐ Sidepass
- ☐ Shoulder in/out

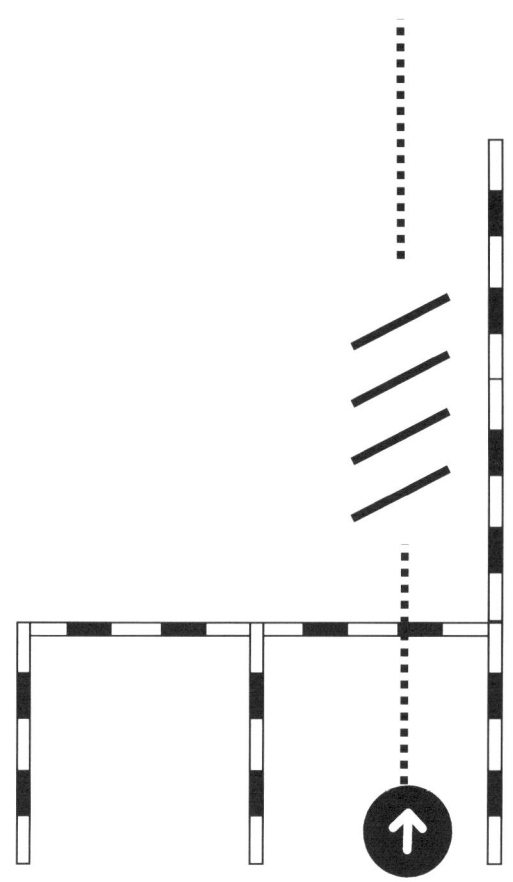

Poles: 7

Level: ★ ★

Benefits:

- ☑ Accuracy
- ☑ Rhythm
- ☑ Impulsion
- ☑ Straightness
- ☐ Suppleness & bend
- ☑ Lateral movement & collection

Gaits:

- ☑ Groundwork
- ☑ Walk
- ☑ Trot
- ☑ Canter

Movements:

- ☐ Backup
- ☐ Leg yield
- ☐ Sidepass
- ☑ Shoulder out

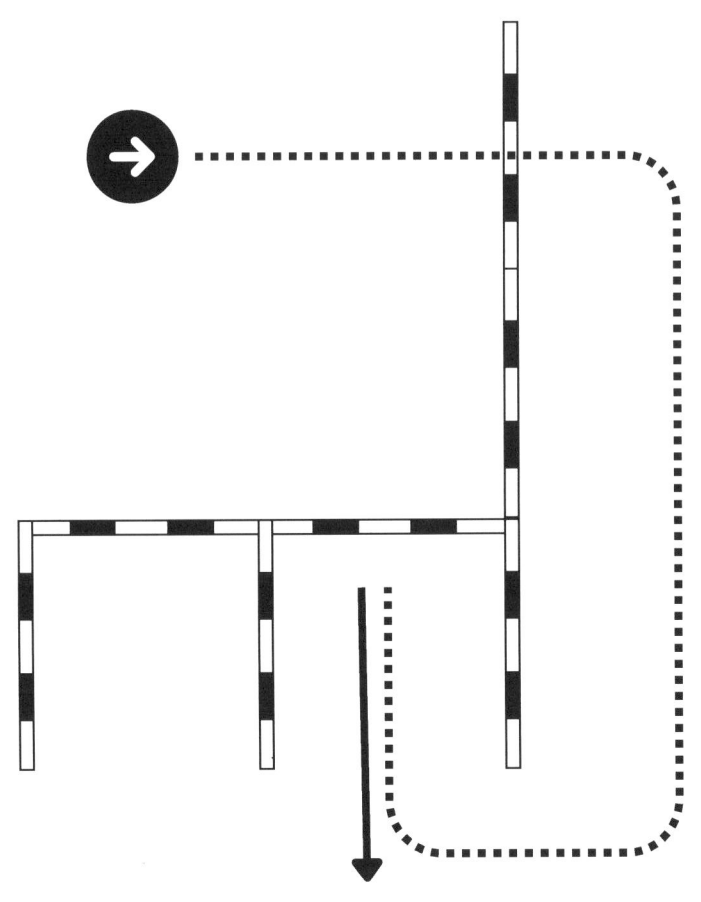

Poles: 7
Level: ★ ★
Benefits:
- ☑ Accuracy
- ☑ Rhythm
- ☑ Impulsion
- ☑ Straightness
- ☑ Suppleness & bend
- ☑ Lateral movement
  & collection

Gaits:
- ☑ Groundwork
- ☑ Walk
- ☑ Trot
- ☑ Canter

Movements:
- ☑ Backup
- ☐ Leg yield
- ☐ Sidepass
- ☐ Shoulder in/out

8 Poles

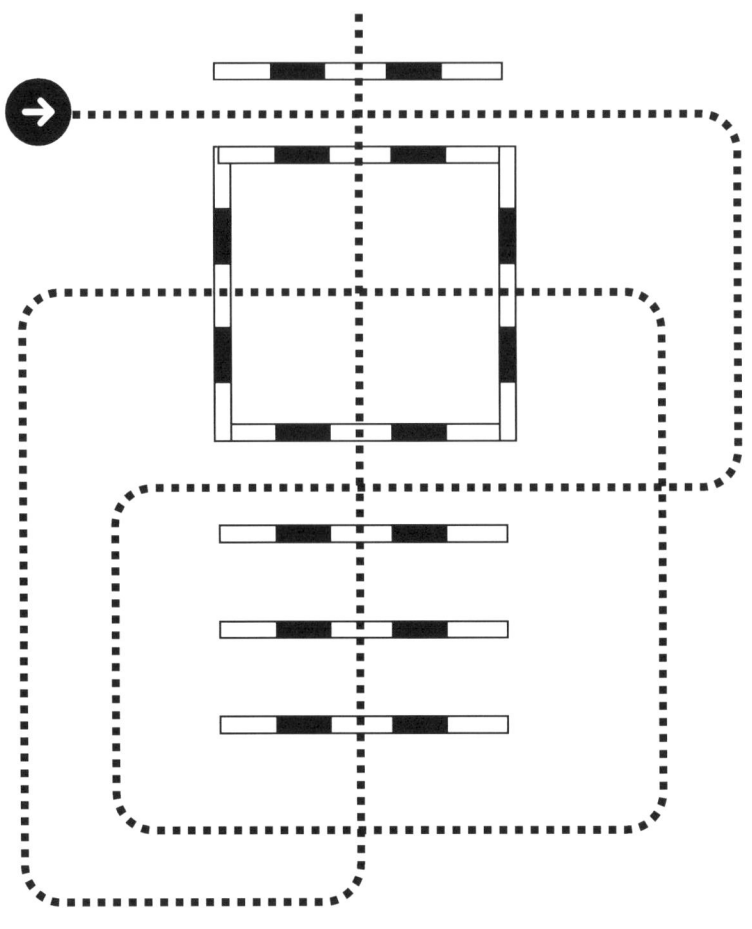

Poles: 8
Level: ★
Benefits:
- ☑ Accuracy
- ☑ Rhythm
- ☑ Impulsion
- ☑ Straightness
- ☑ Suppleness & bend
- ☐ Lateral movement & collection

Gaits:
- ☑ Groundwork
- ☑ Walk
- ☑ Trot
- ☑ Canter

Movements:
- ☐ Backup
- ☐ Leg yield
- ☐ Sidepass
- ☐ Shoulder in/out

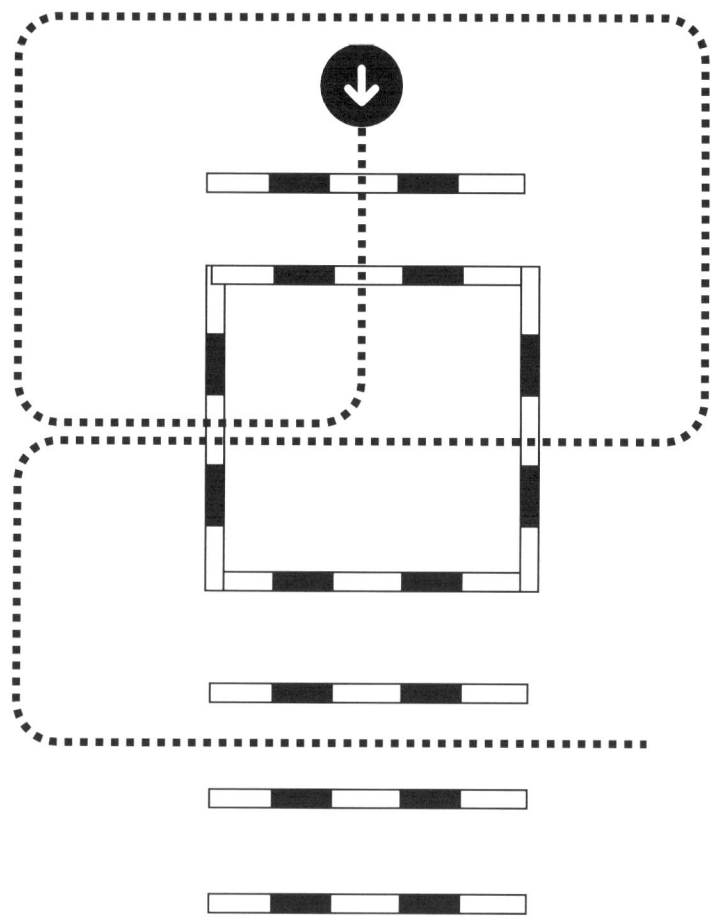

Poles: 8

Level: ⭐

Benefits:

- ☑ Accuracy
- ☑ Rhythm
- ☑ Impulsion
- ☑ Straightness
- ☑ Suppleness & bend
- ☐ Lateral movement & collection

Gaits:

- ☑ Groundwork
- ☑ Walk
- ☑ Trot
- ☐ Canter

Movements:

- ☐ Backup
- ☐ Leg yield
- ☐ Sidepass
- ☐ Shoulder in/out

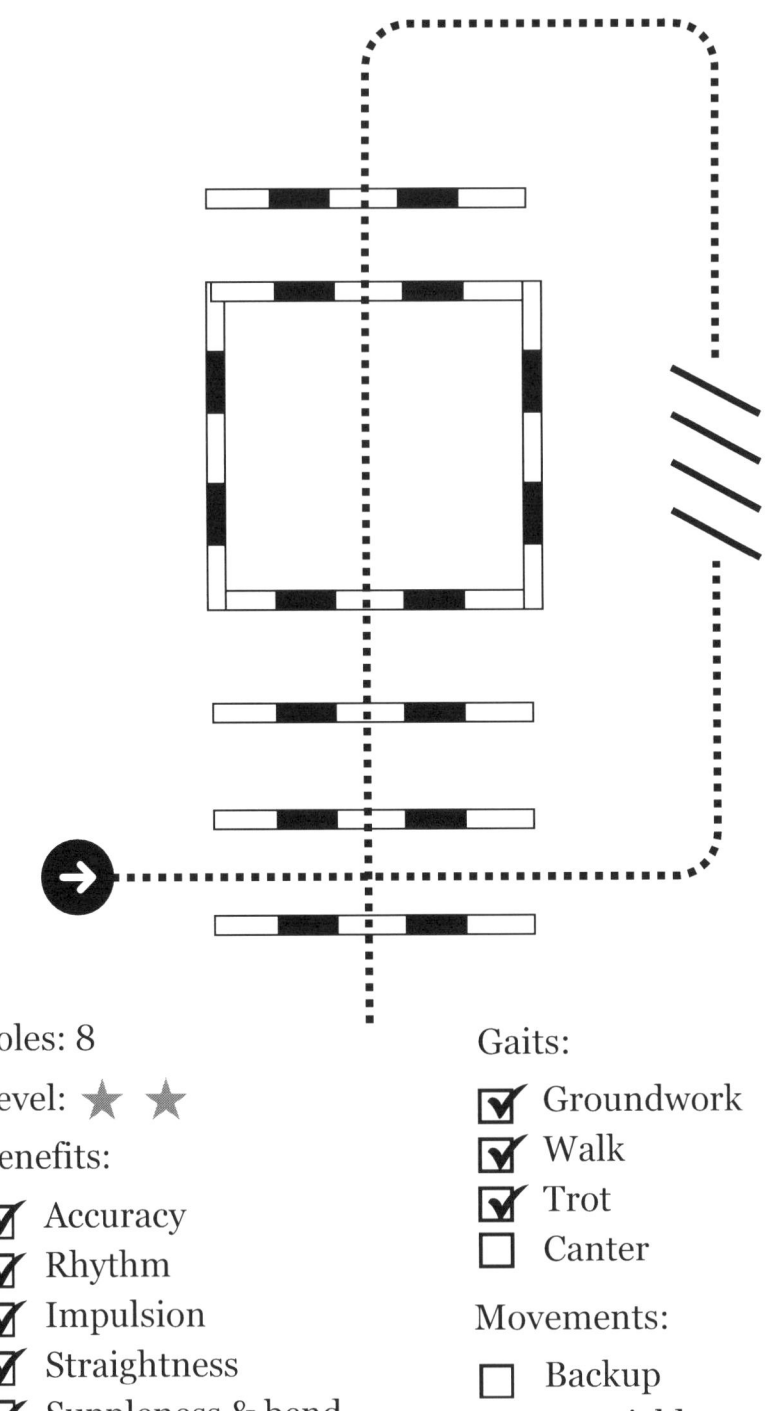

Poles: 8
Level: ★ ★
Benefits:
- ☑ Accuracy
- ☑ Rhythm
- ☑ Impulsion
- ☑ Straightness
- ☑ Suppleness & bend
- ☑ Lateral movement & collection

Gaits:
- ☑ Groundwork
- ☑ Walk
- ☑ Trot
- ☐ Canter

Movements:
- ☐ Backup
- ☐ Leg yield
- ☐ Sidepass
- ☑ Shoulder in

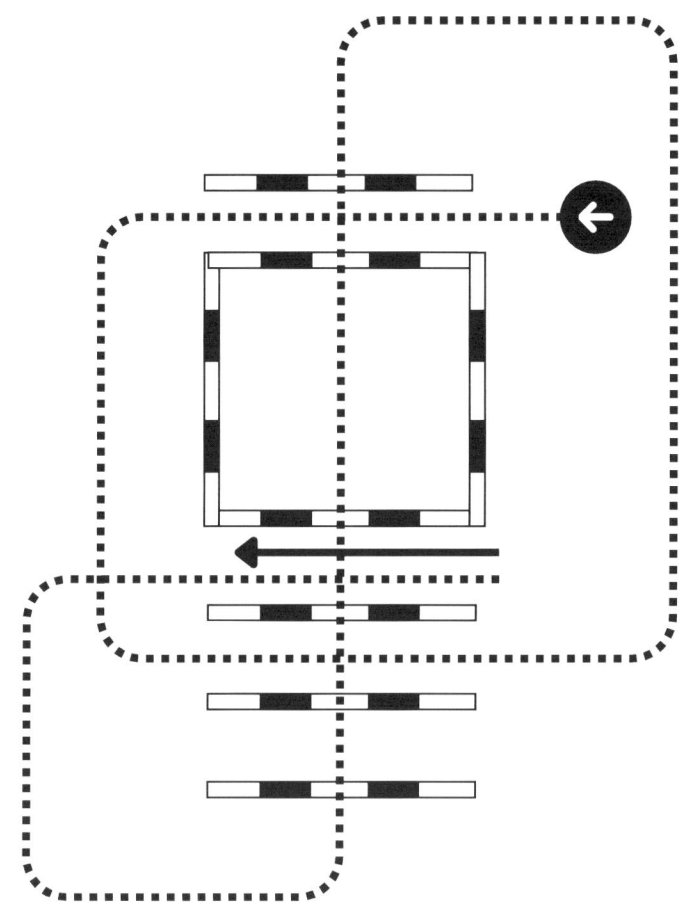

Poles: 8
Level: ★ ★
Benefits:
- ☑ Accuracy
- ☑ Rhythm
- ☑ Impulsion
- ☑ Straightness
- ☑ Suppleness & bend
- ☑ Lateral movement & collection

Gaits:
- ☑ Groundwork
- ☑ Walk
- ☑ Trot
- ☐ Canter

Movements:
- ☑ Backup
- ☐ Leg yield
- ☐ Sidepass
- ☐ Shoulder in/out

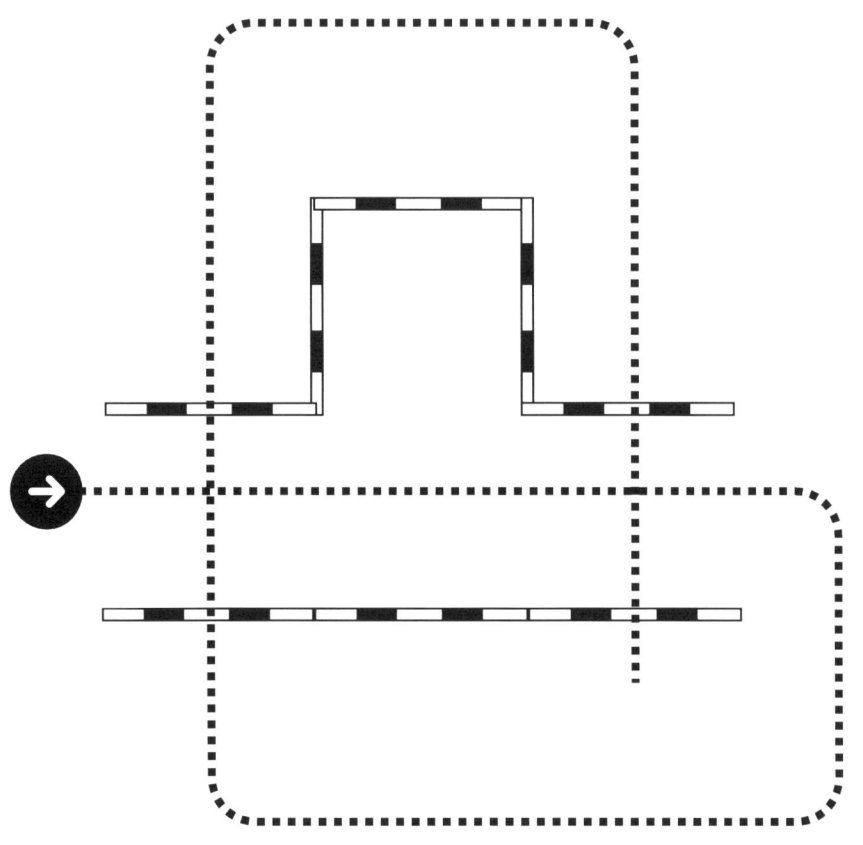

Poles: 8

Level: ★

Benefits:

- ☑ Accuracy
- ☑ Rhythm
- ☑ Impulsion
- ☑ Straightness
- ☑ Suppleness & bend
- ☐ Lateral movement & collection

Gaits:

- ☑ Groundwork
- ☑ Walk
- ☑ Trot
- ☑ Canter

Movements:

- ☐ Backup
- ☐ Leg yield
- ☐ Sidepass
- ☐ Shoulder in/out

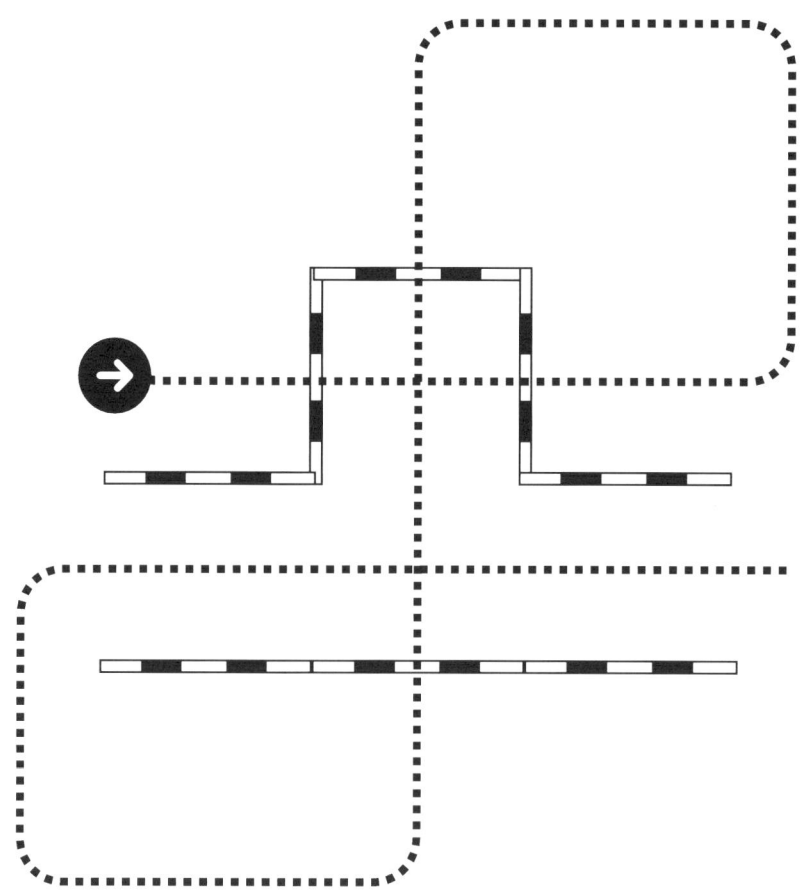

Poles: 8
Level: ★
Benefits:
- ☑ Accuracy
- ☑ Rhythm
- ☑ Impulsion
- ☑ Straightness
- ☑ Suppleness & bend
- ☐ Lateral movement & collection

Gaits:
- ☑ Groundwork
- ☑ Walk
- ☑ Trot
- ☑ Canter

Movements:
- ☐ Backup
- ☐ Leg yield
- ☐ Sidepass
- ☐ Shoulder in/out

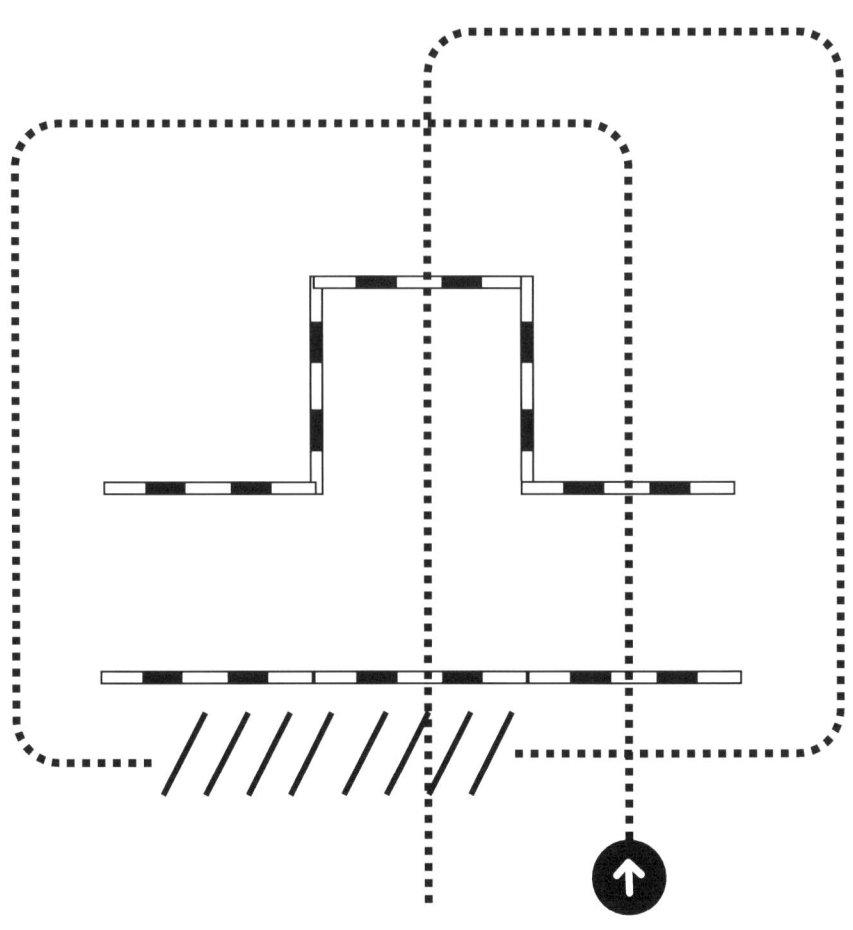

Poles: 8
Level: ★ ★
Benefits:
- ☑ Accuracy
- ☑ Rhythm
- ☑ Impulsion
- ☑ Straightness
- ☑ Suppleness & bend
- ☑ Lateral movement & collection

Gaits:
- ☑ Groundwork
- ☑ Walk
- ☑ Trot
- ☑ Canter

Movements:
- ☐ Backup
- ☐ Leg yield
- ☐ Sidepass
- ☑ Shoulder in

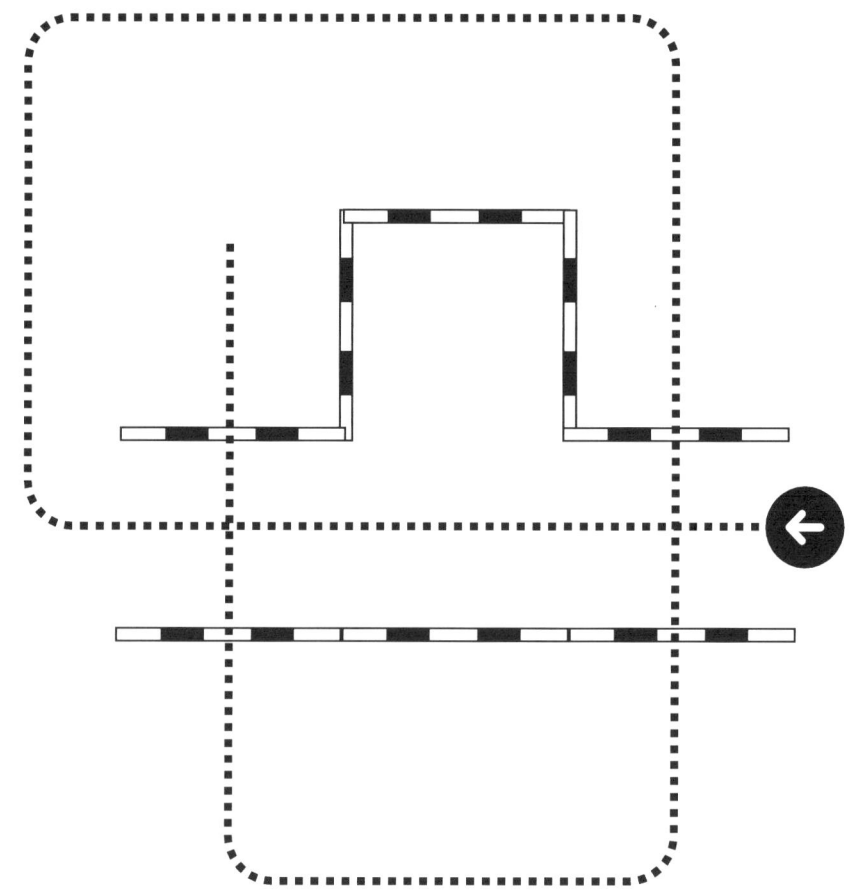

Poles: 8
Level: ★
Benefits:
- ☑ Accuracy
- ☑ Rhythm
- ☑ Impulsion
- ☑ Straightness
- ☑ Suppleness & bend
- ☐ Lateral movement & collection

Gaits:
- ☑ Groundwork
- ☑ Walk
- ☑ Trot
- ☑ Canter

Movements:
- ☐ Backup
- ☐ Leg yield
- ☐ Sidepass
- ☐ Shoulder in/out

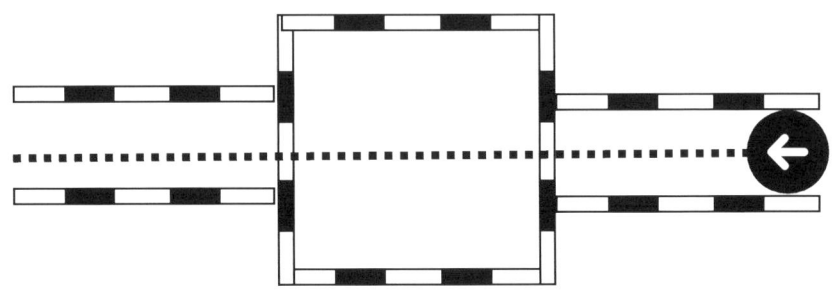

Poles: 8
Level: ★
Benefits:
- ☑ Accuracy
- ☑ Rhythm
- ☑ Impulsion
- ☑ Straightness
- ☐ Suppleness & bend
- ☐ Lateral movement & collection

Gaits:
- ☑ Groundwork
- ☑ Walk
- ☑ Trot
- ☑ Canter

Movements:
- ☐ Backup
- ☐ Leg yield
- ☐ Sidepass
- ☐ Shoulder in/out

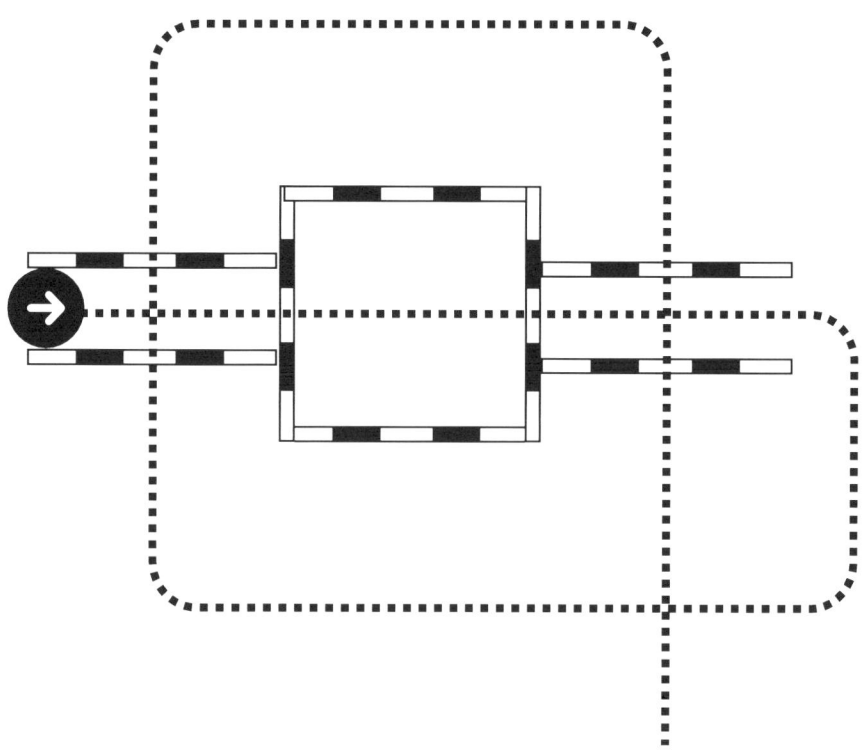

Poles: 8

Level: ★

Benefits:

- ☑ Accuracy
- ☑ Rhythm
- ☑ Impulsion
- ☑ Straightness
- ☑ Suppleness & bend
- ☐ Lateral movement & collection

Gaits:

- ☑ Groundwork
- ☑ Walk
- ☑ Trot
- ☐ Canter

Movements:

- ☐ Backup
- ☐ Leg yield
- ☐ Sidepass
- ☐ Shoulder in/out

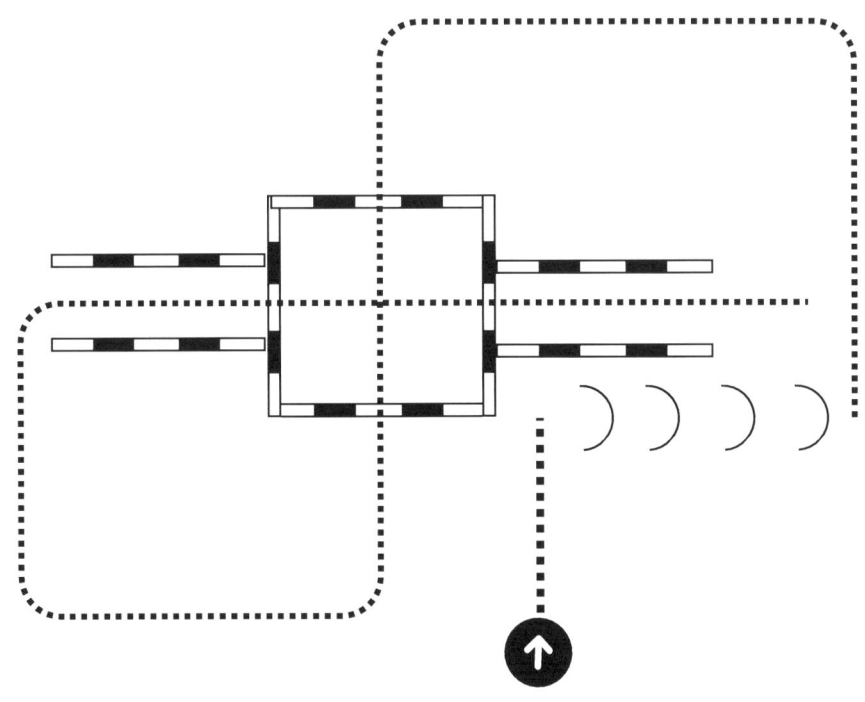

Poles: 8
Level: ★ ★
Benefits:
- ☑ Accuracy
- ☑ Rhythm
- ☑ Impulsion
- ☑ Straightness
- ☑ Suppleness & bend
- ☑ Lateral movement & collection

Gaits:
- ☑ Groundwork
- ☑ Walk
- ☑ Trot
- ☑ Canter

Movements:
- ☐ Backup
- ☐ Leg yield
- ☑ Sidepass
- ☐ Shoulder in/out

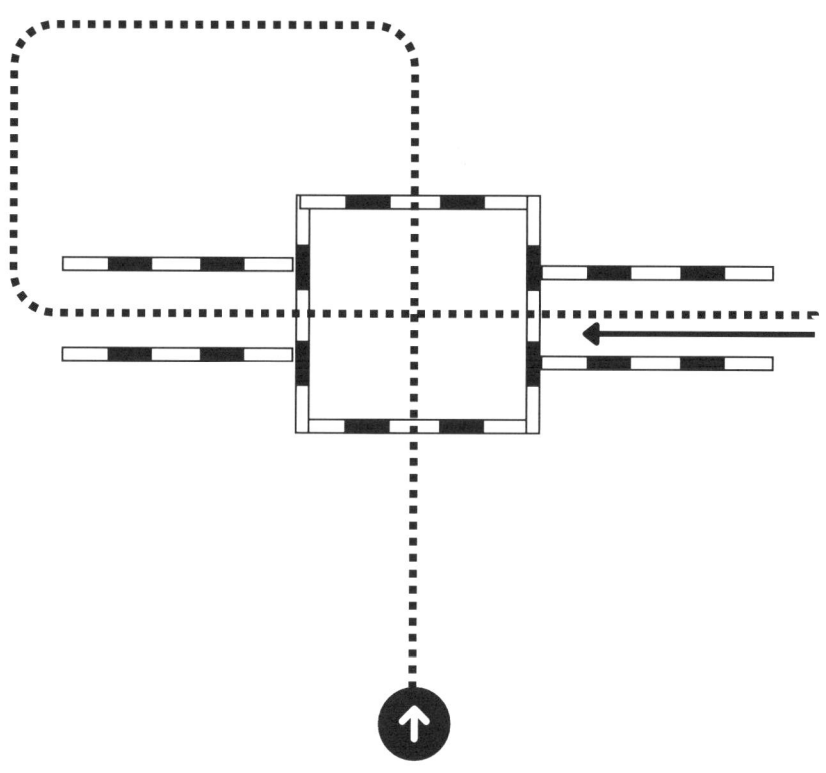

Poles: 8

Level: ★ ★

Benefits:
- ☑ Accuracy
- ☑ Rhythm
- ☑ Impulsion
- ☑ Straightness
- ☑ Suppleness & bend
- ☑ Lateral movement & collection

Gaits:
- ☑ Groundwork
- ☑ Walk
- ☑ Trot
- ☑ Canter

Movements:
- ☑ Backup
- ☐ Leg yield
- ☐ Sidepass
- ☐ Shoulder in/out

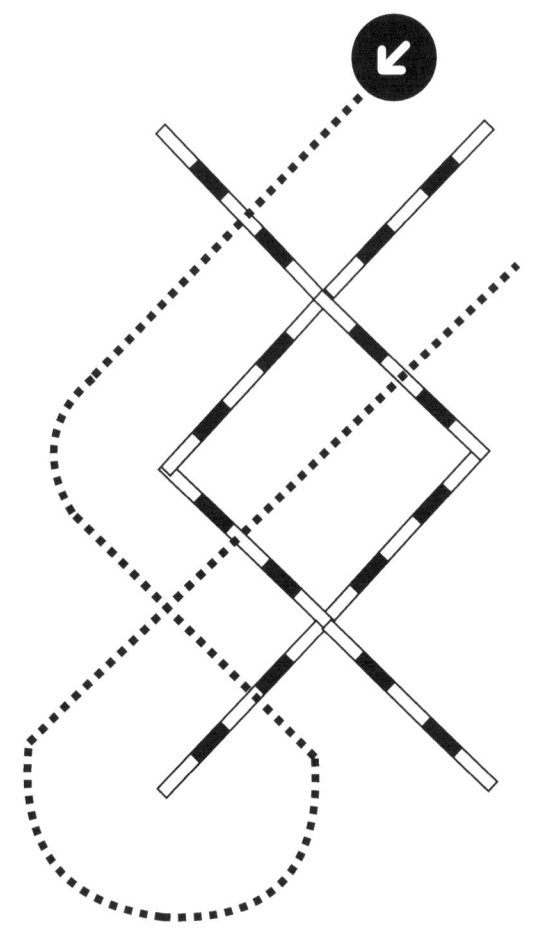

Poles: 8
Level: ★
Benefits:
- ☑ Accuracy
- ☑ Rhythm
- ☑ Impulsion
- ☑ Straightness
- ☑ Suppleness & bend
- ☐ Lateral movement & collection

Gaits:
- ☑ Groundwork
- ☑ Walk
- ☑ Trot
- ☑ Canter

Movements:
- ☐ Backup
- ☐ Leg yield
- ☐ Sidepass
- ☐ Shoulder in/out

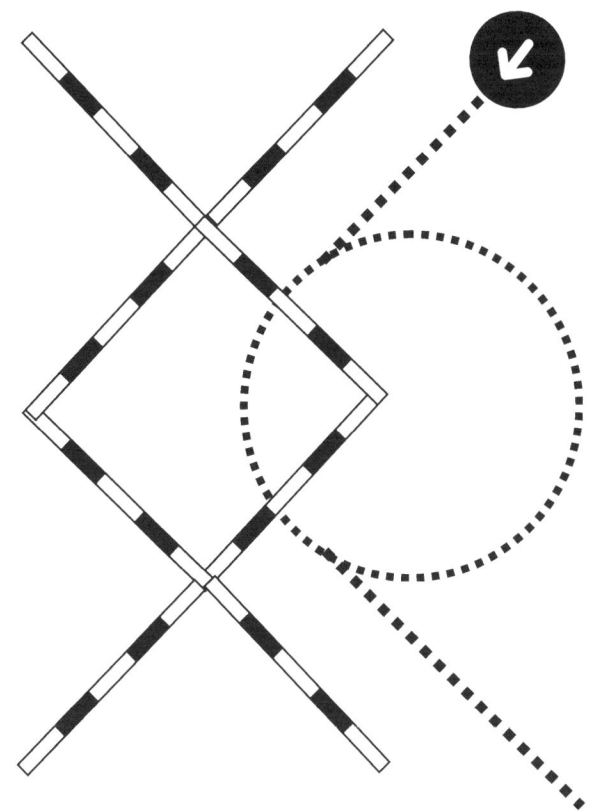

Poles: 8
Level: ★
Benefits:
- ☑ Accuracy
- ☑ Rhythm
- ☑ Impulsion
- ☐ Straightness
- ☑ Suppleness & bend
- ☐ Lateral movement & collection

Gaits:
- ☑ Groundwork
- ☑ Walk
- ☑ Trot
- ☐ Canter

Movements:
- ☐ Backup
- ☐ Leg yield
- ☐ Sidepass
- ☐ Shoulder in/out

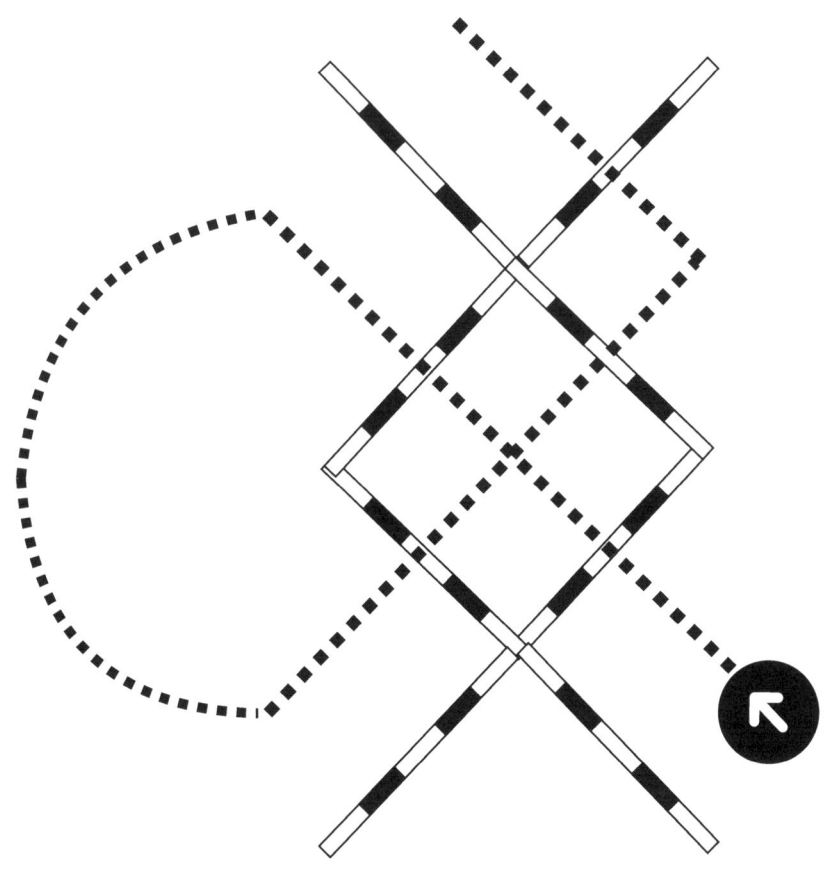

Poles: 8
Level: ★
Benefits:
- ☑ Accuracy
- ☑ Rhythm
- ☑ Impulsion
- ☑ Straightness
- ☑ Suppleness & bend
- ☐ Lateral movement & collection

Gaits:
- ☑ Groundwork
- ☑ Walk
- ☑ Trot
- ☐ Canter

Movements:
- ☐ Backup
- ☐ Leg yield
- ☐ Sidepass
- ☐ Shoulder in/out

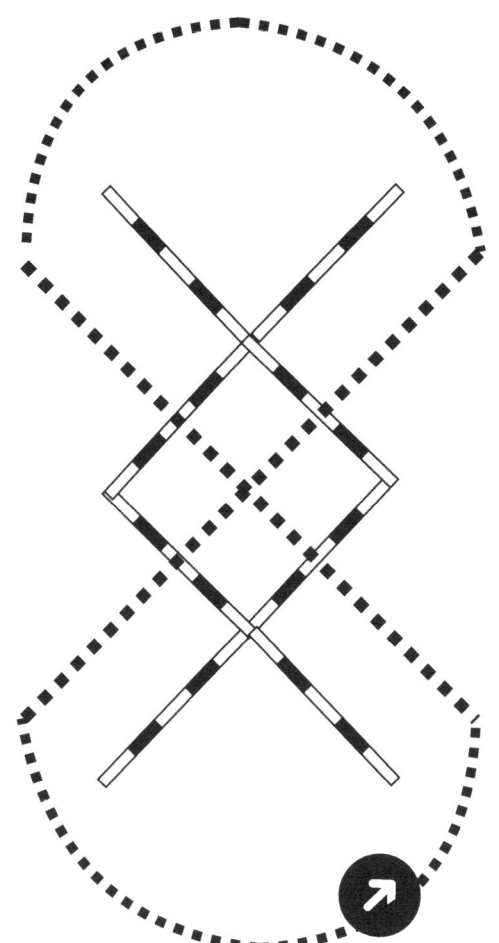

Poles: 8
Level: ★
Benefits:
- ☑ Accuracy
- ☑ Rhythm
- ☑ Impulsion
- ☑ Straightness
- ☑ Suppleness & bend
- ☐ Lateral movement & collection

Gaits:
- ☑ Groundwork
- ☑ Walk
- ☑ Trot
- ☑ Canter

Movements:
- ☐ Backup
- ☐ Leg yield
- ☐ Sidepass
- ☐ Shoulder in/out

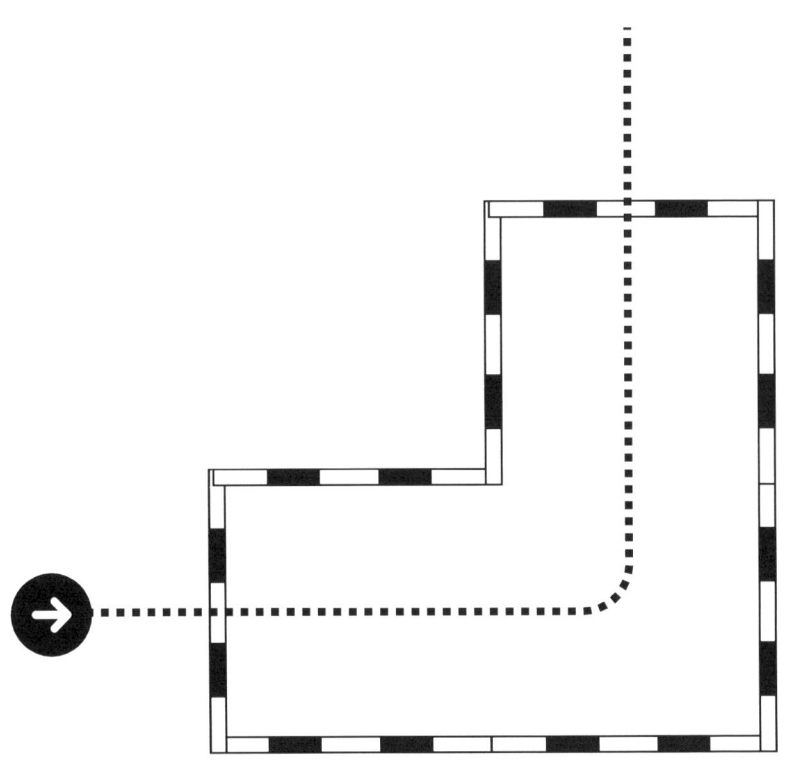

Poles: 8
Level: ★
Benefits:
- ☑ Accuracy
- ☑ Rhythm
- ☑ Impulsion
- ☑ Straightness
- ☑ Suppleness & bend
- ☐ Lateral movement & collection

Gaits:
- ☑ Groundwork
- ☑ Walk
- ☑ Trot
- ☐ Canter

Movements:
- ☐ Backup
- ☐ Leg yield
- ☐ Sidepass
- ☐ Shoulder in/out

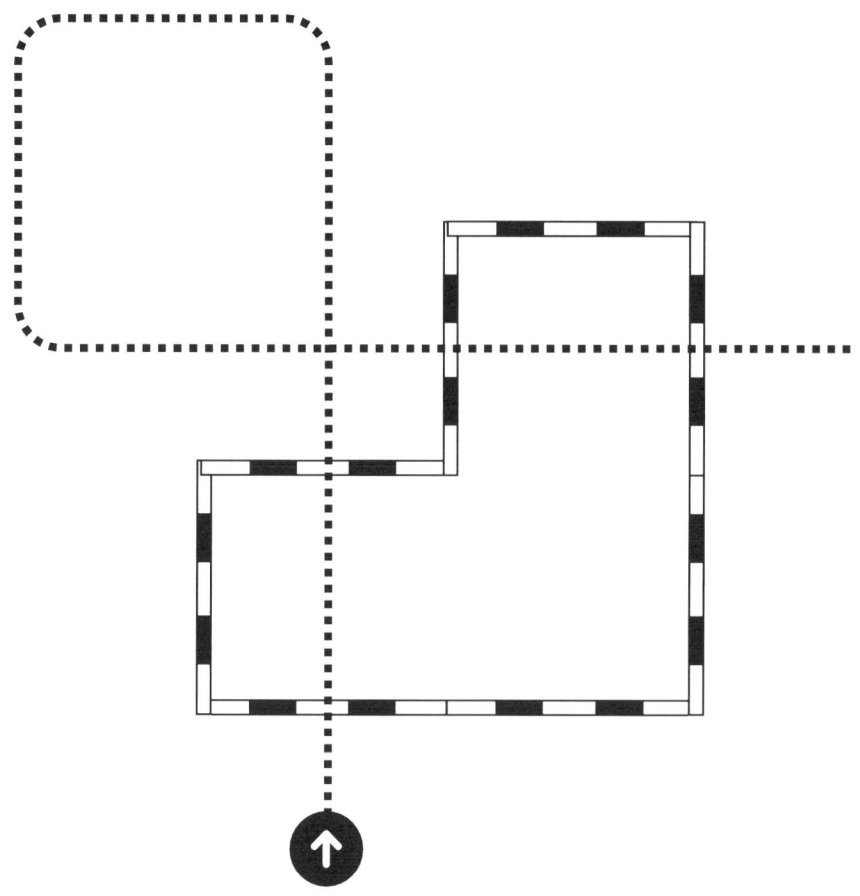

Poles: 8
Level: ★
Benefits:
- ☑ Accuracy
- ☑ Rhythm
- ☑ Impulsion
- ☑ Straightness
- ☑ Suppleness & bend
- ☐ Lateral movement & collection

Gaits:
- ☑ Groundwork
- ☑ Walk
- ☑ Trot
- ☑ Canter

Movements:
- ☐ Backup
- ☐ Leg yield
- ☐ Sidepass
- ☐ Shoulder in/out

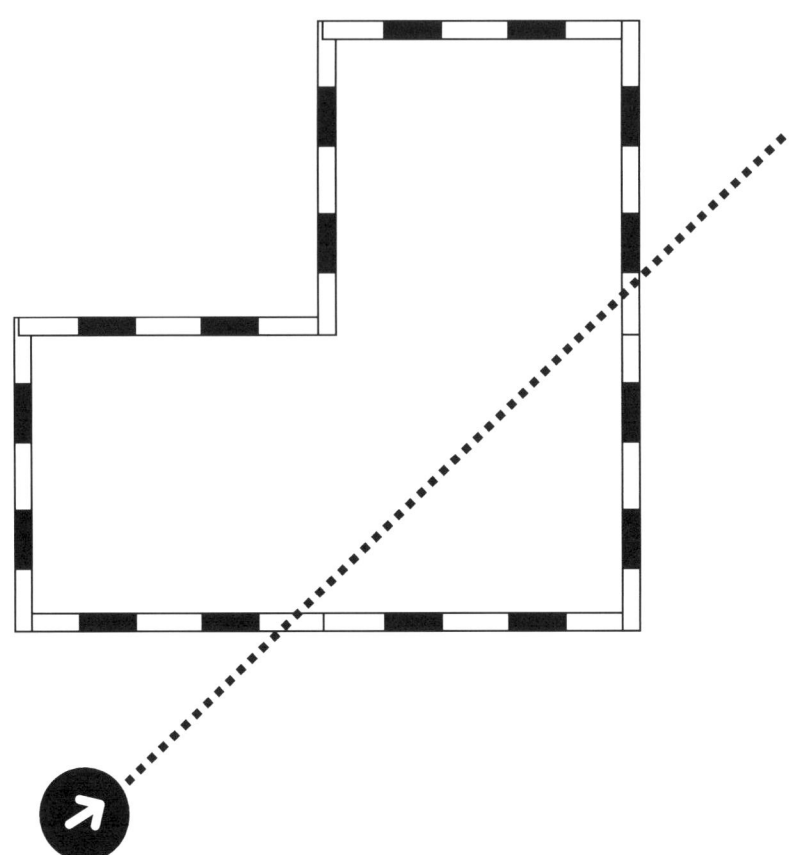

Poles: 8
Level: ★
Benefits:
- ☑ Accuracy
- ☑ Rhythm
- ☑ Impulsion
- ☑ Straightness
- ☐ Suppleness & bend
- ☐ Lateral movement & collection

Gaits:
- ☑ Groundwork
- ☑ Walk
- ☑ Trot
- ☑ Canter

Movements:
- ☐ Backup
- ☐ Leg yield
- ☐ Sidepass
- ☐ Shoulder in/out

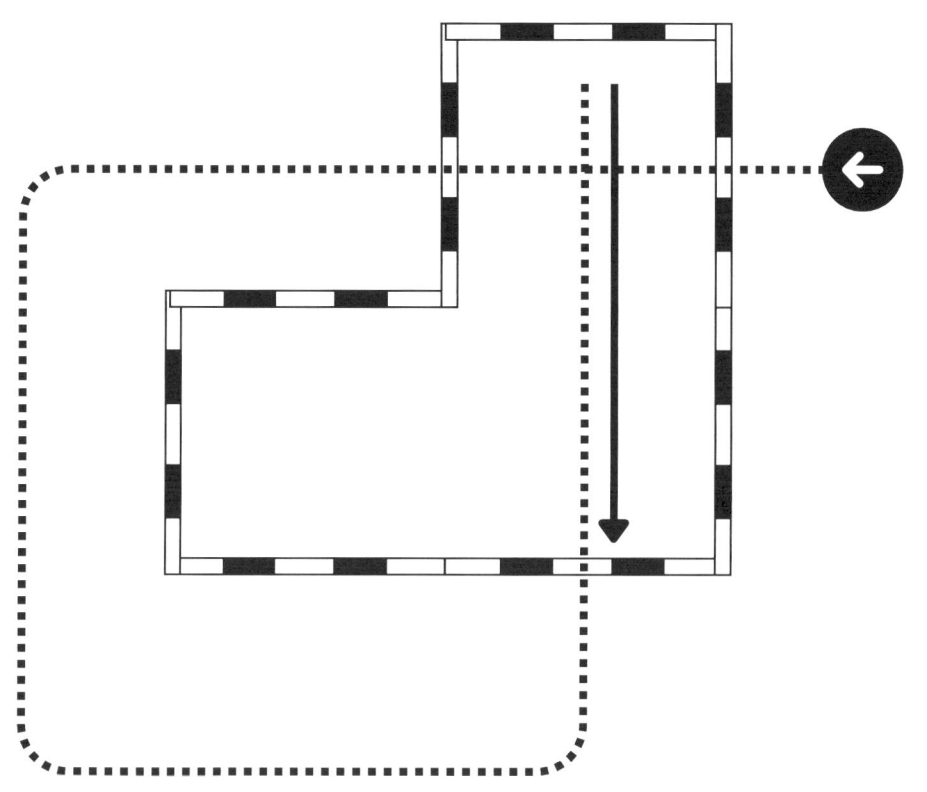

Poles: 8
Level: ★ ★
Benefits:
- ☑ Accuracy
- ☑ Rhythm
- ☑ Impulsion
- ☑ Straightness
- ☑ Suppleness & bend
- ☑ Lateral movement & collection

Gaits:
- ☑ Groundwork
- ☑ Walk
- ☑ Trot
- ☑ Canter

Movements:
- ☑ Backup
- ☐ Leg yield
- ☐ Sidepass
- ☐ Shoulder in/out

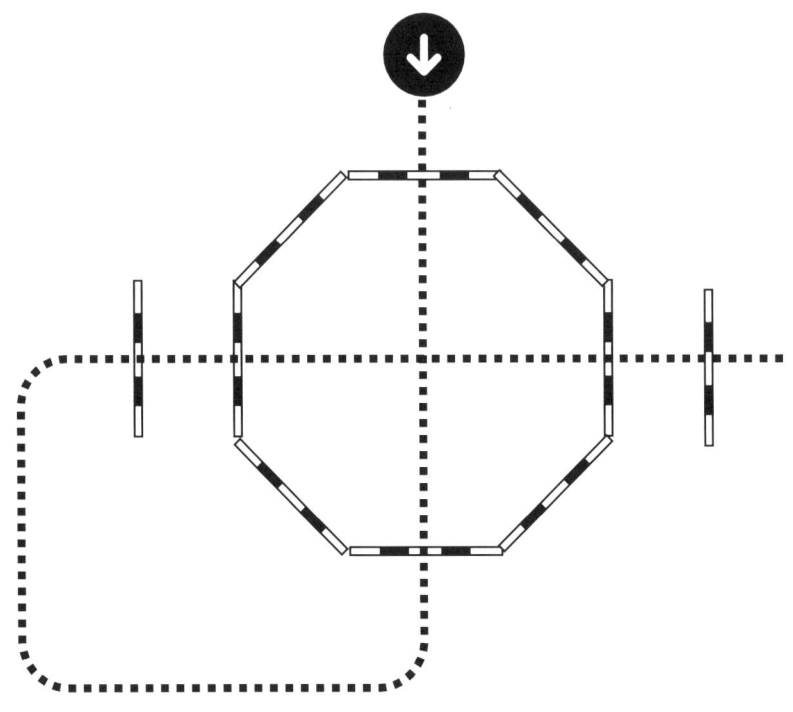

Poles: 8
Level: ⭐
Benefits:
- ☑ Accuracy
- ☑ Rhythm
- ☑ Impulsion
- ☑ Straightness
- ☑ Suppleness & bend
- ☐ Lateral movement & collection

Gaits:
- ☑ Groundwork
- ☑ Walk
- ☑ Trot
- ☑ Canter

Movements:
- ☐ Backup
- ☐ Leg yield
- ☐ Sidepass
- ☐ Shoulder in/out

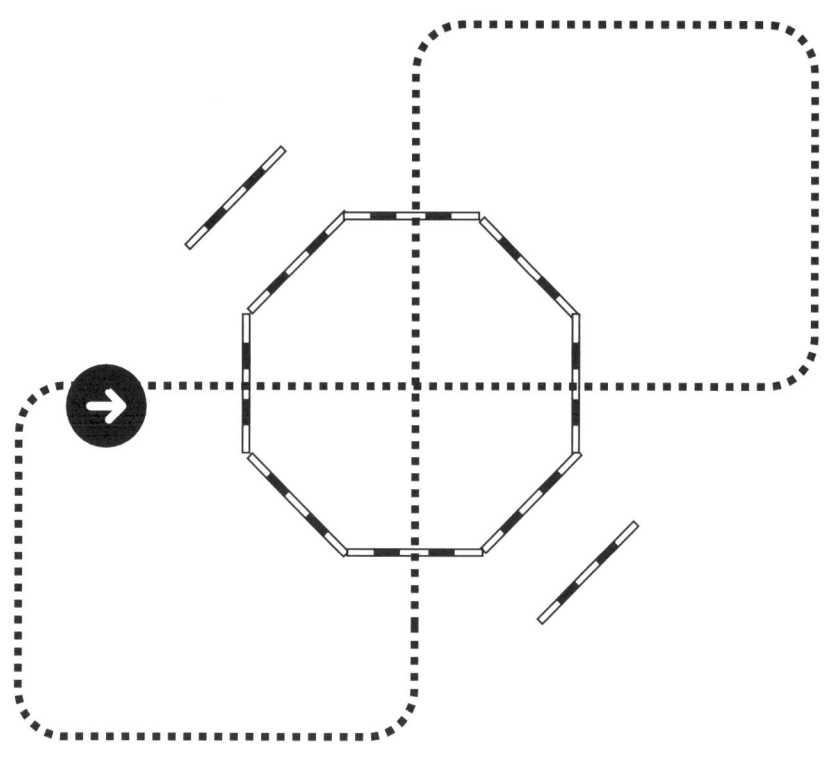

Poles: 8
Level: ★
Benefits:
- ☑ Accuracy
- ☑ Rhythm
- ☑ Impulsion
- ☑ Straightness
- ☑ Suppleness & bend
- ☐ Lateral movement & collection

Gaits:
- ☑ Groundwork
- ☑ Walk
- ☑ Trot
- ☑ Canter

Movements:
- ☐ Backup
- ☐ Leg yield
- ☐ Sidepass
- ☐ Shoulder in/out

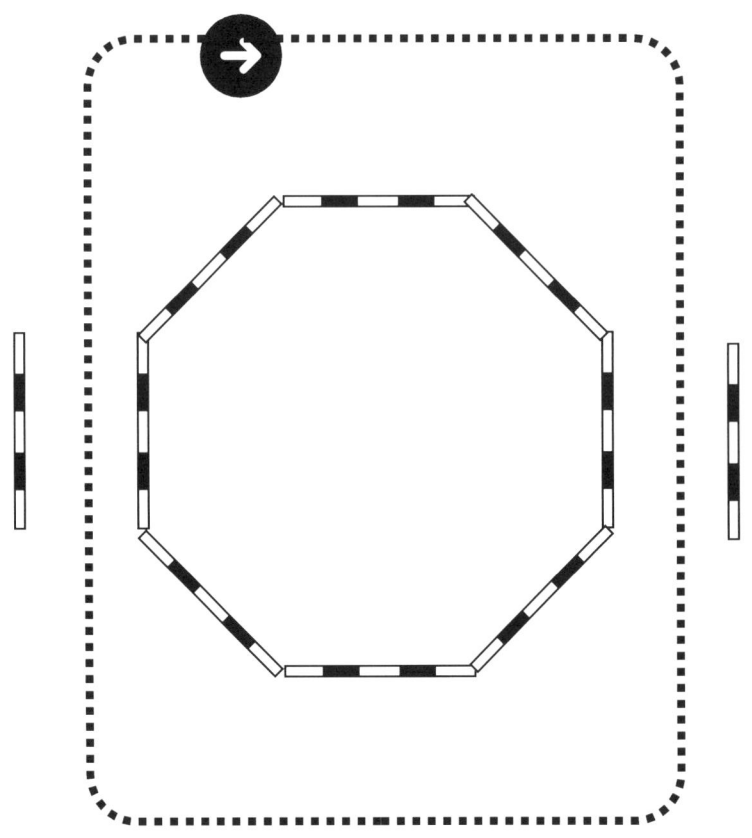

Poles: 8
Level: ★
Benefits:
- ☑ Accuracy
- ☑ Rhythm
- ☑ Impulsion
- ☑ Straightness
- ☑ Suppleness & bend
- ☐ Lateral movement & collection

Gaits:
- ☑ Groundwork
- ☑ Walk
- ☑ Trot
- ☑ Canter

Movements:
- ☐ Backup
- ☐ Leg yield
- ☐ Sidepass
- ☐ Shoulder in/out

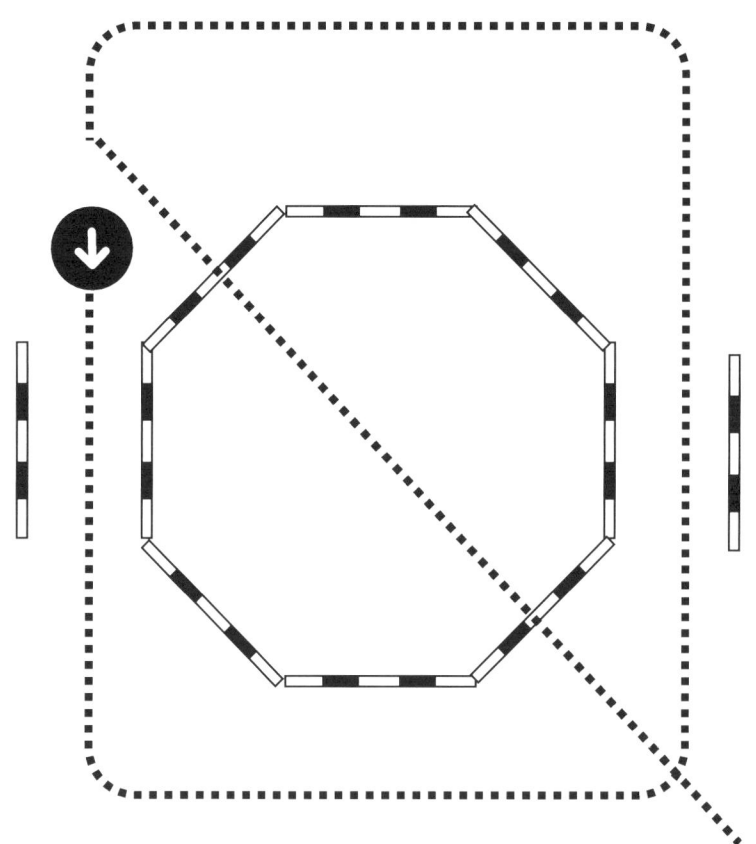

Poles: 8
Level: ★
Benefits:
- ☑ Accuracy
- ☑ Rhythm
- ☑ Impulsion
- ☑ Straightness
- ☑ Suppleness & bend
- ☐ Lateral movement & collection

Gaits:
- ☑ Groundwork
- ☑ Walk
- ☑ Trot
- ☑ Canter

Movements:
- ☑ Backup
- ☐ Leg yield
- ☐ Sidepass
- ☐ Shoulder in/out

10 Poles

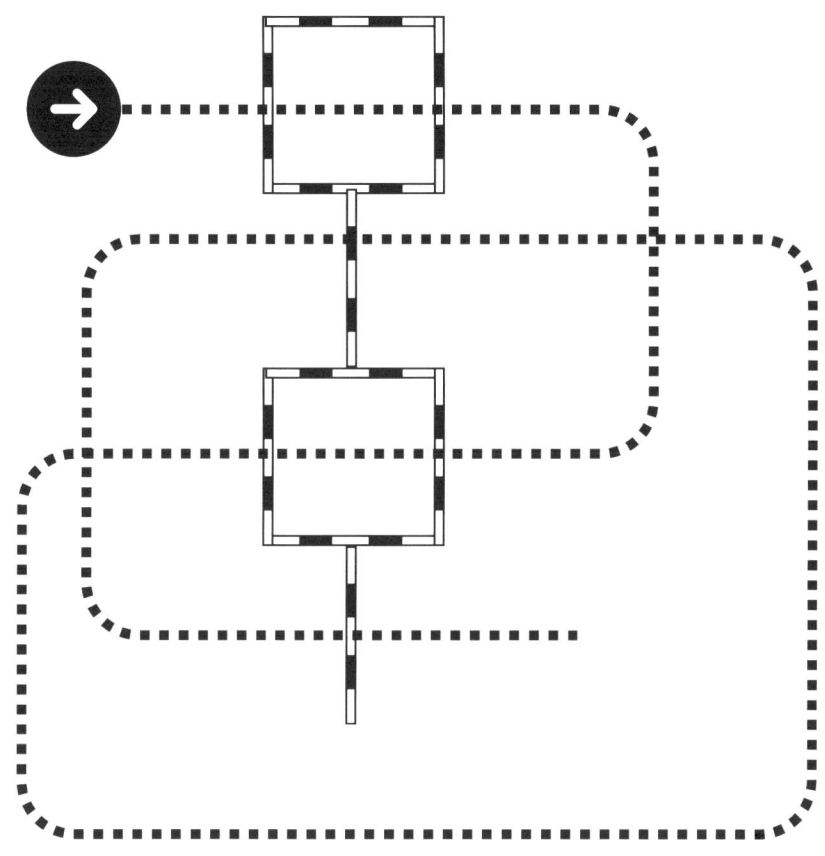

Poles: 10
Level: ★
Benefits:

- ☑ Accuracy
- ☑ Rhythm
- ☑ Impulsion
- ☑ Straightness
- ☑ Suppleness & bend
- ☐ Lateral movement & collection

Gaits:

- ☑ Groundwork
- ☑ Walk
- ☑ Trot
- ☑ Canter

Movements:

- ☐ Backup
- ☐ Leg yield
- ☐ Sidepass
- ☐ Shoulder in/out

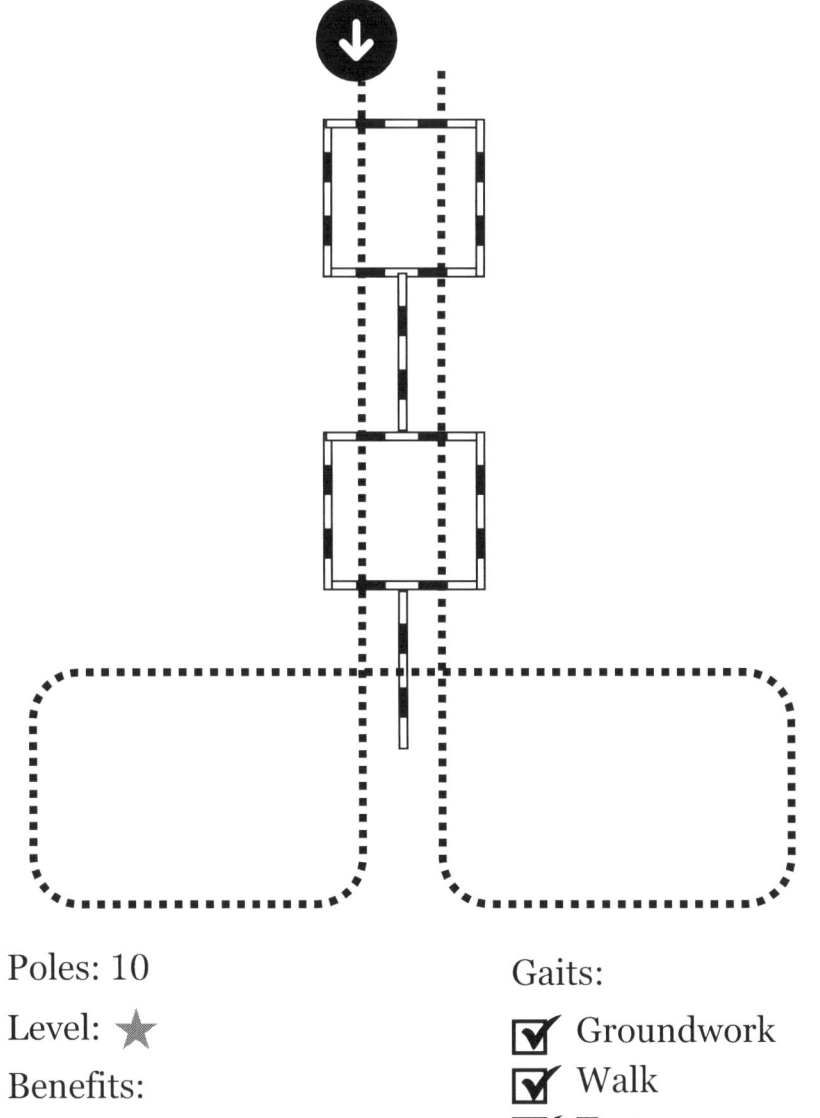

Poles: 10
Level: ★
Benefits:
- ☑ Accuracy
- ☑ Rhythm
- ☑ Impulsion
- ☑ Straightness
- ☑ Suppleness & bend
- ☐ Lateral movement & collection

Gaits:
- ☑ Groundwork
- ☑ Walk
- ☑ Trot
- ☐ Canter

Movements:
- ☐ Backup
- ☐ Leg yield
- ☐ Sidepass
- ☐ Shoulder in/out

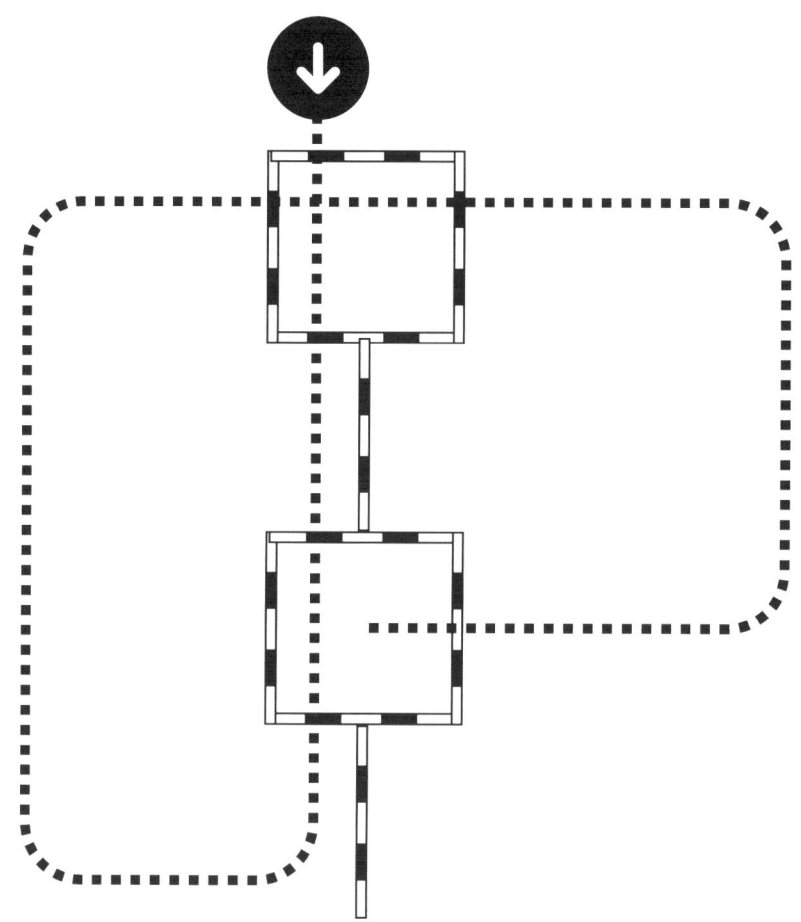

Poles: 10
Level: ★
Benefits:

- ☑ Accuracy
- ☑ Rhythm
- ☑ Impulsion
- ☑ Straightness
- ☑ Suppleness & bend
- ☐ Lateral movement & collection

Gaits:

- ☑ Groundwork
- ☑ Walk
- ☑ Trot
- ☐ Canter

Movements:

- ☐ Backup
- ☐ Leg yield
- ☐ Sidepass
- ☐ Shoulder in/out

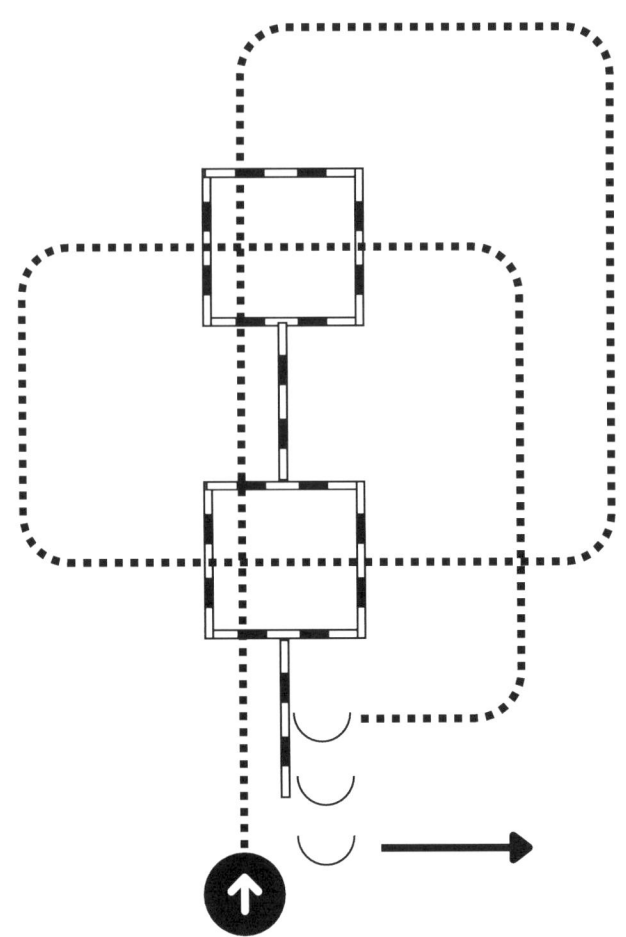

Poles: 10

Level: ★ ★ ★

Benefits:
- ☑ Accuracy
- ☑ Rhythm
- ☑ Impulsion
- ☑ Straightness
- ☑ Suppleness & bend
- ☑ Lateral movement & collection

Gaits:
- ☑ Groundwork
- ☑ Walk
- ☑ Trot
- ☐ Canter

Movements:
- ☑ Backup
- ☐ Leg yield
- ☑ Sidepass
- ☐ Shoulder in/out

12 Poles

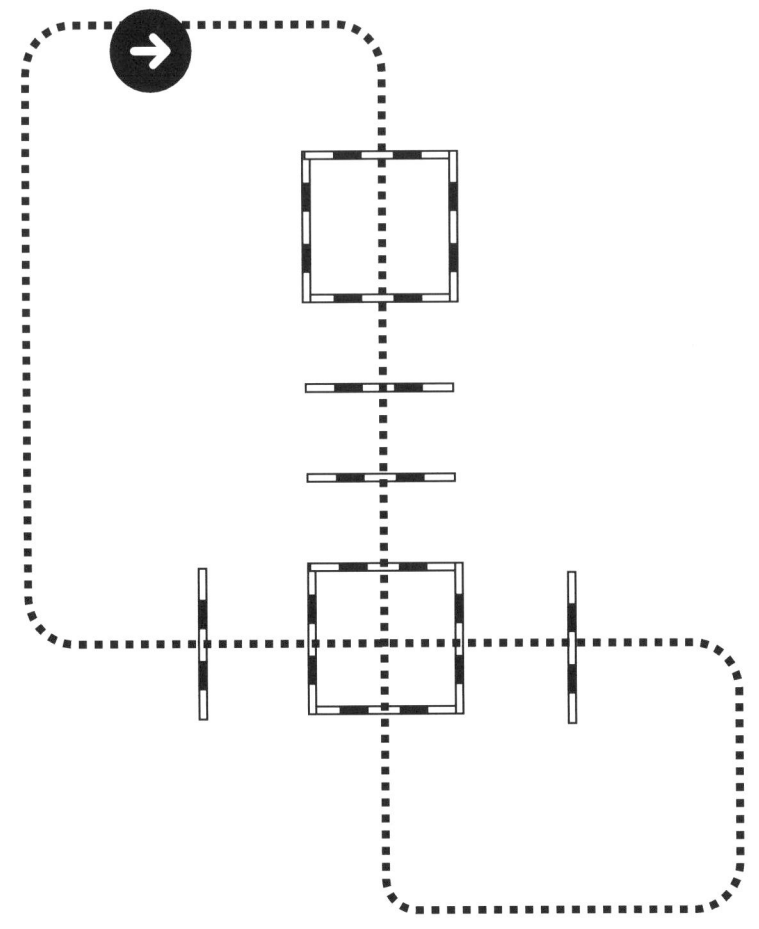

Poles: 12
Level: ⭐
Benefits:
- ☑ Accuracy
- ☑ Rhythm
- ☑ Impulsion
- ☑ Straightness
- ☑ Suppleness & bend
- ☐ Lateral movement & collection

Gaits:
- ☑ Groundwork
- ☑ Walk
- ☑ Trot
- ☑ Canter

Movements:
- ☐ Backup
- ☐ Leg yield
- ☐ Sidepass
- ☐ Shoulder in/out

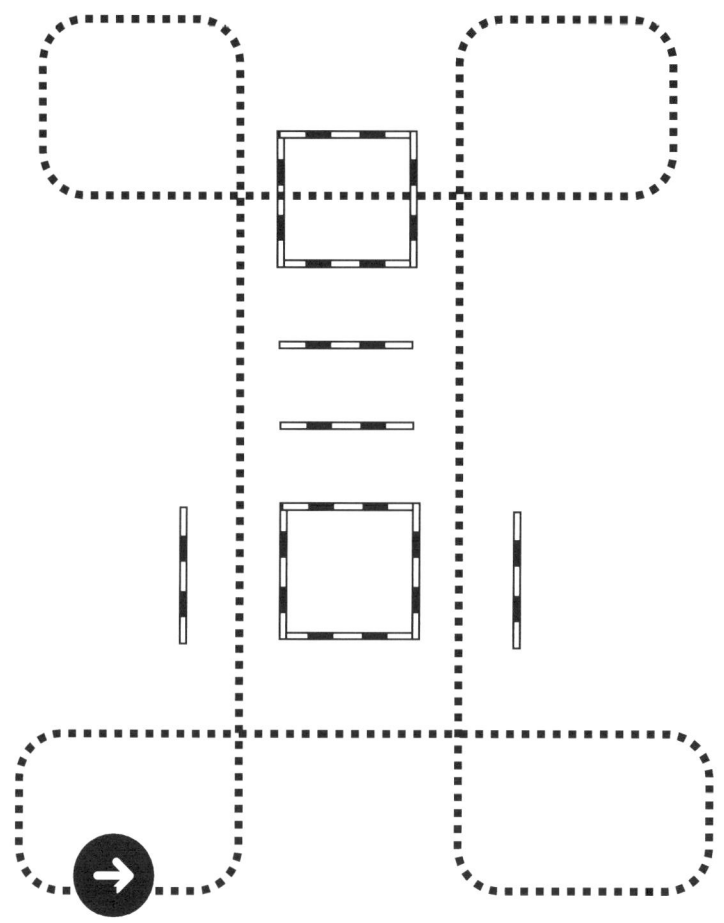

Poles: 12
Level: ★
Benefits:
- [x] Accuracy
- [x] Rhythm
- [x] Impulsion
- [x] Straightness
- [x] Suppleness & bend
- [ ] Lateral movement & collection

Gaits:
- [x] Groundwork
- [x] Walk
- [x] Trot
- [x] Canter

Movements:
- [ ] Backup
- [ ] Leg yield
- [ ] Sidepass
- [ ] Shoulder in/out

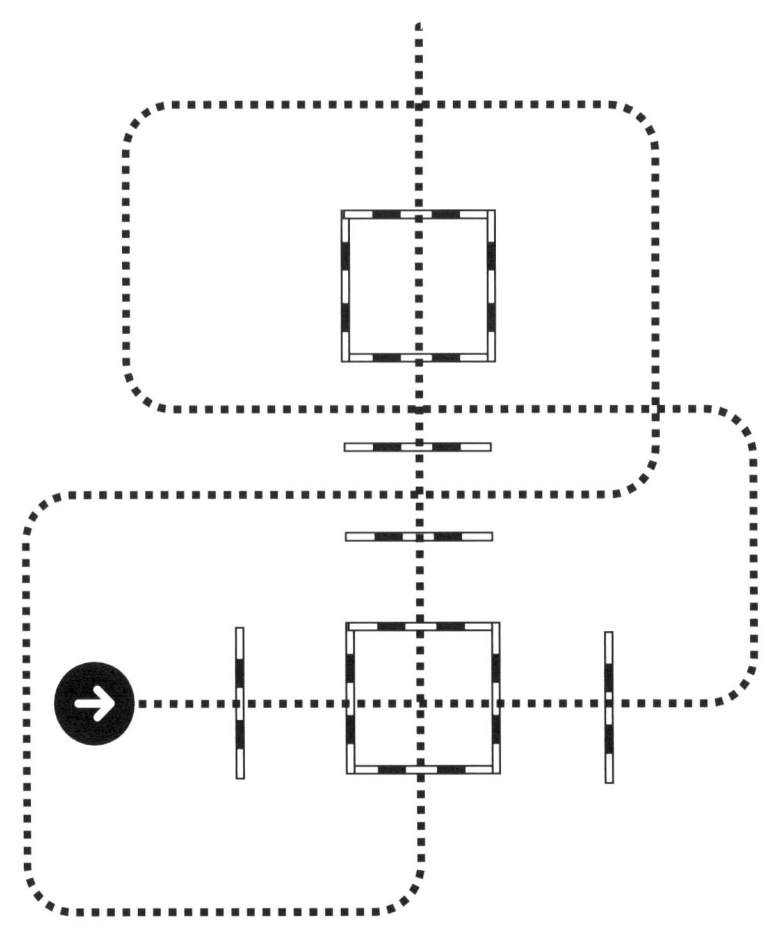

Poles: 12
Level: ★
Benefits:
- ☑ Accuracy
- ☑ Rhythm
- ☑ Impulsion
- ☑ Straightness
- ☑ Suppleness & bend
- ☐ Lateral movement & collection

Gaits:
- ☑ Groundwork
- ☑ Walk
- ☑ Trot
- ☐ Canter

Movements:
- ☐ Backup
- ☐ Leg yield
- ☐ Sidepass
- ☐ Shoulder in/out

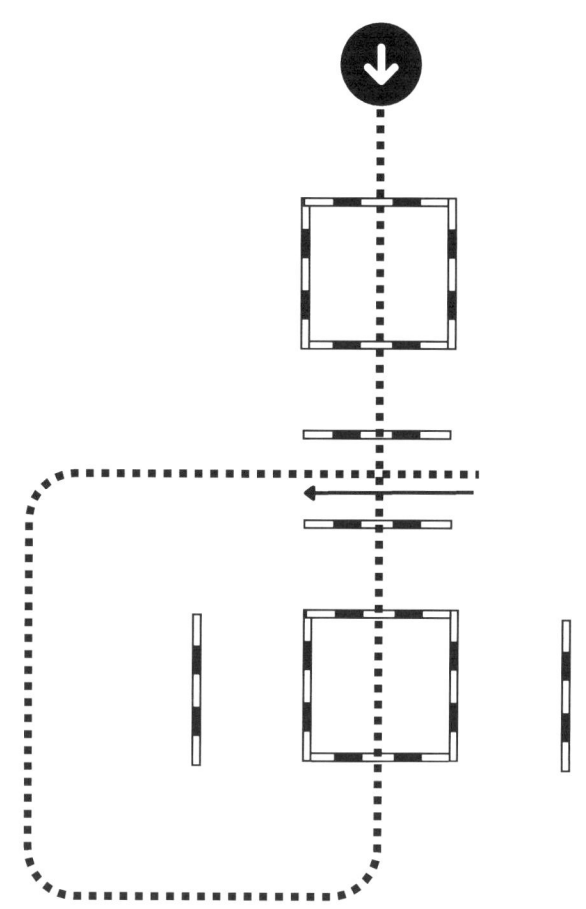

Poles: 12
Level: ★ ★
Benefits:
- ☑ Accuracy
- ☑ Rhythm
- ☑ Impulsion
- ☑ Straightness
- ☑ Suppleness & bend
- ☑ Lateral movement & collection

Gaits:
- ☑ Groundwork
- ☑ Walk
- ☑ Trot
- ☐ Canter

Movements:
- ☑ Backup
- ☐ Leg yield
- ☐ Sidepass
- ☐ Shoulder in/out

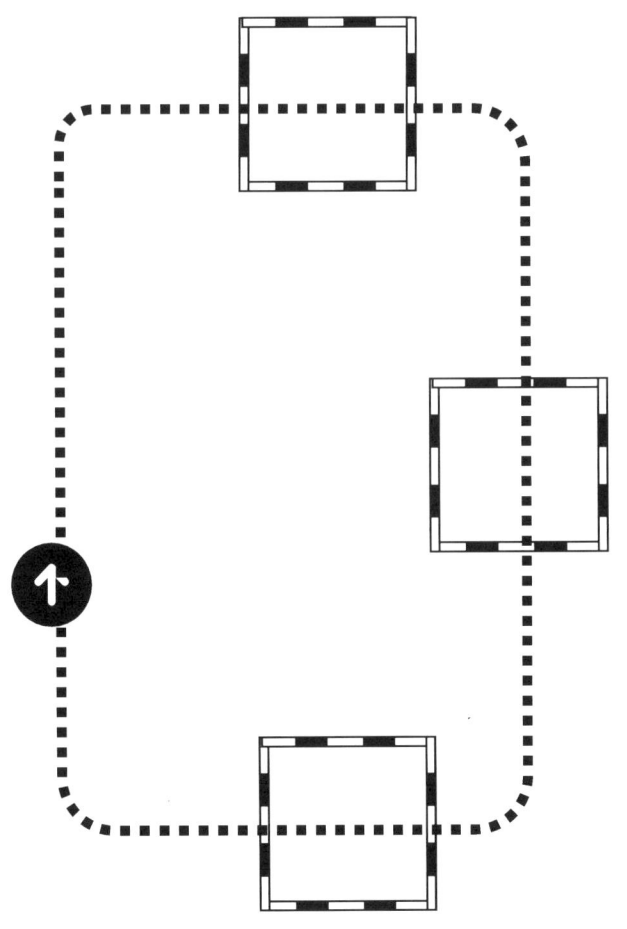

Poles: 12

Level: ★

Benefits:

- ☑ Accuracy
- ☑ Rhythm
- ☑ Impulsion
- ☑ Straightness
- ☑ Suppleness & bend
- ☐ Lateral movement & collection

Gaits:

- ☑ Groundwork
- ☑ Walk
- ☑ Trot
- ☑ Canter

Movements:

- ☐ Backup
- ☐ Leg yield
- ☐ Sidepass
- ☐ Shoulder in/out

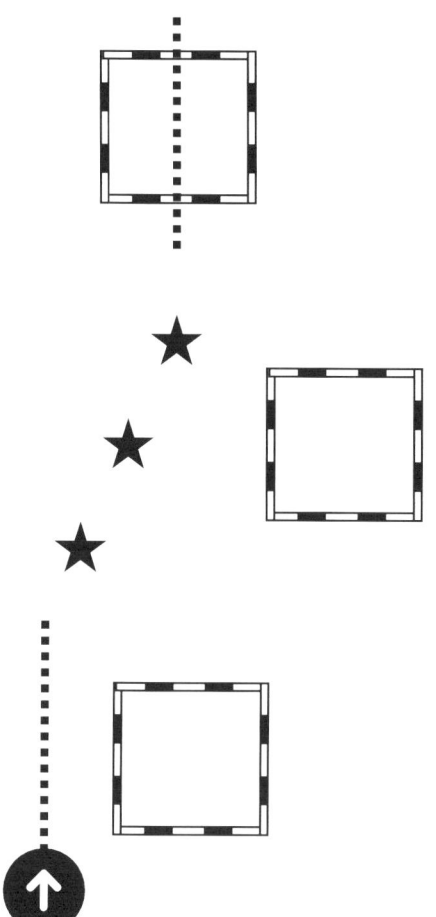

Poles: 12
Level: ★ ★
Benefits:
- ☑ Accuracy
- ☑ Rhythm
- ☑ Impulsion
- ☑ Straightness
- ☐ Suppleness & bend
- ☑ Lateral movement & collection

Gaits:
- ☑ Groundwork
- ☑ Walk
- ☑ Trot
- ☑ Canter

Movements:
- ☐ Backup
- ☑ Leg yield
- ☐ Sidepass
- ☐ Shoulder in/out

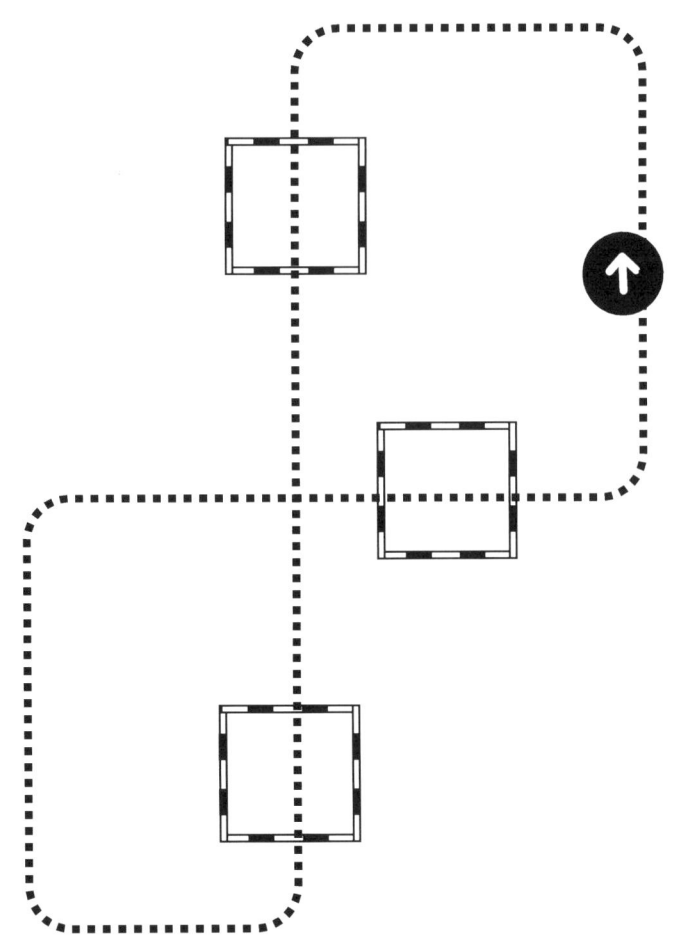

Poles: 12
Level: ★
Benefits:
- ☑ Accuracy
- ☑ Rhythm
- ☑ Impulsion
- ☑ Straightness
- ☑ Suppleness & bend
- ☐ Lateral movement & collection

Gaits:
- ☑ Groundwork
- ☑ Walk
- ☑ Trot
- ☑ Canter

Movements:
- ☐ Backup
- ☐ Leg yield
- ☐ Sidepass
- ☐ Shoulder in/out

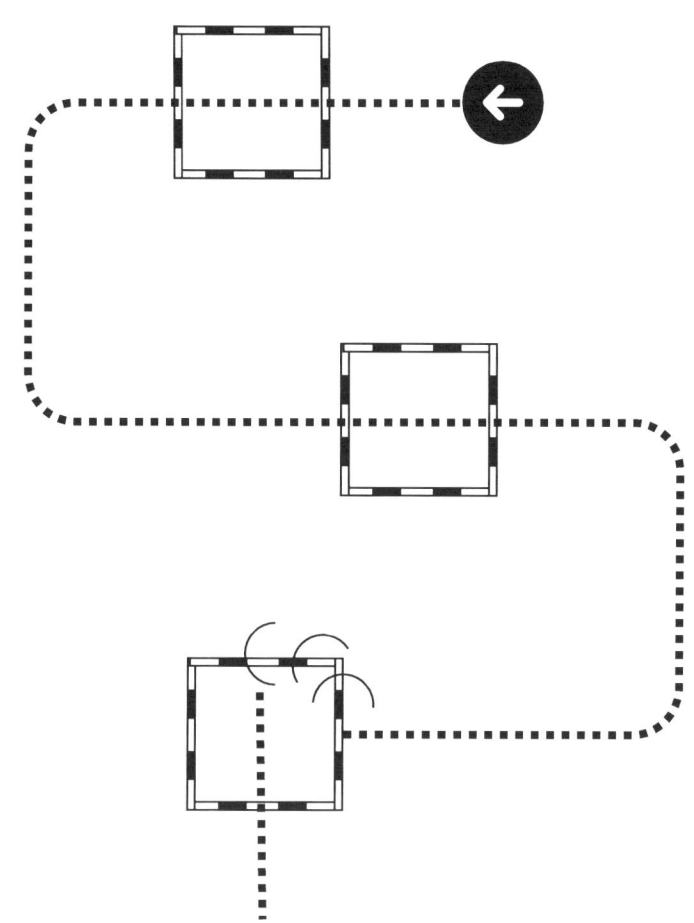

Poles: 12
Level: ★ ★
Benefits:
- ☑ Accuracy
- ☑ Rhythm
- ☑ Impulsion
- ☑ Straightness
- ☑ Suppleness & bend
- ☑ Lateral movement & collection

Gaits:
- ☑ Groundwork
- ☑ Walk
- ☑ Trot
- ☑ Canter

Movements:
- ☐ Backup
- ☐ Leg yield
- ☑ Sidepass
- ☐ Shoulder in/out

13 Poles

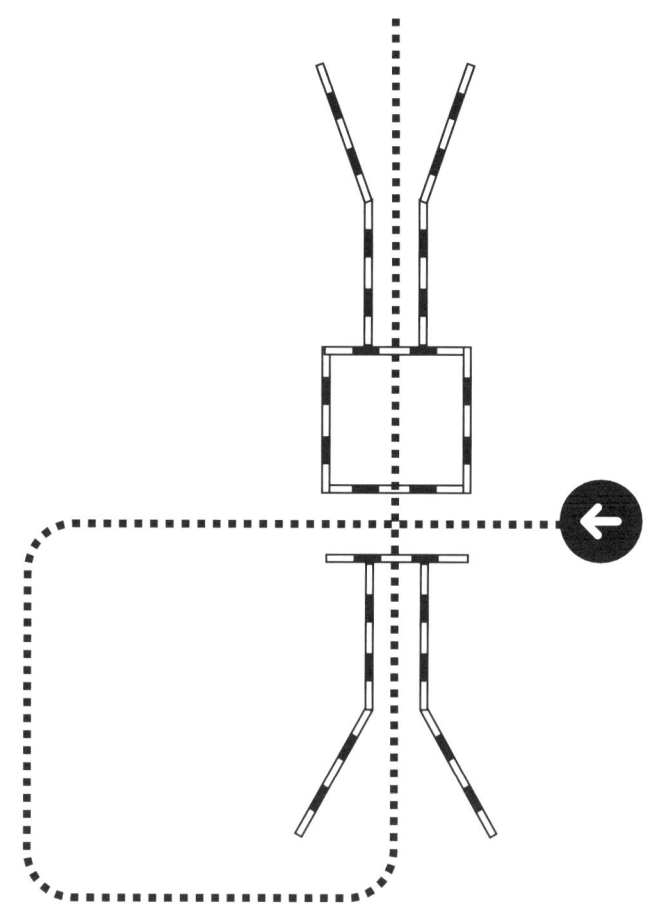

Poles: 13
Level: ⭐
Benefits:
- ☑ Accuracy
- ☑ Rhythm
- ☑ Impulsion
- ☑ Straightness
- ☑ Suppleness & bend
- ☐ Lateral movement & collection

Gaits:
- ☑ Groundwork
- ☑ Walk
- ☑ Trot
- ☐ Canter

Movements:
- ☐ Backup
- ☐ Leg yield
- ☐ Sidepass
- ☐ Shoulder in/out

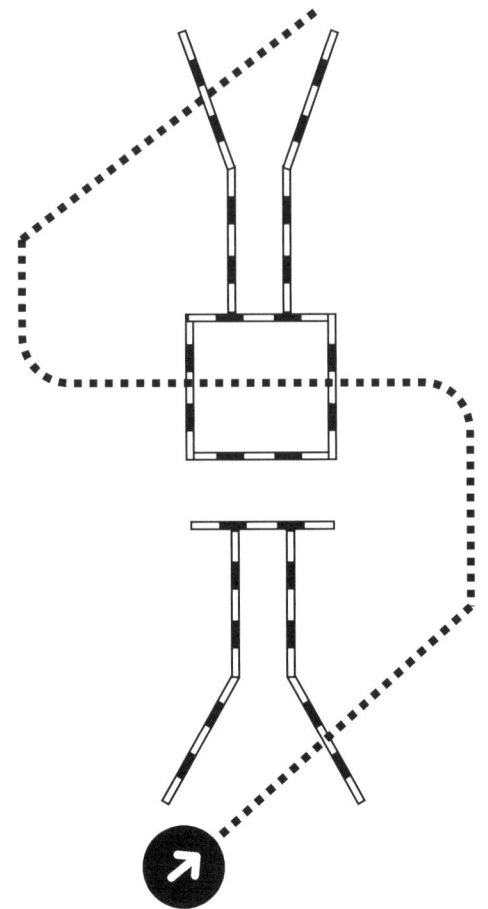

Poles: 13
Level: ★
Benefits:
- ☑ Accuracy
- ☑ Rhythm
- ☑ Impulsion
- ☑ Straightness
- ☑ Suppleness & bend
- ☐ Lateral movement & collection

Gaits:
- ☑ Groundwork
- ☑ Walk
- ☑ Trot
- ☑ Canter

Movements:
- ☐ Backup
- ☐ Leg yield
- ☐ Sidepass
- ☐ Shoulder in/out

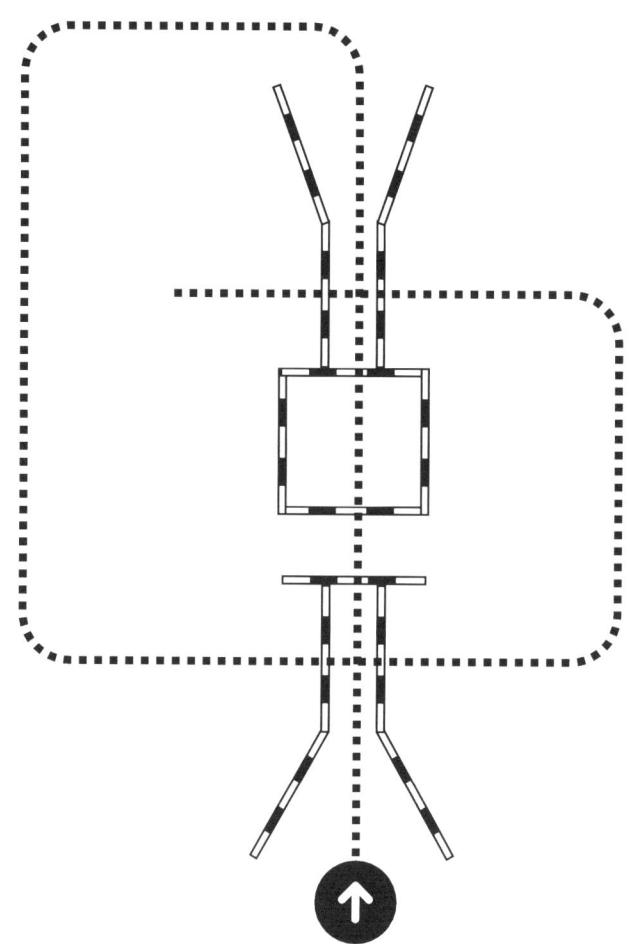

Poles: 13
Level: ★
Benefits:

- ☑ Accuracy
- ☑ Rhythm
- ☑ Impulsion
- ☑ Straightness
- ☑ Suppleness & bend
- ☐ Lateral movement & collection

Gaits:

- ☑ Groundwork
- ☑ Walk
- ☑ Trot
- ☐ Canter

Movements:

- ☐ Backup
- ☐ Leg yield
- ☐ Sidepass
- ☐ Shoulder in/out

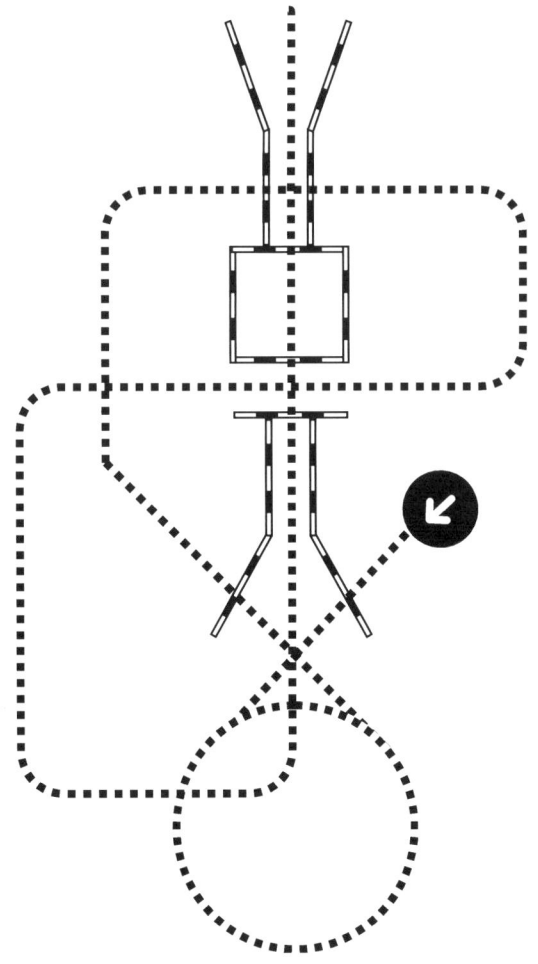

Poles: 13
Level: ⭐
Benefits:

- ☑ Accuracy
- ☑ Rhythm
- ☑ Impulsion
- ☑ Straightness
- ☑ Suppleness & bend
- ☐ Lateral movement & collection

Gaits:

- ☑ Groundwork
- ☑ Walk
- ☑ Trot
- ☐ Canter

Movements:

- ☐ Backup
- ☐ Leg yield
- ☐ Sidepass
- ☐ Shoulder in/out

14 Poles

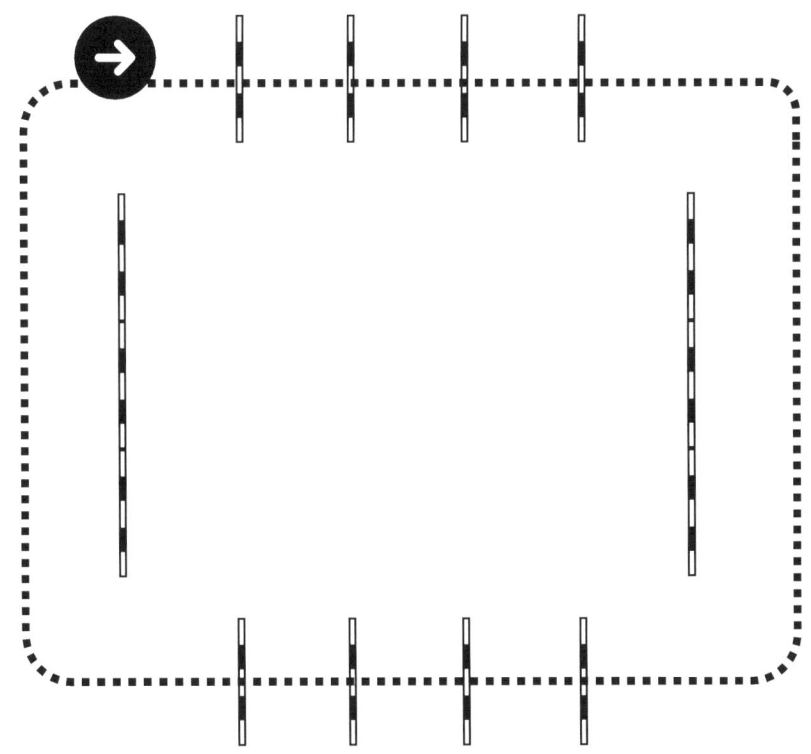

Poles: 14
Level: ★
Benefits:
- ☑ Accuracy
- ☑ Rhythm
- ☑ Impulsion
- ☑ Straightness
- ☑ Suppleness & bend
- ☐ Lateral movement & collection

Gaits:
- ☑ Groundwork
- ☑ Walk
- ☑ Trot
- ☑ Canter

Movements:
- ☐ Backup
- ☐ Leg yield
- ☐ Sidepass
- ☐ Shoulder in/out

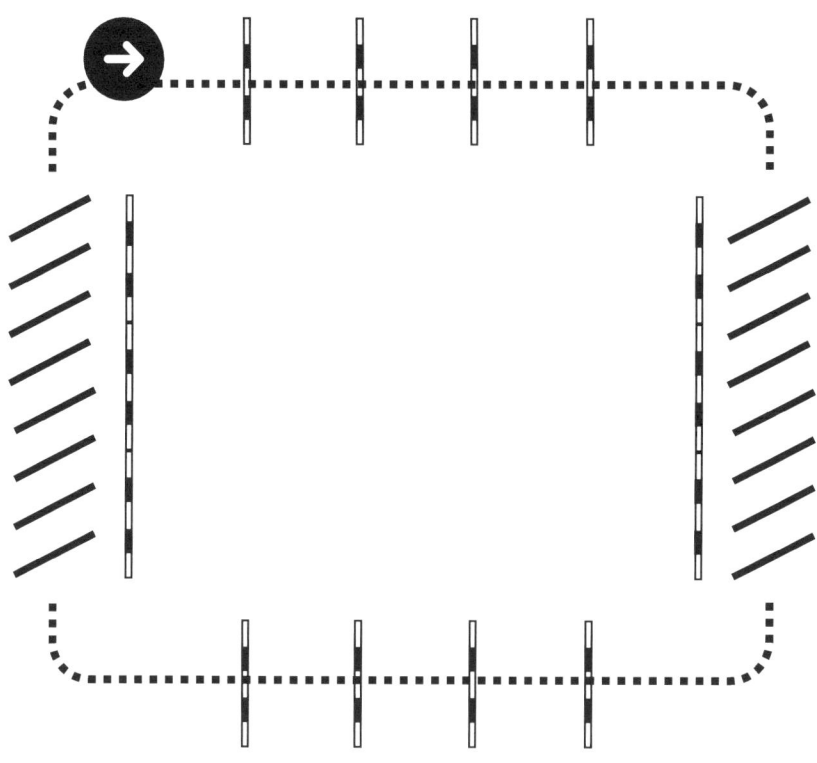

Poles: 14
Level: ★ ★
Benefits:
- ☑ Accuracy
- ☑ Rhythm
- ☑ Impulsion
- ☑ Straightness
- ☑ Suppleness & bend
- ☑ Lateral movement & collection

Gaits:
- ☑ Groundwork
- ☑ Walk
- ☑ Trot
- ☐ Canter

Movements:
- ☐ Backup
- ☐ Leg yield
- ☐ Sidepass
- ☑ Shoulder in/out

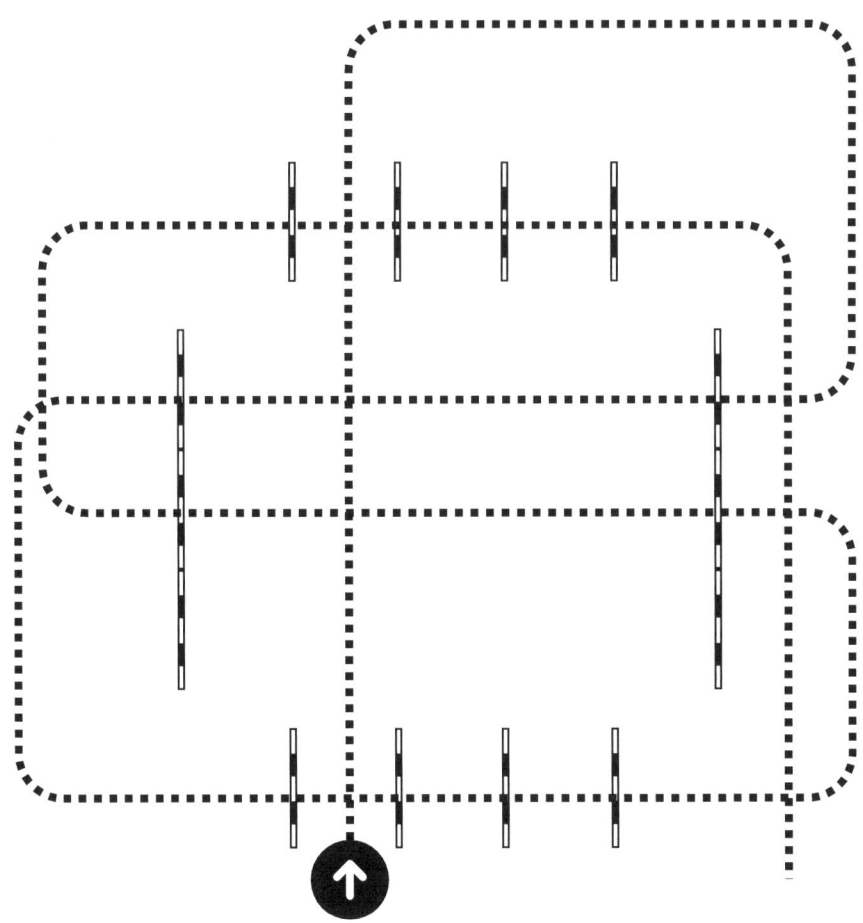

Poles: 14
Level: ★
Benefits:
- ☑ Accuracy
- ☑ Rhythm
- ☑ Impulsion
- ☑ Straightness
- ☑ Suppleness & bend
- ☐ Lateral movement & collection

Gaits:
- ☑ Groundwork
- ☑ Walk
- ☑ Trot
- ☑ Canter

Movements:
- ☐ Backup
- ☐ Leg yield
- ☐ Sidepass
- ☐ Shoulder in/out

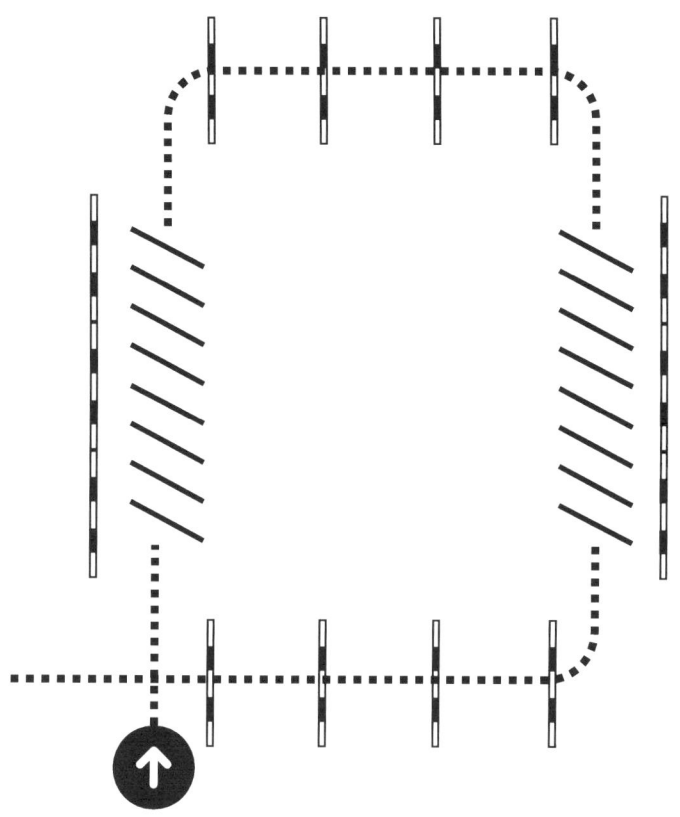

Poles: 14
Level: ★ ★
Benefits:
- ☑ Accuracy
- ☑ Rhythm
- ☑ Impulsion
- ☑ Straightness
- ☑ Suppleness & bend
- ☑ Lateral movement & collection

Gaits:
- ☑ Groundwork
- ☑ Walk
- ☑ Trot
- ☐ Canter

Movements:
- ☐ Backup
- ☐ Leg yield
- ☐ Sidepass
- ☑ Shoulder out

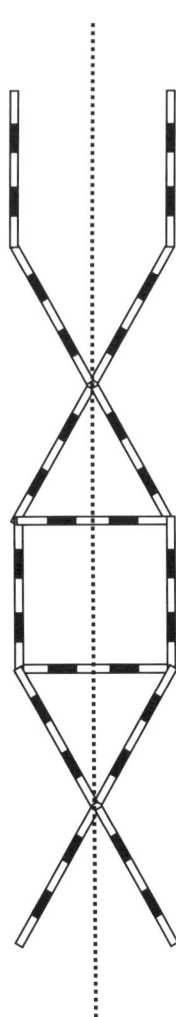

Poles: 14
Level: ★ ★
Benefits:
- ☑ Accuracy
- ☑ Rhythm
- ☑ Impulsion
- ☑ Straightness
- ☐ Suppleness & bend
- ☐ Lateral movement & collection

Gaits:
- ☑ Groundwork
- ☑ Walk
- ☑ Trot
- ☐ Canter

Movements:
- ☐ Backup
- ☐ Leg yield
- ☐ Sidepass
- ☐ Shoulder in/out

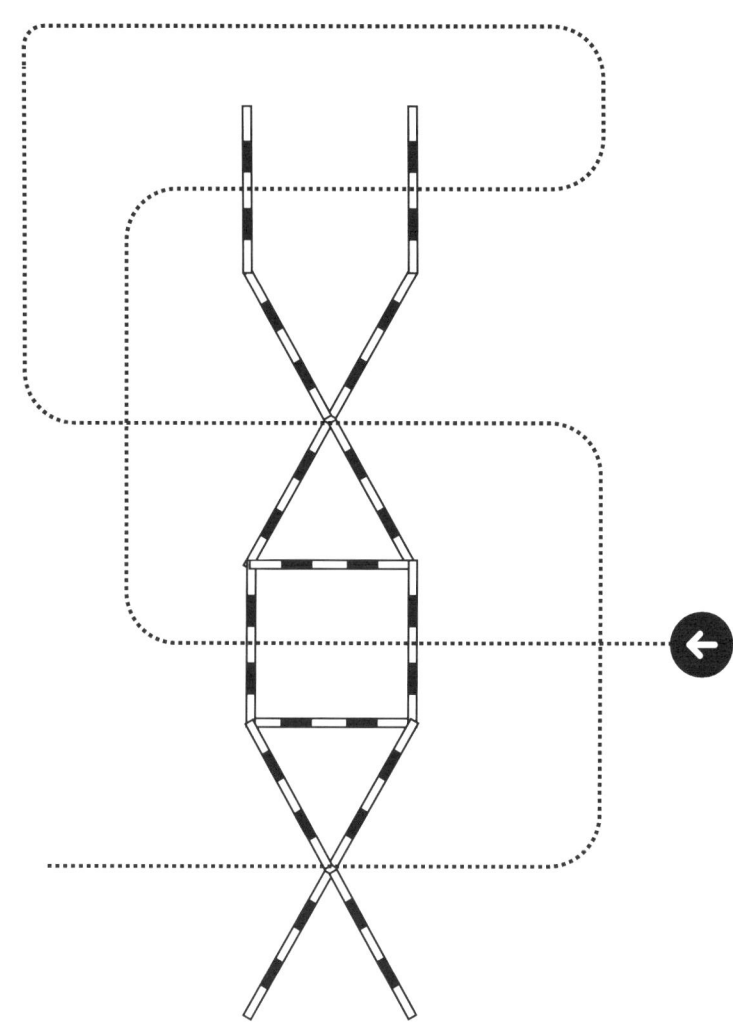

Poles: 14
Level: ★ ★
Benefits:
- ☑ Accuracy
- ☑ Rhythm
- ☑ Impulsion
- ☑ Straightness
- ☑ Suppleness & bend
- ☐ Lateral movement & collection

Gaits:
- ☑ Groundwork
- ☑ Walk
- ☑ Trot
- ☑ Canter

Movements:
- ☐ Backup
- ☐ Leg yield
- ☐ Sidepass
- ☐ Shoulder in/out

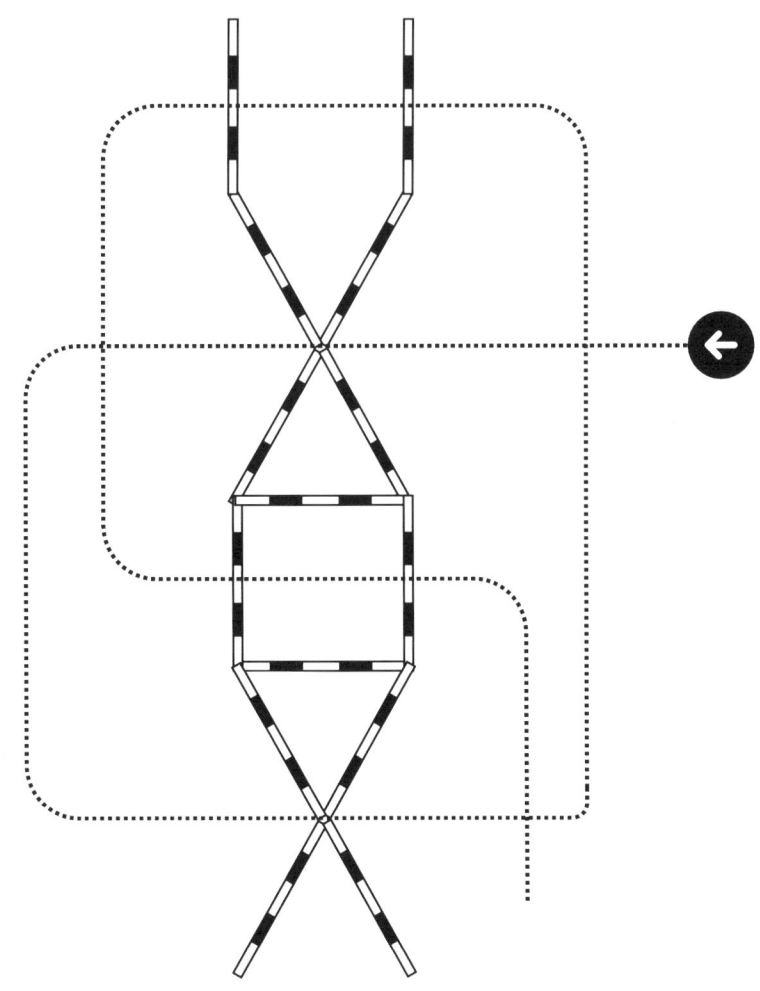

Poles: 14
Level: ★ ★
Benefits:
- ☑ Accuracy
- ☑ Rhythm
- ☑ Impulsion
- ☑ Straightness
- ☑ Suppleness & bend
- ☐ Lateral movement & collection

Gaits:
- ☑ Groundwork
- ☑ Walk
- ☑ Trot
- ☑ Canter

Movements:
- ☐ Backup
- ☐ Leg yield
- ☐ Sidepass
- ☐ Shoulder in/out

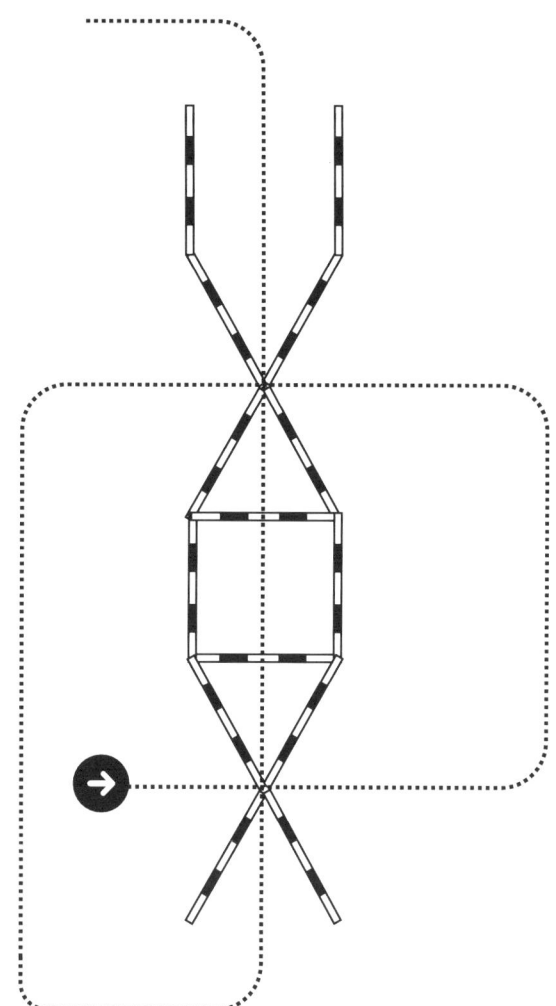

Poles: 14
Level: ★ ★
Benefits:
- ☑ Accuracy
- ☑ Rhythm
- ☑ Impulsion
- ☑ Straightness
- ☑ Suppleness & bend
- ☐ Lateral movement & collection

Gaits:
- ☑ Groundwork
- ☑ Walk
- ☑ Trot
- ☐ Canter

Movements:
- ☐ Backup
- ☐ Leg yield
- ☐ Sidepass
- ☐ Shoulder in/out

16 Poles

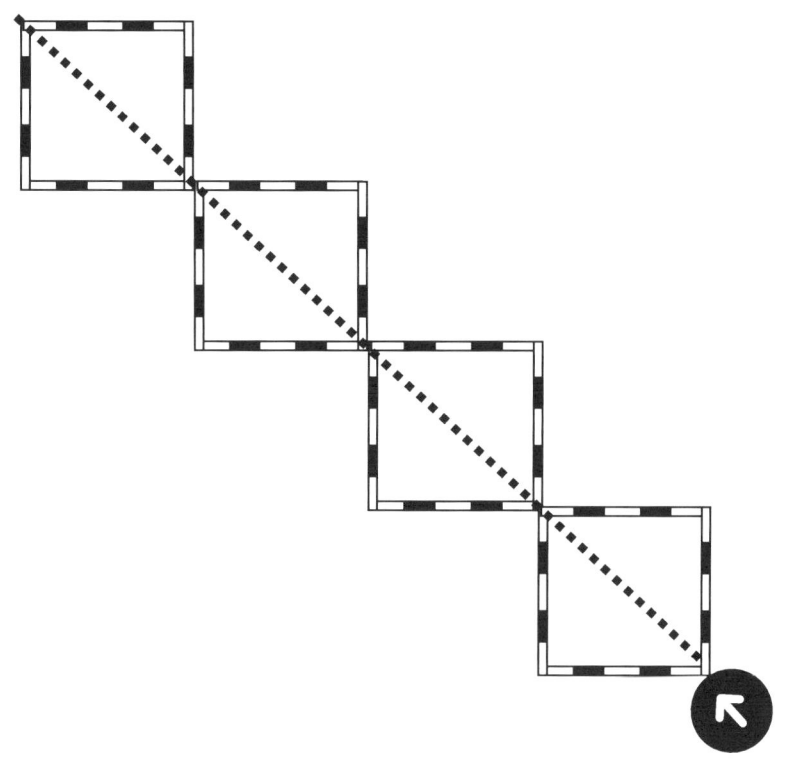

Poles: 16

Level: ★ ★

Benefits:

- ☑ Accuracy
- ☑ Rhythm
- ☑ Impulsion
- ☑ Straightness
- ☑ Suppleness & bend
- ☐ Lateral movement & collection

Gaits:

- ☑ Groundwork
- ☑ Walk
- ☑ Trot
- ☐ Canter

Movements:

- ☐ Backup
- ☐ Leg yield
- ☐ Sidepass
- ☐ Shoulder in/out

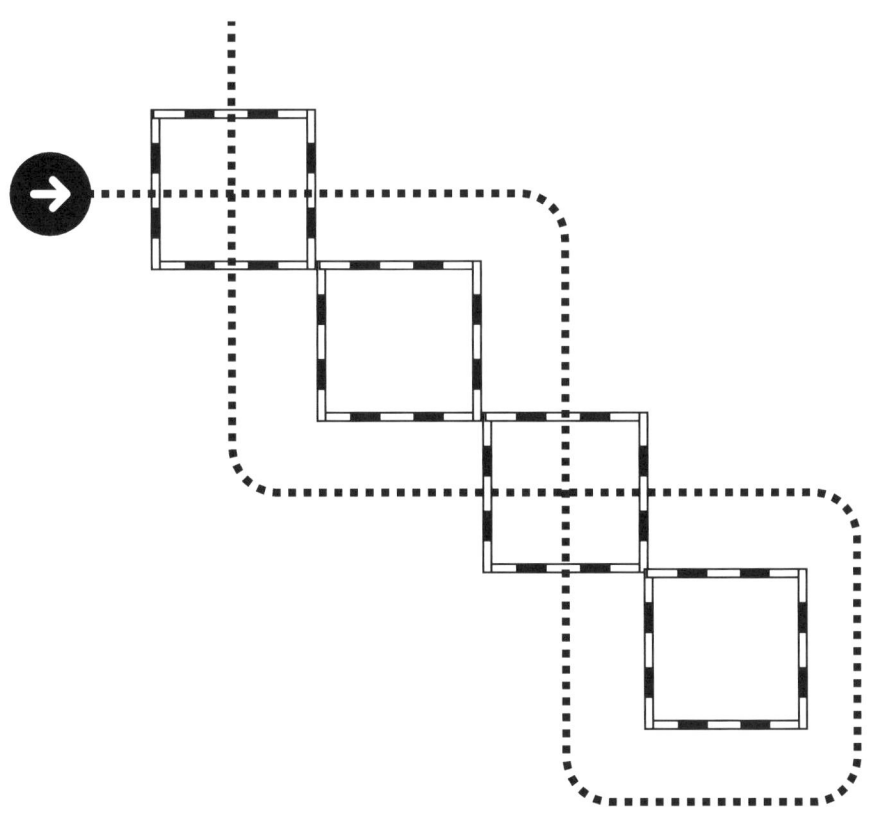

Poles: 16
Level: ★
Benefits:
- ☑ Accuracy
- ☑ Rhythm
- ☑ Impulsion
- ☑ Straightness
- ☑ Suppleness & bend
- ☐ Lateral movement & collection

Gaits:
- ☑ Groundwork
- ☑ Walk
- ☑ Trot
- ☑ Canter

Movements:
- ☐ Backup
- ☐ Leg yield
- ☐ Sidepass
- ☐ Shoulder in/out

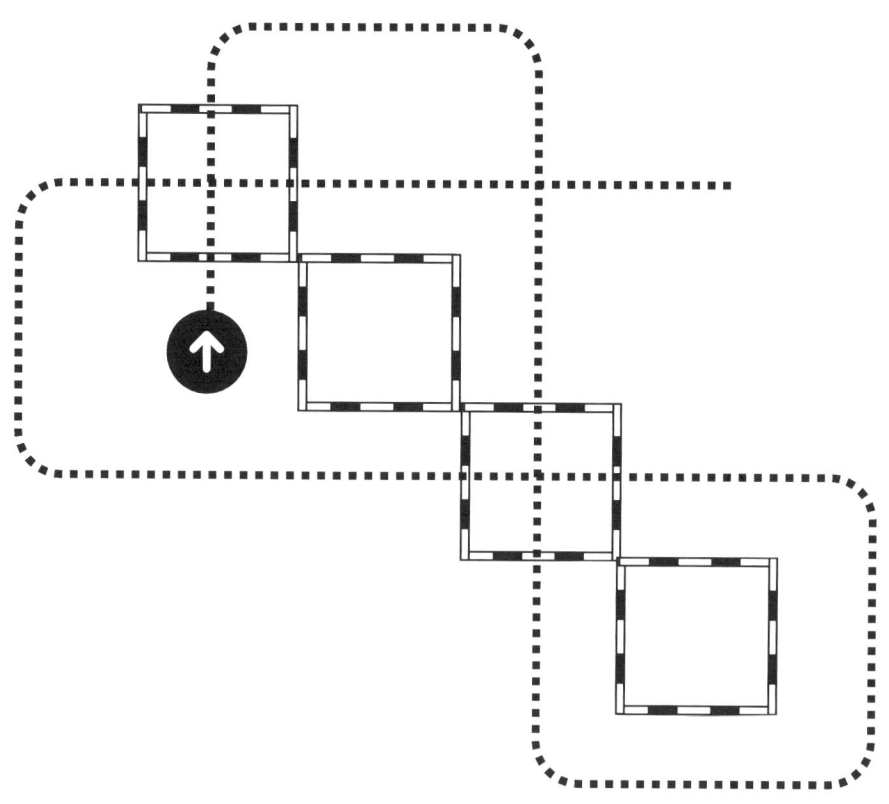

Poles: 16
Level: ★
Benefits:

- ☑ Accuracy
- ☑ Rhythm
- ☑ Impulsion
- ☑ Straightness
- ☑ Suppleness & bend
- ☐ Lateral movement & collection

Gaits:

- ☑ Groundwork
- ☑ Walk
- ☑ Trot
- ☑ Canter

Movements:

- ☐ Backup
- ☐ Leg yield
- ☐ Sidepass
- ☐ Shoulder in/out

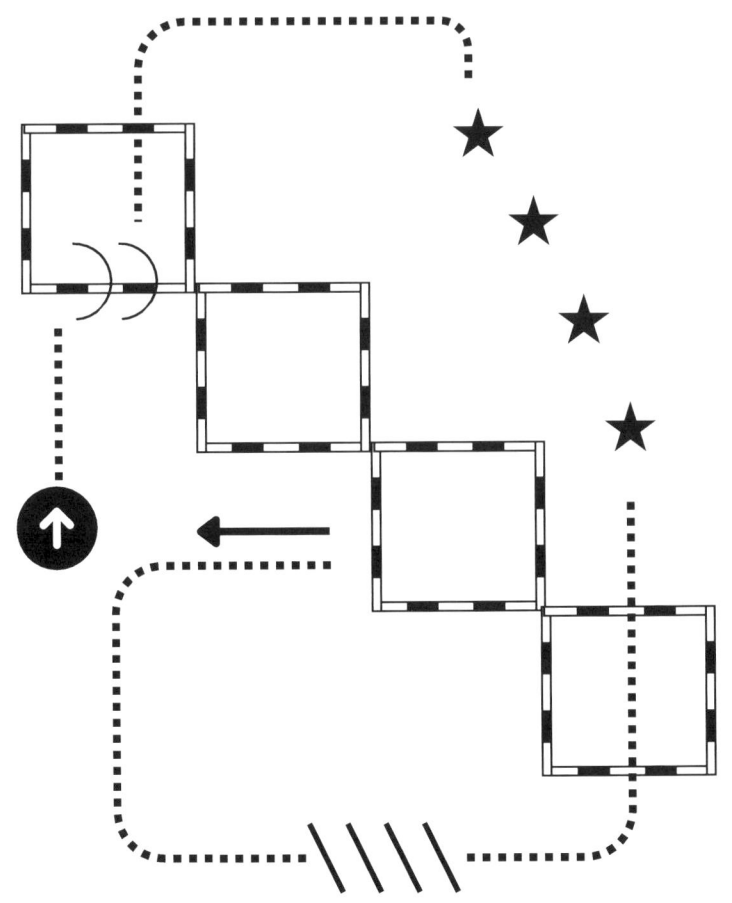

Poles: 16
Level: ★ ★ ★
Benefits:
- ☑ Accuracy
- ☑ Rhythm
- ☑ Impulsion
- ☑ Straightness
- ☑ Suppleness & bend
- ☑ Lateral movement & collection

Gaits:
- ☑ Groundwork
- ☑ Walk
- ☑ Trot
- ☑ Canter

Movements:
- ☑ Backup
- ☑ Leg yield
- ☑ Sidepass
- ☑ Shoulder in/out

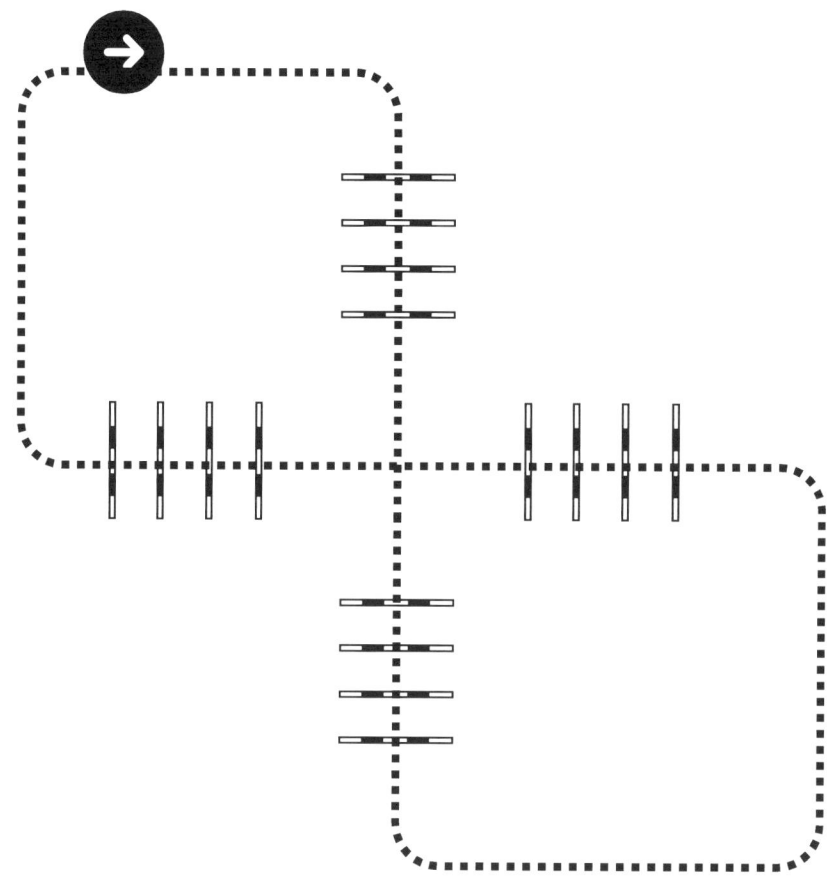

Poles: 16
Level: ★
Benefits:
- ☑ Accuracy
- ☑ Rhythm
- ☑ Impulsion
- ☑ Straightness
- ☑ Suppleness & bend
- ☐ Lateral movement & collection

Gaits:
- ☑ Groundwork
- ☑ Walk
- ☑ Trot
- ☑ Canter

Movements:
- ☐ Backup
- ☐ Leg yield
- ☐ Sidepass
- ☐ Shoulder in/out

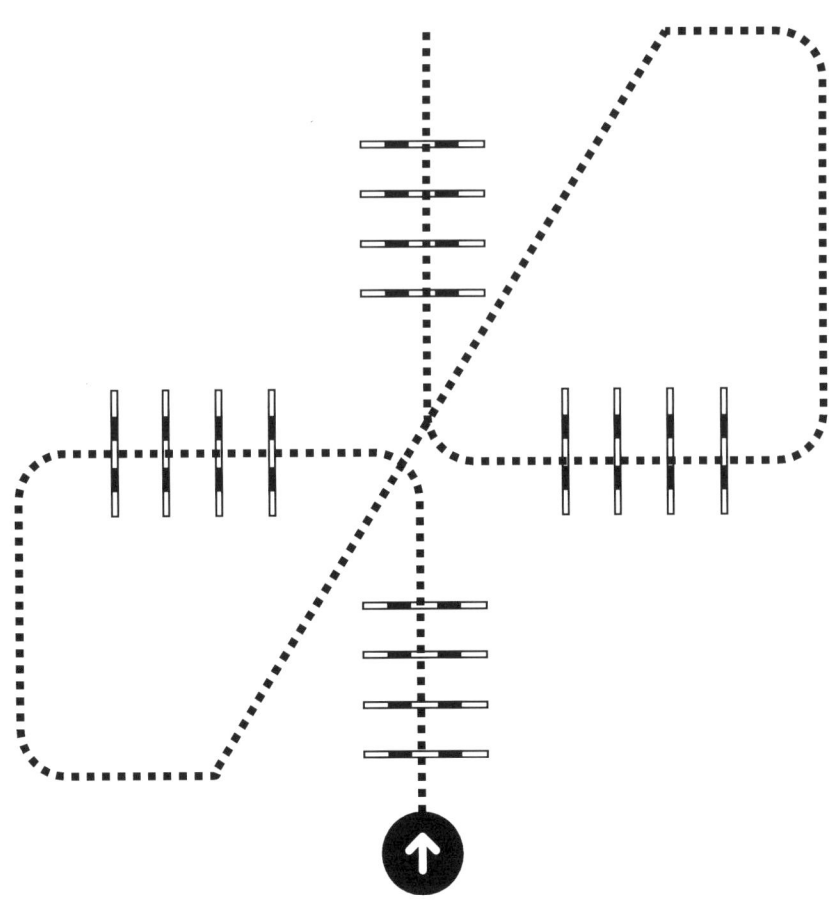

Poles: 16
Level: ★
Benefits:
- ☑ Accuracy
- ☑ Rhythm
- ☑ Impulsion
- ☑ Straightness
- ☑ Suppleness & bend
- ☐ Lateral movement & collection

Gaits:
- ☑ Groundwork
- ☑ Walk
- ☑ Trot
- ☐ Canter

Movements:
- ☐ Backup
- ☐ Leg yield
- ☐ Sidepass
- ☐ Shoulder in/out

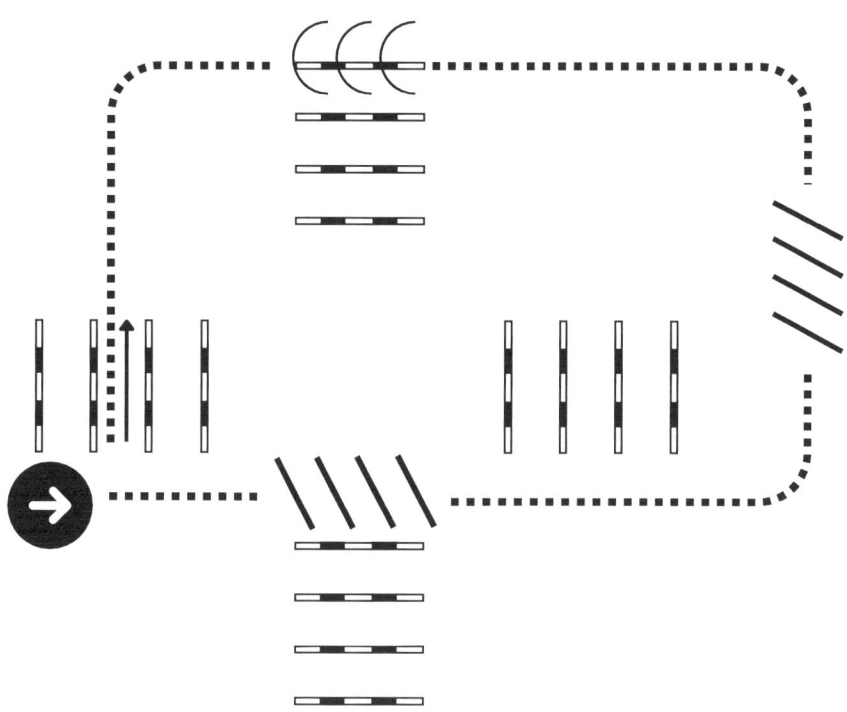

Poles: 16
Level: ★ ★ ★
Benefits:

- ☑ Accuracy
- ☑ Rhythm
- ☑ Impulsion
- ☐ Straightness
- ☑ Suppleness & bend
- ☑ Lateral movement & collection

Gaits:

- ☑ Groundwork
- ☑ Walk
- ☑ Trot
- ☐ Canter

Movements:

- ☑ Backup
- ☐ Leg yield
- ☑ Sidepass
- ☑ Shoulder out & in

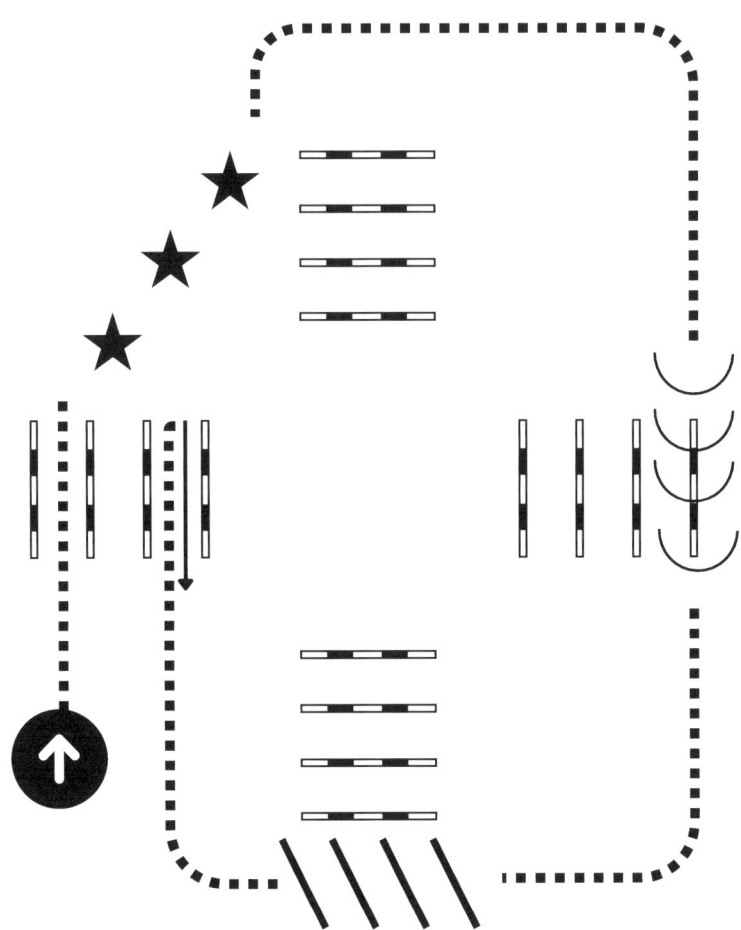

Poles: 16
Level: ★ ★ ★
Benefits:
- ☑ Accuracy
- ☑ Rhythm
- ☑ Impulsion
- ☑ Straightness
- ☑ Suppleness & bend
- ☑ Lateral movement & collection

Gaits:
- ☑ Groundwork
- ☑ Walk
- ☑ Trot
- ☑ Canter

Movements:
- ☑ Backup
- ☑ Leg yield
- ☑ Sidepass
- ☑ Shoulder in/out

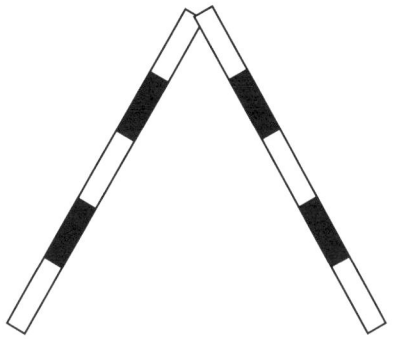

I hope you have enjoyed all the polework exercises in this book. Every horse and rider is on their own journey, at their own speed.

At the heart of all this training is the joy and happiness of spending time with your horse, a horse who is trying their very best for you.

Remember to approach each training session with an open heart and a curious mind. Stay patient, keep it fun, and cherish every moment you get to spend with your horse.

Here's to many more hours of joyful learning and to the endless possibilities that lie ahead in your polework adventures. Happy riding!

Elaine Heney.

HORSE BOOKS
by #1 best-selling author
ELAINE HENEY

www.elaineheneybooks.com

Saddlestone
Connemara Pony Listening School

by #1 best-selling author
Elaine Heney

Made in the USA
Columbia, SC
30 November 2024

6a54bb19-e221-4ca7-9f0d-86d8c4a43c86R01